CAMBRIDGE Professional English

for work and life
English 365

Student's Book 2

Bob Dignen Steve Flinders Simon Sweeney

CAMBRIDGE
UNIVERSITY PRESS

PUBLISHED BY THE PRESS SYNDICATE OF THE UNIVERSITY OF CAMBRIDGE
The Pitt Building, Trumpington Street, Cambridge, United Kingdom

CAMBRIDGE UNIVERSITY PRESS
The Edinburgh Building, Cambridge CB2 2RU, UK
40 West 20th Street, New York, NY 10011–4211, USA
477 Williamstown Road, Port Melbourne, VIC 3207, Australia
Ruiz de Alarcón 13, 28014 Madrid, Spain
Dock House, The Waterfront, Cape Town 8001, South Africa

http://www.cambridge.org
http://www.cambridge.org/elt/english365

First published 2004

Printed in Dubai by Oriental Press

Typeface Swift *System* QuarkXpress® [HMCL]

A catalogue record for this book is available from the British Library

ISBN 0 521 75367 8 Student's Book 2
ISBN 0 521 75368 6 Teacher's Book 2
ISBN 0 521 75369 4 Personal Study Book 2 with Audio CD
ISBN 0 521 75370 8 Student's Book 2 Audio Cassette Set
ISBN 0 521 75371 6 Student's Book 2 Audio CD Set

Thanks and acknowledgements

The authors would like to thank:

- Will Capel and Sally Searby of Cambridge University Press for their unflinching support from start to finish;
- Alison Silver for her eagle eye for detail, for her good sense and good cheer throughout the editorial and proofreading process;
- Sue Nicholas for the picture research and Ruth Carim for proofreading;
- James Richardson for producing the recordings at The Soundhouse Ltd, London;
- Hart McLeod for the design and page make-up;
- Sue Evans; Lorenza, Mathieu, Jérôme and Michael Flinders; and Lyn, Jude, Ruth and Neil Sweeney for their continuing patience;
- colleagues and friends at York Associates and in the School of Management, Community and Communication at York St John College for their tolerance of authorial distraction;
- and Chris Capper of Cambridge University Press for his immeasurable contribution to the project. It is above all his huge efforts which have made this book possible.

The authors and publishers would like to thank:

- Iyad Takrouri (Syngenta), Ablaziz Esseid (Total), Joanna Baker (Edinburgh International Festival), Judy Irigoin, Gerry Kregor (York St John College), Javier Alvarez (Henkel), Zac Goldsmith (The Ecologist), Elaine Williams, Henry de Montebello (Russell Reynolds Associates), Chris Wait, Harald Peterssen (Statoil), Gwenaëlle Puntous (Alstom Power Centrales), Christophe Lehy and Bernard Gaudiez (HP), Susanna Longley, Vanessa Chen (Sherwood Taipei Hotel), Nicholas Bate (Strategic Edge Ltd), Richard Scase (University of Kent), Sylvia Heinzen (Bombardier Flexjet Europe), Clare Abbott, Anna Teevan, Ron Ragsdale, Jenny Cutler (Image Counts), Anke Schweikart (Lafarge Zement), Arnauld Schwalm (Douwe Egberts), Lesley Downer, Janie O'Connor (Events Promotions Casting), Tony Weston (the Vegan Society) for their help with the interviews;
- John Davidson of BCD, Paris, for providing the introduction to Henry de Montebello;
- the interviewees for their photographs; Joanna Baker – photographer Douglas Robertson;
- Tim Banks, Gareth Davies, Helena Sharman, George Tomaszewski and Julian Wheatley for reviewing the material in its early stages.

The authors and publishers are grateful to the following for permission to use copyright material. While every effort has been made, it has not been possible to identify the sources of all the material used and in such cases the publishers would welcome information from the copyright owners.

The publishers are grateful to the following for permission to reproduce copyright photographs and material:

Key: l = left, c = centre, r = right, t = top, b = bottom, back = background

p.9: back ©Syngenta, cr ©Syngenta; p.10: tr ©Ralf-Finn Hestoft/Corbis; p.11: back ©Peter Turnley/Corbis; p.12: cr ©Tom Tracy Photography/alamy.com, Total logo ©courtesy of Total; p.13: rt ©Bettmann/Corbis, rb ©Mark Scheuern/alamy.com; p.14: tr ©John Springer Collection/Corbis; p.15: back ©Dominic Twist/alamy.com, bl ©PEPE/alamy.com, bcl ©Photodisc Green/Getty Images, bc ©aophotography.com/alamy.com, br ©Brian Horisk/alamy.com; p.16: cr ©Leslie Garland/LGPL/alamy.com, back ©Kevin Fleming/Corbis; p.18: cl ©Michael Boys/Corbis; p.19: back ©Topfoto/UPPA; p.20: b ©Leo Dennis Productions/Brand X Pictures/alamy.com; p.21: tl and tr ©Gareth Boden; p.22: cr ©Gareth Boden; p.23: tr ©Charles Gupton/Corbis; p.24: back and t ©Will Capel, all b ©Gareth Boden; p.25: cr ©Profimedia.CZ s.r.o./alamy.com, bl ©Bill Bachmann/alamy.com; p.26: ctl ©Justin Kase/alamy.com, cbl ©Peter Johnson/Corbis, cr ©Andy Marshall/alamy.com, b ©Max Earey/alamy.com; p.27: back ©Peter M. Wilson/alamy.com, cr ©courtesy of Henkel; p.29: b ©Rubberball/alamy.com; p.30: r cover provided with kind permission of The Economist ©The Economist; p.31: tr ©Bettmann/Corbis; p.31: b ©Reuters/Corbis; p.33: back and t ©Joseph Sohm/ChromoSohm Inc./Corbis, all b ©Gareth Boden; p.34: crt ©Tougig Sion/Corbis Sygma, crb ©UPPA Ltd, clb ©Comstock Images/alamy.com; p.35: br ©Royalty Free/Corbis; p.37: back ©Vodafone/with the kind permission of Vodafone; p.39: t ©SuperStock/alamy.com; p.40: r ©Bettmann/Corbis; p.41: t ©John Foxx/alamy.com, cr ©Gordon R. Gainer/Corbis, br ©Bettmann/Corbis; p.42: back and t ©Caron Philippe/Corbis Sygma, br ©John Angerson Yorkshire Sculpture Park/alamy.com, bcl, bcr, br ©Gareth Boden; p.43: cr ©Powered by Light/Alan Spencer/alamy.com, br ©David Hoffman/David Hoffman Photo Library/alamy.com; p.44: back ©Justin Kase/alamy.com; p.45: tl ©Royalty Free/Corbis, tr ©Jim Boorman/Pixland/alamy.com, cr ©MedioImages/alamy.com; text ©Andrew Osborn, The Guardian Online; p.47: b ©Phil Boorman/ImageState/alamy.com; p.48: text and t and cr ©2004Wal*Mart Stores, Inc, USA/courtesy of Wal*Mart Stores.com; p.49: tr ©Dave G. Houser/Corbis, cr ©Bettmann/Corbis; p.51: back and t ©Trevor Smithers ARPS/alamy.com, all b ©Gareth Boden; p.52: t and c ©Will Capel; p.56: cl ©Courtesy of the Sherwood Taipei Hotel, cr ©Tom Wagner/Corbis Sygma; p.57: b ©Michael S. Yamashita/Corbis; p.59: text and t and cr and p.60 tr courtesy of Nick Wirth ©2000-2003 RoboScience Ltd, www.roboscience.com; p.60: b Aiptek PenCam used by kind permission of Aiptek International GmbH ©Aiptek International; p.62: back and t ©BananaStock/alamy.com, bl ©Image100/alamy.com, bc ©Gareth Boden; p.63: t ©Ronald Chapple/Thinkstock/alamy.com, c ©Webphotographer/alamy.com; p.67: b ©UPPA.co.uk; p.68: cl and cr courtesy of Bombardier Inc.; p.69: cl ©Alan Schein Photography/Corbis; p.70: t ©Corbis; p.71: back and t ©Bettmann/Corbis, bl ©Hulton-Deutsch Collection/Corbis, bcl ©Bettmann/Corbis, bcr ©Bettmann/Corbis, br ©Bettmann/Corbis; p.72: tr ©Pictor International/ImageState/alamy.com, ctr ©Everett collection/Rex Features, cbr ©Nils Jorgnesen/Rex Features, br ©Lord of the Rings/©New Line Productions; p.73: tr ©Sunset Boulevard/Corbis Sygma; p.74: cl ©Alex Berliner/BEI/ Rex Features, cr ©R. Hepler/Everett (EVT)/Rex Features; p.77: cr ©Ed Wheeler/Corbis; p.78: tr ©Royalty Free/Corbis, br ©Bettmann/Corbis; p.79: tr ©Bettmann/Corbis; p.80: back and t ©Popperfoto/alamy.com, all b ©Gareth Boden; p.81: tl ©Mark Anderson/RubberBall/alamy.com, tcl ©ImageState Royalty Free/alamy.com, tc ©Mark Anderson/RubberBall/alamy.com, tcr ©BananaStock/alamy.com, tr ©BananaStock/alamy.com, cr ©David Montford/Photofusion Picture Library/alamy.com, bl ©Pictor International/ImageState/alamy.com, br ©Reuters/Corbis; p.82: b ©Motoring Picture Library/alamy.com, p.83: cr ©Comstock Images/alamy.com, cl ©Ricardo Azoury/Corbis; p.84: cr ©Catherine Karnow/Corbis; p.85: b ©Imagina The Image Maker/alamy.com; p.86: text and t Shannon Bentley, Discovery Channel Canada, www.exn.ca, cr and br ©Head/courtesy of Head.com; p.87: cr ©Hewlett-Packard/used with kind permission of Hewlett-Packard/www.hp.com; p.88: tr ©H. Armstrong Roberts/Corbis; p.89: back ©Linda Burgess/Anthony Blake Picture Library, bl ©James Murphy/Anthony Blake Picture Library, bcl ©Stock Connection Inc./alamy.com, bcr ©Guy Moberly/Anthony Blake Picture Library, br ©BCA&D Photo Illustration/alamy.com; p.90: cr ©Royalty Free/Corbis, bl ©Harry Bradley/Corbis; p.92: br ©Lisa O'Connor/ZUMA/Corbis; p.93: br ©David Cumming/Eye Ubiquitous/Corbis; p.94: bl ©James Leynse/Corbis; p.95: tl ©Jackson Smith/alamy.com, tr ©John Foxx/alamy.com, ctl ©Robert Llewellyn/alamy.com, ctr ©Shout/alamy.com, cb ©Tom and Dee Ann McCarthy/Corbis; p.96: tr ©Lex van Lieshout/imageshop-zefa visual media uk ltd/alamy.com; p.97: tr ©Royalty Free/Corbis, br ©Everett Collection/Rex Features; p.98: br ©Lois Ellen Frank/Corbis; p.100: back Owen Franken/Corbis, all c ©Gareth Boden; p.106: tr ©Hewlett-Packard/used with kind permission of Hewlett-Packard/www.hp.com; p.110: tr ©Sony UK Ltd, used with kind permission/sony.co.uk.

Illustrations:
Louise Wallace: pages 53 and 90
Tim Oliver: pages 108 and 111
Rupert Besley: pages 10,17, 28, 34, 39, 46, 60, 65, 66 and 76
Linda Combi: page 36

Contents

Thanks and acknowledgements 3   To the student 8

1 Working internationally 9

Listening
From Jordan to Switzerland
Grammar
Present simple and present continuous
Pronunciation
Strong and weak stress
Speaking
Working life

4 Changing direction 18

Listening
Change is fun
Grammar
Past simple and past continuous
Pronunciation
Using intonation to show interest
Speaking
Describing past experiences

7 From Mexico to Germany 27

Listening
Work is fun
Grammar
Adjectives and adverbs: comparative, superlative and as … as
Pronunciation
Stress patterns in long words
Speaking
Making comparisons

2 Power for life 12

Reading
Total – in the energy business
Vocabulary
Business and business organisation
Speaking
Profiling your organisation
Communicating at work
Telephoning 1: Getting through / Leaving a message

5 Job swap 21

Reading
Job swapping
Vocabulary
Jobs and personal development
Speaking
Explaining professional responsibilities
Communicating at work
Presenting 1: Welcoming visitors

8 Globalisation 30

Reading
Can Zac save the planet?
Vocabulary
Trade and the economy
Speaking
Presenting an argument
Communicating at work
Emails 1: Formal and informal writing

3 Edinburgh – the festival city 15

Social phrases
Arriving in a place you don't know
Listening
The festival city
Vocabulary
Music, theatre, dance and opera
Speaking
Likes and preferences

6 Tourist attraction 24

Social phrases
Health and feeling ill
Listening
Are you looking for somewhere different?
Vocabulary
Tourist attractions and accommodation
Speaking
Talking about tourist attractions and locations

9 Here is the news 33

Social phrases
Talking about news
Listening
Finding out what's going on
Vocabulary
The news and news media
Speaking
News and current affairs

10 Executive search   36

Listening
Finding the right people
Grammar
Past simple, present perfect
simple and present perfect
continuous; *for*, *since* and *ago*
Pronunciation
Weak forms of *have* and *for* with
the present perfect
Speaking
Describing work experience

11 Making money   39

Reading
Alternative investments
Vocabulary
Finance and investments
Speaking
Personal finance
Communicating at work
Meetings 1: Asking for and
giving opinions

12 Ecotourism   42

Social phrases
Getting directions
Listening
Tourism and the environment:
the Eden Project
Vocabulary
Environmental problems
Speaking
The environment

13 Changing culture   45

Listening
Norway sets female quota for
boardrooms
Grammar
Future 1: *will*, *going to* and the
present continuous
Pronunciation
Contractions with pronouns and
auxiliary verbs
Speaking
Discussing future plans

14 The customer is   48
always right

Reading
Ten foot attitude
Vocabulary
Customer service
Speaking
Customer satisfaction
Communicating at work
Telephoning 2: Making and
changing arrangements

15 An interesting place   51
to live

Social phrases
Visiting someone's home for dinner
Listening
Living in a windmill
Vocabulary
Houses and homes
Speaking
Homes

Revision 1 Units 1–15   54

16 Taiwan – still a tiger 56

Listening
Real competitive advantage
Grammar
Quantifiers: *all, every, each, most, much, many, a few, a little, no, any, some*
Pronunciation
Linking
Speaking
Describing quantities

17 RoboDog 59

Reading
Barks and bytes
Vocabulary
Technology and gadgets
Speaking
Technology
Communicating at work
Emails 2: Handling customer enquiries

18 Learning styles 62

Social phrases
Asking for and giving help
Listening
Teaching people how to learn
Vocabulary
Learning a language
Speaking
Developing a learning action plan

19 Britain at work in 2010 65

Listening
Vision of the future
Grammar
Future 2: *will, can, may, might* and the first conditional
Pronunciation
Using stress when giving opinions
Speaking
Predicting the future

20 How the rich travel 68

Reading
Selling jet travel for €8,000 an hour
Vocabulary
Sales and selling
Speaking
Selling and the sales process
Communicating at work
Meetings 2: Leading a meeting

21 Great cinema 71

Social phrases
Making recommendations and giving advice
Listening
The big screen experience
Vocabulary
Film and cinema
Speaking
Cinema and favourite films

22 Your personal brand image 74

Listening
Image Counts
Grammar
Must, have to and *need to*
Pronunciation
Strong and weak stress with modal verbs
Speaking
Personal image

23 Managing people 77

Reading
We listen to what they say
Vocabulary
Managing people
Speaking
Human resources
Communicating at work
Emails 3: Making travel arrangements

24 Social issues 80

Social phrases
Receiving international colleagues
Listening
Social issues in Britain
Vocabulary
Social problems and solutions
Speaking
Discussing social problems

25 The coffee business   83

Listening
Douwe Egberts – coffee producer
and seller
Grammar
The second conditional
Pronunciation
Silent letters and difficult words
Speaking
Discussing possibilities

26 Intelligent skis   86

Reading
Intelligent ski technology
Vocabulary
Products
Speaking
Describing products and their
selling points
Communicating at work
Telephoning 3: Handling complaints

27 You are what
you eat   89

Social phrases
Food talk
Listening
How do you like our food?
Vocabulary
Food and cooking
Speaking
Discussing local specialities

28 That's entertainment!   92

Listening
From strongmen to look-alikes
Grammar
The passive
Pronunciation
Corrective stress
Speaking
Processes

29 Life coaching   95

Reading
Do you need a change?
Vocabulary
Changes and trends
Speaking
Describing change
Communicating at work
Presenting 2: Handling questions
effectively

30 Work or lifestyle?   98

Social phrases
Saying goodbye
Listening
Work, belief and lifestyle
Vocabulary
Continuous learning
Speaking
Discussing work and lifestyle

Revision 2 Units 16–30   101

File cards   104
Grammar reference   112
Tapescripts   120
Answer key   136

To the student

Who is *English365* for?

Welcome to *English365* Book 2. You may already know *English365* from Book 1, but if not, this brief introduction explains some key features of the series. *English365* is for people who need English for their jobs and for their free time. If you use English at work and also when you travel and meet people, *English365* is for you. The book is for and about real working people and every unit gives you English which you can use straightaway at work or in your free time.

What is *English365*?

There are two main parts to this course:

The **Student's Book**, which you are reading now. There are also classroom cassettes or audio CDs for the listening exercises in this book. As well as the core material in each unit, there is support material to help your learning in the Grammar reference section.

The **Personal Study Book with Audio CD** is to help you remember the English which you learn in the classroom. It provides important support, consolidation and extra practice material to help your learning. The more you work outside the classroom, the better your English.
- The Personal Study Book has important information about the language, and exercises for you to practise.
- The Audio CD gives you extra listening practice. You can also practise the pronunciation exercises and social English dialogues from the Student's Book on your own.

What's in the Student's Book?

With the Student's Book, you can work on:
- the **grammar** which you need to make English work for you
- the **vocabulary** you need for your job and for your free time
- the **phrases** you need for your free time – getting directions, welcoming visitors, etc.
- the **phrases** you need for your work – telephoning, emailing, etc.
- **pronunciation** rules to help you speak better and understand better too.

There are 30 units in the book (plus two revision units, one after Unit 15 and one after Unit 30), and there are three types of unit:
Type 1 units (Units 1, 4, 7, etc. – the purple units)
Type 2 units (Units 2, 5, 8, etc. – the blue units)
Type 3 units (Units 3, 6, 9, etc. – the green units)

In **type 1** units you work mainly on:
- Listening
- Grammar
- Pronunciation.

In **type 2** units, you work mainly on:
- Reading
- Vocabulary for **work**
- Communication skills for **work** – for telephoning, writing emails, presenting information and taking part in meetings.

In **type 3** units, you work mainly on:
- Phrases for **travel and socialising**
- Listening
- Vocabulary for your **free time**.

You practise **speaking** in every unit!

At the back of the book, there are also:
- File cards for pairwork exercises (page 104)
- Grammar notes (page 112)
- The tapescripts for the classroom cassettes/audio CDs (page 120)
- Answers to all the exercises (page 136).

English365 Book 2

English365 Book 2 is for learners who have already completed Book 1 or who are at lower-intermediate to intermediate level. Book 2 consolidates what you already know and takes you forward.

In Book 2 the listening and reading tasks are more challenging and they will help you to develop a better all-round level of confidence and competence in understanding English, as well as, of course, speaking the language.

Book 2 also introduces a wider range of communication skills, including presenting information and taking part in meetings and simple discussions. Another difference between Book 1 and Book 2 is that a larger number of new words are introduced in each unit.

We hope you enjoy learning with *English365* Book 2. Good luck with your English.

Bob Dignen   Steve Flinders

Simon Sweeney

On the agenda

Speaking
Working life

Grammar
Present simple and present continuous

Pronunciation
Strong and weak stress

Meet Iyad Takrouri. He's from Jordan and works for Syngenta, a Swiss company which makes crop protection products for farmers across the world.

1 Working internationally

Warm up

Would you like to work in another country?
What would you enjoy about working abroad?
What would you find difficult?

Listen to this

From Jordan to Switzerland

1 Listen to Iyad talking about working in Switzerland. Are these sentences true or false? ▶▶|1.1

1 He works in Geneva as a technical manager.   **T**   **F**

2 Business is increasing a lot at the moment.   **T**   **F**

3 He has responsibility for the Middle East and North Africa regions.   **T**   **F**

4 He finds Swiss German difficult to understand. **T**   **F**

5 His team is not very international.   **T**   **F**

2 Listen again and answer these questions. ▶▶|1.1

1 What is Iyad's main responsibility?
2 Why are big European farming organisations moving into Egypt and Morocco?
3 How often does Iyad visit the countries for which he is responsible?
4 What does Iyad like most about Switzerland?
5 Why does Iyad prefer to speak English at work?

What do you think? How international are you? Would you like a job with a lot of travel? Would you like to work in an international team? Why? Why not?

Check your grammar

Present simple and present continuous

Look at the examples (a–f) of the present simple and present continuous.

a I *work* in Zurich for Syngenta as a technical manager.
b Business *is* really *increasing* a lot.
c I *visit* all the countries once a year for business meetings.
d *Do* you *enjoy* living in Switzerland?
e Everybody *speaks* English.
f He's *staying* in your hotel.

Match these two descriptions with each of the sentences (a–f).

1 Temporary actions and situations which are happening now, for example, current trends and short-term events in progress.
2 Actions and situations which are not temporary, for example, general and personal facts, regular events, likes and dislikes.

Which description (1 or 2) describes the present simple tense and which one describes the present continuous?

Note We do not normally use continuous tenses with 'state' verbs, for example:
believe, know, think, understand, feel, smell, taste, look, want, like, love, hate, need, prefer.

Grammar reference pages 112–113 ▶

Do it yourself

1 Correct the mistakes in these sentences.

1 He work in Madrid.
2 Where do you coming from originally? Are you German?
3 Sales increase a lot at the moment in China.
4 I'm usually going to work by car.
5 This meal is delicious. The meat is tasting really good.

2 Choose the correct question from the two options (present simple or present continuous) for each answer.

1 Q: *What do you do? / What are you doing?*
  A: I'm a consultant.

2 Q: *What do you do? / What are you doing?*
  A: I'm helping with a project in China at the moment.

3 Q: *Do you specialise in project work? / Are you specialising in project work?*
  A: No, I don't. I work in a lot of different areas.

4 Q: *How often do you come to Zurich? / How often are you coming to Zurich?*
  A: This is my first time!

5 Q: *Where do you stay? / Where are you staying?*
  A: I'm in a hotel near the railway station.

6 Q: *Does your business expand at the moment? / Is your business expanding at the moment?*
  A: Absolutely. The market is fantastic right now.

Work with a partner and practise asking and answering the questions.

I'm in a hotel near the railway station.

3 Two former colleagues meet at an airport. Complete their conversation using the words in brackets.

A: Hi, Marina. Surprise, surprise.

B: Karl! Good to see you. What (1) (you / do) .... here?

A: I'm on my way to Nairobi for a business meeting.

B: Really? (2) (I / go) .... to Paris to meet my brother for the weekend.

A: Oh, (3) (he / work) .... in Paris?

B: No. He works in Budapest. Paris is just an easy place for us to meet.

A: OK. (4) (How often / you / see) .... him?

B: (5) (We / try / meet) .... twice a year in Paris.

A: Sounds good.

B: It is. (6) (You / know) .... Paris?

A: Not very well. (7) (I / not / go) .... there very much. Anyway, how's work?

B: Good. (8) (I / work) .... on a new product at the moment. And you?

A: Well, (9) (things / not / go / well) .... , you know, because it's a very difficult market situation. Oh, I think (10) (your plane / board) ....

B: You're right. I've got to go. Bye.

A: Bye. Have a good trip! Really good to see you again.

Listen and check your answers. ▶▶|1.2

Strong and weak stress

1 Listen to these short dialogues. The stressed words are underlined. ▶▶|1.3

A: <u>Where</u> do you <u>work</u>?
B: I <u>work</u> in <u>Geneva</u>. And <u>you</u>?

A: <u>What</u> do you <u>do</u>?
B: I'm a <u>journalist</u>.

A: <u>Where</u> are you <u>staying</u>?
B: In the <u>Hilton</u>. Where are <u>you</u> staying?

Listen again. Why do the speakers stress the underlined words? Why does the speaker stress 'you' in two of the questions? ▶▶|1.3

When speaking, we place strong stress on syllables or words which carry the main meaning or focus. Other words have weak stress. In present simple and present continuous questions, the auxiliary verbs and pronouns normally have weak stress. However, in short questions and reply questions we change the stress, e.g. 'And <u>you</u>?'

Work with a partner and practise asking and answering the questions.

2 Underline the words which have the main stress in the following short dialogues.

A: How often do you travel on business?
B: About once a month. And you?

A: Are you busy?
B: Yes, I'm working on a big project in China.

A: Do you know Madrid?
B: No, I don't. Do you?

A: What are you working on at the moment?
B: A report – the deadline is next week.

A: Did you have a good weekend?
B: Great, thanks. How was yours?

Listen and check your answers. ▶▶|1.4

Work with a partner and practise asking and answering the questions.

It's time to talk

Dynamic communication

1 In Do it yourself exercise **3**, Marina and Karl created a dynamic conversation using two simple techniques:

- asking a lot of questions
- using short phrases like 'OK' to show interest when listening.

Read the dialogue again and find different questions and short phrases you can use to build a dynamic conversation.

2 You meet a former colleague (your partner) in an airport departure lounge. Start and maintain a short conversation by asking questions about the following. Make notes about yourself below, and prepare questions to ask your partner before you start talking. Try to make your conversation dynamic.

<u>My profile</u>

Job responsibilities ....

Current projects ....

Current situation of the business or sector ....
....

Business travel ....

Family ....

Weather at home ....

Remember

- We can use the present simple tense to talk about personal details, habits and routines, and likes or dislikes.
- We can use the present continuous tense to talk about personal projects, current changes and temporary situations.
- We build a dynamic conversation by asking lots of questions, and showing interest when listening by responding with short phrases.

On the agenda

Speaking
Profiling your organisation

Vocabulary
Business and business organisation

Communicating at work
Telephoning 1: Getting through /
Leaving a message

**Meet Ablaziz Esseid.
He works for Total.
His company's
headquarters is at
La Défense in Paris.**

2 Power for life

Warm up

How many oil companies can you name?
Which countries do they come from?
Which one sells the most petrol in your country?
Do you always buy the same brand of petrol?

TOTAL

Read on

Total – in the energy business

Total is France's biggest oil company and Ablaziz Esseid works for it. He is based in Paris but he travels all over the world. We interviewed Ablaziz about his company.

1 Match our questions to the answers which Ablaziz gives. There are two questions which do not match an answer.

1 What does the company do exactly?
2 What do you do at Total?
3 How big is the company?
4 Do you ever feel lost in such a large organisation?
5 Where is the company based?
6 What's the history behind Total?

We need energy to live and we depend on oil. Without it, our jobs, our free time and our mobility would all be very different. Every day we consume 70 million barrels of oil. Every year we consume 2,200 million tonnes of coal and 2,500 billion cubic metres of gas.

It's a long story! Total was founded in 1924, and for many years it was a French state oil company. In 1999 Total joined Petrofina, the Belgian oil and gas company, and in 2000 Totalfina merged with its main French competitor, Elf Aquitaine, and the name became Totalfinaelf. Now it's called Total again, and it's France's biggest company.

2 What do the following figures in the article refer to?

1 70 million
2 2,500 billion
3 1924
4 700 billion
5 50 billion
6 120

As a company, Total is organised into three areas. Firstly, Upstream, which means oil and gas exploration and production. This also covers electricity production where we have investments in nuclear, solar and wind energy. Then there's Downstream, which includes refining gasoline for cars. The third area is Chemicals. But our core business is supplying energy for people to live: to run a car, to light offices, schools and homes. We provide power for life.

Total is huge. The turnover is around $700 billion per annum, with profit after tax at around $50 billion. In terms of staff, we employ over 120,000 people in more than 120 countries. It's massive, but it's incredible to think that Exxon, the biggest oil company, has twice our total sales!

Never! The headquarters at La Défense is enormous, but I work in a small team of just 20 people. It's really good fun and we have a great working atmosphere. And, for everyone, it's very motivating to be at the centre of a truly global business doing something that's necessary for everyone to live their lives.

3 The article mentions several forms of power. How many can you find?

What do you think? Which do you think is the most important form of energy for the future? Why?

In American English the words 'gas' or 'gasoline' are used for the fuel for cars.

In British English it is called 'petrol'.

The words you need ... to talk about business and business organisation

1 Use words from the box to complete the profile of General Motors.

Factfile – General Motors

(1) .... in 1908 by Billy Durant, General Motors, the world's largest vehicle manufacturer, designs, builds and (2) .... cars and trucks worldwide, and has been the global automotive (3) .... since 1931.

GM today (4) .... cars in factories in over 30 countries and sells them in about 200 countries. The company is (5) .... six major regional (6) ....: North America, Western Europe, Eastern Europe, Asia/Pacific, Latin America and Africa/Middle East. GM (7) .... about 355,000 people around the world.

Last year GM sold over 8.5 million cars and trucks (8) ...., more than any other automaker. It has a 15.1 per cent (9) .... of the global vehicle market. In 2002 (10) .... reached $186,763 million.

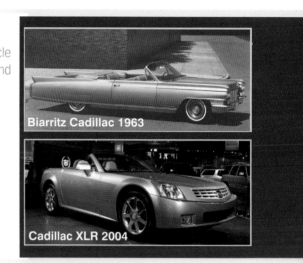

Biarritz Cadillac 1963

Cadillac XLR 2004

How many of the words in the box can you use to talk about your own organisation or an organisation you know?

produces   worldwide   markets

organised into   turnover   employs

share   market leader   founded   sells

2 Look at the business mind map below. Complete the sentences using words from the mind map.

1 We .... a lot of business in Germany.

2 We sell worldwide. We're a .... business.

3 Our .... business is writing software but we also do some consultancy.

4 Unfortunately, pirate software is .... business in some parts of the world.

5 Our union has members in a number of business .... including cars, food and engineering.

6 Do you give people your business .... when you first meet them or when you say goodbye?

7 In my new job I'm going to have to .... business a lot more than before.

8 OK, we've only got a couple of hours. Let's .... business.

Can you add any more words to the mind map? Can you make your own sentences for the words you add?

The business mind map

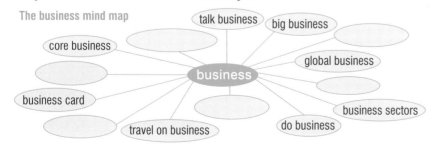

core business   talk business   big business   global business   business   business card   business sectors   travel on business   do business

It's time to talk

A new organisation

You work for an energy business (which you are going to invent). Make notes about the organisation under each of these headings.

Name
Core business
Founded
Number of employees
Organised into
Number of countries
Market share in home country
Turnover
Strong points
Weak points

Work with a partner. Ask each other questions about your organisations.

Communicating at work

Telephoning 1: Getting through / Leaving a message

Do you use the phone in English? If so, what do you use it for?

1 Listen to four phone calls and match each call to one of the headings. ▶▶|2.1

Call 1   Waiting on line

Call 2   The person called is not available

Call 3   Getting through

Call 4   Leaving a message

2 Now listen again and complete the dialogues below. ▶▶|2.1

<u>Call 1</u>

You've (1) .... the voicemail of Eve Warner. Please (2) ....
and I'll (3) .... as soon as I can.

<u>Call 2</u>

A: Hello, I'd like (4) .... Helen Foster, please. Is she (5) .... ?

B: I'll (6) .... to her department. One (7) .... , please.

<u>Call 3</u>

A: Would you like to (8) .... ?

B: Well, no, I (9) .... to him personally. Perhaps he could
(10) .... Can I (11) .... ?

A: Yes, of course, please do.

<u>Call 4</u>

We are (12) ....high call load at the current time. For web support,
please visit our website at www.supex.com/technical. Otherwise, please
(13) .... and an operator will be with you as soon as one (14) ....

Is he getting through?

3 Work in pairs. Use this flowchart to build a short conversation with your partner. Then change roles.

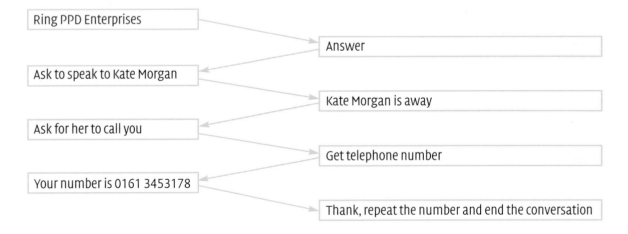

Ring PPD Enterprises

Answer

Ask to speak to Kate Morgan

Kate Morgan is away

Ask for her to call you

Get telephone number

Your number is 0161 3453178

Thank, repeat the number and end the conversation

4 Work in pairs. Student A should look at the information
on page 104, and Student B should look at page 108.

Remember

On the phone:
- Speak slowly and clearly.
- Repeat all key information.
- Always be polite.

On the agenda

Speaking
Likes and preferences

Social phrases
Arriving in a place you don't know

Vocabulary
Music, theatre, dance and opera

Warm up

Do you ever have problems finding your way around new places that you visit? What kinds of problem?

3 Edinburgh
— the festival city

Arriving in a place you don't know

1 Complete the dialogues with phrases (a–h) below.

At left luggage

A: Excuse me, (1) .... ?
B: Yes, what have you got?
A: We've got a backpack and a large suitcase.
B: OK. That's £4 for the suitcase and £3 for the backpack. The ticket's valid for 24 hours.
A: Fine, thanks. (2) ....
B: That'll be fine. Have a nice morning.

At the accommodation bureau

A: Hello, we've just arrived and (3) .... , please.
B: Singles or double?
A: Double, please.
B: OK. Edinburgh's very full but I can phone one in Leith for you.
A: Thank you. How far is it and (4) .... ?
B: It's about half an hour by bus.

At tourist information

A: Hello, can you help us? (5) ....
B: Yes, here you are.
A: And (6) .... the festival?
B: This tells you about the official festival. And this has information about the Fringe – the unofficial festival.
A: Thanks. And one last thing: do you have a bus timetable for Leith?
B: Yes, here you are.
A: Thanks for your help.

Getting there

A: Excuse me, we want to get to Leith. (7) .... , please?
B: Yes, you want a number 37. The stop is just down the road there.
A: (8) .... ?
B: You don't need to get a ticket in advance. You can pay on the bus.
A: Thank you.
B: You're welcome.

a We'd like a map of the city
b Where does the bus leave from
c Where do we buy the tickets
d can we leave our bags here
e can you give us some information about
f how do we get there
g We'll come and get them around 2 this afternoon
h we'd like a bed and breakfast for two for three nights

Have a go

Cover the dialogues above and make your own, starting with the words below.

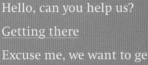

At left luggage

Excuse me, ...

At the accommodation bureau

Hello, we've just arrived and ...

At tourist information

Hello, can you help us?

Getting there

Excuse me, we want to get to ...

2 Now listen and check. ▶▶3.1

3 Practise reading the dialogues with a partner.

Listen to this

The festival city

Which towns and cities do you think of when you hear the word 'festival'? Do you ever go to festivals? Have you heard of the Edinburgh Festival?

1 Listen to Joanna Baker talking about the Edinburgh Festival. Are these sentences true or false? ▶▶|3.2

  1 The Edinburgh International Festival is an arts festival.   T   F

  2 The different festivals last five weeks.   T · F

  3 The International Festival is quite formal.   T   F

  4 Joanna's personal favourite is opera.   T   F

Joanna Baker is the marketing and public affairs director for the Edinburgh International Festival. We interviewed her about the festival and about her work.

2 Listen again and answer the questions. ▶▶|3.2

  1 How many different performances does the International Festival have?

  2 How many visitors come to the festival?

  3 Complete what Joanna says about her job: 'My job is to make sure we .... and that we bring in ....'

  4 How much do the 10.30 pm shows cost to attend?

  5 What does Joanna enjoy doing during the rest of the year?

Joanna says: '... it's perfect. Job and hobby together.' Can you say the same? What is your main hobby? Would you like to have your job and hobby together? If you could do this, what would you do?

The words you need ... to talk about music, theatre, dance and opera

Going out 1: The performing arts

The performing arts are arts like music, dance, opera and theatre which are performed live by people on the stage of a concert hall or theatre. Add an ending from the box to the words in the sentences below.

> -ector   -et   -orary   -ion   -estra   -ing
> -ographer   -wright   -ume   -cert   -ance
> -erina   -ress   -ign   -ition   -or

The performing arts (general)

1 The Comédie Française's product.......... of Molière's *Tartuffe* is perhaps their best version of this great play in the last 20 years.

2 We are sorry to announce that Barbara Bonney has a heavy cold and is unable to appear in tonight's perform.......... of *The Marriage of Figaro*.

3 I couldn't see what was happening on the stage half the time! The light.......... was very poor.

4 The stage des........... for this *Hamlet* was excellent and made the opening scene with the castle at night very dramatic.

Music

5 The wonderful Octet is a relatively early compos......... of Mendelssohn's: he wrote it when he was only 16.

6 Sir Simon Rattle is the first conduct......... to become music director of the Berlin Philharmoniker in its history.

7 The Berlin Philharmoniker is thought by many to be the best orch.......... in the world today.

8 We went to a marvellous con.......... at the Théâtre des Champs-Elysées last weekend – Mitzuko Uchida at her best, playing Schubert.

Theatre

9 People who have seen the theatre work of dir.......... Peter Brook can often remember it years afterwards.

10 Shakespeare is rightly thought to be the greatest play.......... in the English language but we should not forget that there were many other interesting dramatists living at the same time as him.

11 The play was very well done but I don't think it was a good idea to do this eighteenth century piece in modern cost.......... .

12 She wants to be an act....... when she grows up.

Dance

13 The Bolshoi Ball............ is still one of the leading companies in the world, with a history going back to the eighteenth century.

14 She's the leading ball............ at the Bolshoi.

15 The chore.......... is the person who designs the dances which dance companies put on.

16 I prefer contemp............. dance to classical dance because I think there is more creativity and variety in what the dancers do.

Going out 2: What you like

1 Put these phrases in order from most positive to most negative.

I love ...	`1` I like ...
I really like ...	I can't stand ...
I'm not very keen on ...	I quite like ...
I don't really like ...	`8` I hate ...

Note: All the above take the *-ing* form of any following verb.

Example:

 I love going to festivals but I'm not very keen on queuing for tickets.

2 Talk to your partner. What do you like to do when you go out? What's on at the moment where you live? What do you recommend? Use some of this language as a model.

You either love it or ...

Questions
Do you (ever) go ... to the theatre?
How often do you go ... to the opera?
Do you like ... ballet?
What sort/type/kind of ... music do you listen to?

Answers
I love ... → I hate ...

Responses

They say:	You say:
I like ...	Me too. (Agreeing with a positive sentence)
I don't like ...	Me neither / Nor me. (Agreeing with a negative sentence)

If you have another opinion, you can say:
Really? Actually I like ... / I don't like ...

It's time to talk

You and your partner have a free evening in Edinburgh after a business meeting. The Festival is on. Decide from this evening's programme what you are going to do. Will you go out together or will you have different plans? Or would you prefer to do something completely different?

You can start by saying, for example:

A: What would you like to do tonight?

B: I don't know. What's on?

A: They're doing *The Seagull* at the King's Theatre ...

DANCE. Cullberg Ballet. The Edinburgh Playhouse.
Cullberg Ballet combines brilliant dancing with great theatricality, making it one of the most innovative modern ballet companies performing today.
A must for all lovers of dance and theatre. The two works tonight are:
Home and Home
Choreography: Johan Inger. Music: JS Bach / Tobin / Ferrari / Raczynski. *Home and Home* is a dreamy work by the new Artistic Director of Cullberg Ballet, Johan Inger.
Fluke
Choreography: Mats Ek. Music: Flesh Quartet. Fluke is contemporary dance at its most entertaining and satisfying.
    Price: £6.00–£25.00. *Running time: approx 2hrs.*

OPERA. Das Rheingold by Richard Wagner. Scottish Opera. Edinburgh Festival Theatre. Staged production sung in German with English supertitles. Wagner's story of gods and mortals, good and bad, life and death takes us on an extraordinary musical and emotional journey. The Ring Cycle is one of the most complex studies of the human condition ever written and Scottish Opera's production is a brilliant success.
    Price: not available. *Running time: approx 2hrs 45mins.*

THEATRE. The Seagull by Anton Chekhov. King's Theatre.
A major production of *The Seagull* created specially for the Festival, performed in English by a cast which includes Fiona Shaw as Arkadina. Peter Stein's productions of Chekhov's *Three Sisters*, *Uncle Vanya* and *The Cherry Orchard* are among the most famous of modern times.
    Price: £6.50–£26.00. *Running time: 3hrs 30 mins including one interval.*

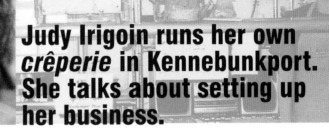

On the agenda

Speaking
Describing past experiences

Grammar
Past simple and past continuous

Pronunciation
Using intonation to show interest

Judy Irigoin runs her own *crêperie* in Kennebunkport. She talks about setting up her business.

4 Changing direction

Warm up

Would you like a career change?
Would you like to run a restaurant?
Why? Why not?

Listen to this

Change is fun

1 Judy Irigoin runs a *crêperie*, a restaurant that specialises in *crêpes* (the French word for pancakes). Listen and choose the correct details. ▶▶ **4.1**

1 Judy opened her restaurant in: the USA ▢   the UK ▢

2 Judy set up the restaurant:
to give her children a new life ▢
because she was bored with teaching ▢

3 Judy designed her restaurant:
with a small consulting company ▢   with a friend ▢

4 Judy's children: like the *crêperie* ▢   don't like the *crêperie* ▢

5 The restaurant:
didn't make a profit last year ▢   made a good profit last year ▢

2 Listen again and answer the questions. ▶▶ **4.1**

1 Why did she set up the restaurant near Boston?
2 How long did it take Judy to set up the business?
3 Why do so many visitors come to Kennebunkport in June?
4 How did the *crêperie* change Judy's children?
5 Why is it difficult to make a profit?

What do you think? Judy says: 'Change is fun. Everyone should have a small business.' How far do you agree? Would you like to set up your own business? If so, what kind of business would you like to start?

Check your grammar

Past simple and past continuous

We can use the past simple and past continuous when we talk about the past, especially when discussing life experiences.

1 Look at the sentences below and underline the verbs in the past simple and past continuous.

1 I was working for a language school in France when I had the idea.
2 When my son saw it, he was really excited.
3 We were living in France at the time.
4 After I figured I could make a profit, I set up the place.
5 She was working in the restaurant business and so she came over.
6 Things were not going well for them at school around this time.

We make the past continuous with *was/were* + the *-ing* form of the verb. When do we use *was* and when do we use *were*?

2 Now match sentences 1–6 opposite with the three explanations (a–c) below.

a When describing the past, we can use the simple past to talk about finished and complete actions. We often use the past simple to describe a sequence of completed actions – one after the other.

b We can use the past continuous tense to give background information to main actions which we can describe with the past simple. The past continuous describes a temporary situation, not a finished action. The focus is on something in progress at some point in the past.

c We can use the past continuous and past simple together to say how one action happens during another action. The past continuous action is the background action which starts before (and can continue after) the past simple action.

I was working for a language school in France when I had the idea.

I was working for a language school
(action in progress)

_____ ✕ _ _ _ _ _ _ _ _ _____|NOW

I had the idea
(single action)

Grammar reference pages 113–14

Do it yourself

1 Correct the mistakes in these sentences.

1 James met Sabine in 1998. He living in New York at the time.
2 I wanted to work in marketing. So I was joining a marketing company.
3 I were listening to the radio when you called.
4 I saw Jess a minute ago. She talked to Sam.
5 Why weren't you answer the phone when I called?

2 Nina Simone, the legendary soul jazz and blues singer, died in 2003. Match the main events of her life (1–5) with the correct background situation (a–e).

Main events
1 1950s – She had her first Top Twenty hit with Gershwin's *I Loves You, Porgy* in 1959.
2 1960s – She recorded many powerful songs in the 60s on the issue of racial discrimination.
3 1970s – She decided to leave the US and the record industry in the 1970s for Barbados.
4 1980s – Her song *Baby Just Cares For Me* became a huge hit in 1987.
5 1990s – She published her autobiography *I Put A Spell On You* in 1991.

Background situations
a She was spending less and less time on stage due to ill health.
b Simone was growing increasingly unhappy with show business and continuing racism in the US.
c The civil rights movement was growing in the US at the time.
d She was rapidly developing a reputation as a singer of many styles of music.
e Chanel was using the song for a perfume commercial on television.

3 We interviewed Hilary MacDonald, an expert on Nina Simone, about the early career of this extraordinary artist in the 1960s. Complete the interview extract below, using the verbs in brackets in either the past simple or the past continuous.

INTERVIEWER: How (1) .... Nina Simone's career .... (begin)?

HILARY: Well, she (2) .... (work) in a nightclub when she (3) .... (have) the chance to sign for the Bethlehem record label. She (4) .... (take) her opportunity with both hands and her first hit (5) .... (come) in 1959.

INTERVIEWER: (6) .... (be) Nina part of the black civil rights movement in the US during the 1960s?

HILARY: Absolutely, yes. When the protest actually started she (7) .... (already / write) songs and so she quickly (8) .... (join) the movement.

INTERVIEWER: (9) .... Nina .... (write) any specific songs about the fight for equality?

HILARY: Yes. In fact, *Mississippi Goddam* (10) .... (be) a direct response to the killing of four black children.

INTERVIEWER: And (11) .... her songs .... (have) any impact?

HILARY: Absolutely. At that time people always (12) .... (stop) what they (13) .... (do) and (14) .... (listen) when Nina (15) .... (start) to sing.

Listen and check your answers. ▶▶|4.2

Using intonation to show interest

1 Listen to two versions of the same short conversation about a weekend. Note down any differences you hear. ▶▶| 4.3

Differences: ....

....

Effective listening

Listeners use different responses to show polite interest when listening. They also use intonation to sound polite, for example by increasing the volume and changing the tone a little.

<u>Type 1</u> Using intonation with short phrases, some of which give a positive reaction:
Aha, Oh, Yes, OK, Really, Interesting, Good, Great, Nice, etc.

<u>Type 2</u> Using intonation when repeating key words:
A: Yes, and we saw lots of <u>dolphins</u>.
B: *Dolphins!*

<u>Type 3</u> Using intonation when asking follow-up questions:
A: Yes, and we saw lots of dolphins.
B: *How many?*

2 Listen to five mini-dialogues and decide which type of response (Type 1, Type 2 or Type 3) the listener uses in each dialogue. ▶▶| 4.4

Dialogue 1 ☐
Dialogue 2 ☐
Dialogue 3 ☐
Dialogue 4 ☐
Dialogue 5 ☐

3 Work with a partner. Take it in turns to tell each other your news using the list below. Check that your partner listens effectively by showing interest with polite intonation.

- Your sister is getting married.
- You applied for a job with a company located in New York.
- Your partner has got a promotion.
- You saw an excellent film last week.
- You have decided to travel around the world for a year.
- Your company has just won a new contract in India.
- You would like to change your job.
- You read a very interesting book last week.
- One of your children passed their exams.
- You will get a promotion next month.

It's time to talk

How good are you at building conversations about the past?

Prepare to talk about two of the topics below. Ask your partner as many questions as possible about their topics. Try to keep the conversation going for as long as possible. Remember to show interest when you are listening.

A problem you had with a customer
An interesting training course you did
Something you won
A difficult phone call you had
Something interesting you did last weekend
A famous person you met
A great holiday experience
A bad day at work
A fantastic holiday experience
Something you lost

What did you do after that?

What happened next?

What were you doing at the time?

Something interesting you did last weekend

Remember

- We can use the past simple and past continuous to talk about our past experiences:
  I was just finishing some work when the phone rang. A man was screaming at me on the phone and I realised it was our biggest customer!
- We can use polite intonation and responses to show interest:
  Oh, really! What did he say?

On the agenda

Speaking
Explaining professional
responsibilities

Vocabulary
Jobs and personal development

**Communicating
at work**
Presenting 1: Welcoming visitors

Meet Sonia Griffin, a team coordinator, and Ben Walker, a design director, at Winning Design. They swapped jobs for a day. Find out what they learned.

5 Job swap

Warm up

How many different jobs have you done – in your organisation and outside it? Would you like to try another job in your organisation? What? Why?

Read on

Job swapping

1 Look at the article on the right about job swapping and answer these questions.

1 What is job swapping?
2 What jobs did Sonia and Ben swap?
3 Were they positive about the experience?

2 Read the article again and answer these questions about Sonia and Ben.

1 Why does Sonia think Ben's job is difficult?
2 What did Sonia learn about herself from the job swap?
3 How will the job swap change the way Sonia does her job?
4 Why was Ben worried about swapping jobs with Sonia?
5 What major problem did Ben have during the day?
6 What did Ben learn about himself from his job swap?

What do you think? Do you think job swapping is a good idea? What could you learn from doing a job swap? Who would you like to swap with?

Can you imagine? The boss changes jobs with the receptionist. She runs top management meetings for a day while he answers the phone and handles visitors. Job swaps are becoming popular because organisations believe they can be a great way for staff to share experiences and build new relationships. Two people in the same organisation do each other's jobs for a day and then discuss what they can learn from the experience. Two participants give us their thoughts.

Sonia: Team coordinator – responsibilities include organising meetings, travel and documentation

'Ben's job is tough. He has to work on a lot of different things – everything from the company's publicity material to client Christmas cards. I spent the morning with his team designing a new corporate brochure. Actually, it was a bit depressing at first because most of my ideas were hopeless. But when we discussed the design of next year's Christmas cards, the team decided to take up some of my ideas, which was great. At the end of the day I was happy to go back to my job and what I'm trained to do. But the day did teach me that I could do other things and that I had more creativity than I thought. Now I want to get better and be more creative. So I'll try to contribute more ideas during our team meetings in future.'

Ben: Design director – responsibilities include designing corporate brochures and external documentation

'I was definitely more nervous than Sonia. I knew her job was very different from mine, all about organisation: setting up meetings, getting documentation ready, working to tight deadlines, and so on. In fact, my first task was to organise an internal meeting with eight very senior people. The first thing was to book a limo to pick up people from the airport: that was easy. Next was to update information for the actual meeting. That was a disaster! I couldn't print it out because I had no idea how to use the software. It got really stressful but, fortunately, Sonia came to the rescue. How did I feel at the end of the day? For me, it was a great experience. I learned that organisational skills are essential to achieve targets and I learned more about coping with pressure. And for me, swapping seemed to be a good way to develop confidence, communication and motivation. It's nice to meet new people and fun to try new things. I hope we can do more of it in the future and improve our work skills.'

The words you need ... to talk about jobs and personal development

1 Use verbs from the article to complete this advertisement. The first letter is given for you.

Personal development Human Development Associates (HDA) Ltd *Experts in developing potential*

We can help you to help yourself. We will help you to ...

1 b.................... new relationships and useful networks with people
2 c.................... more ideas in meetings
3 w.................... to tight deadlines
4 a.................... targets which you set yourself
5 c.................... with pressure
6 d.................... greater confidence in what you do
7 i.................... work skills

If you would like details of forthcoming training events, please email us: events@hda.co.uk.
HDA Ltd, PO Box 420, Reading RG63 2TR

2 Choose the correct words in Ben's job profile.

NAME: Ben Walker
TITLE: Design director
AREA: I have (1) *responsible for / responsibility for* new designs for our corporate brochure. I'm also (2) *in charge of / in charge for* specific design projects. I'm (3) *responsible for / responsibility for* 25 people.
MAIN TASKS: (4) My main *objective / object* is to support marketing and sales. One of my other key (5) *tasks / work* is to make sure we present a clear brand identity to the customer in our brochures.
OTHER WORK: Another important part of my job is to (6) *deal with / handle with* stores which display and sell our products. Sometimes I (7) *take care for / take care of* visitors from our Spanish office because I speak good Spanish. I'm also (8) *involved in / involved for* the social club at work.

Ben Walker, raising the quality of design for Winning Design.

Listen and check your answers. ▶▶|5.1
Make similar sentences about yourself.

3 With a partner, discuss which of the ideas in exercise 1 *you* do – or could do in the future – to improve your work. Which are most important for you?

It's time to talk

1 You are going to meet colleagues to discuss a job swap.
Make notes about important information in your job.

	You	Person 1	Person 2
Job title			
Main responsibilities			
Other tasks			
Good things about the job			
Bad things			
Qualities you need for the job			

2 Now work with two other people in the class. Interview them about their jobs and complete your notes. When you have finished, decide which person you would like to swap jobs with.

Communicating at work

Presenting 1: Welcoming visitors

Do you ever give presentations in English? Do you often welcome visitors to your organisation?

1 Listen to a short presentation and circle the correct answers below. ▶▶|5.2

Name	Gemma Wood / Wilkins / Walker
Job	Personnel officer / Information officer / Executive PA
Morning tour	Production area / City centre / Offices
Lunch	12.00 / 12.30 / 13.00
Evening programme	Restaurant / Theatre / Concert

2 Match the phrases (a–i) to the structure of Gemma's presentation. Listen again to check your answers. ▶▶|5.2

Phrases

a Right, now I want to go on to the second part ...
b Thank you for listening.
c Does anyone have any questions ...?
d Now I'm going to hand over to ...
e That's all I want to say about ...
f To begin then, I want first of all to ...
g My name's ... and I work in ...
h Hello and welcome to everyone.
i I'd like to give you a short introduction to ...

Beginning
1 Welcome the visitors
2 Introduce myself
3 Introduce the presentation

Main part
4 Start the first part
5 Finish the first part
6 Move on to the next part

Ending
7 Check for questions at the end
8 Thank the audience
9 Introduce the next speaker

3 You work for Le Chat Bleu SA, a shoe manufacturer in France. You are the HR manager responsible for recruitment and training. Read the email below and use the information to prepare a short welcome presentation to a group of visitors to Le Chat Bleu. You should speak for no more than two minutes.

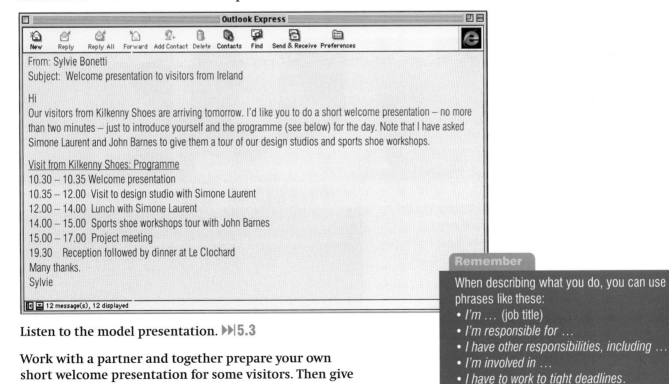

```
┌──────────────────────────  Outlook Express ──────────────────────────┐
│  New   Reply  Reply All  Forward  Add Contact  Delete  Contacts  Find  Send & Receive  Preferences │
├───────────────────────────────────────────────────────────────────────┤
│ From: Sylvie Bonetti                                                    │
│ Subject: Welcome presentation to visitors from Ireland                  │
│                                                                         │
│ Hi                                                                      │
│ Our visitors from Kilkenny Shoes are arriving tomorrow. I'd like you to do a short welcome presentation – no more │
│ than two minutes – just to introduce yourself and the programme (see below) for the day. Note that I have asked │
│ Simone Laurent and John Barnes to give them a tour of our design studios and sports shoe workshops. │
│                                                                         │
│ Visit from Kilkenny Shoes: Programme                                    │
│ 10.30 – 10.35 Welcome presentation                                      │
│ 10.35 – 12.00 Visit to design studio with Simone Laurent                │
│ 12.00 – 14.00 Lunch with Simone Laurent                                 │
│ 14.00 – 15.00 Sports shoe workshops tour with John Barnes               │
│ 15.00 – 17.00 Project meeting                                           │
│ 19.30   Reception followed by dinner at Le Clochard                     │
│ Many thanks.                                                            │
│ Sylvie                                                                  │
│ 12 message(s), 12 displayed                                             │
└───────────────────────────────────────────────────────────────────────┘
```

Listen to the model presentation. ▶▶|5.3

Work with a partner and together prepare your own short welcome presentation for some visitors. Then give your presentation to the class.

> **Remember**
> When describing what you do, you can use phrases like these:
> - *I'm ... (job title)*
> - *I'm responsible for ...*
> - *I have other responsibilities, including ...*
> - *I'm involved in ...*
> - *I have to work to tight deadlines.*

On the agenda

Speaking
Talking about tourist attractions and locations

Social phrases
Health and feeling ill

Vocabulary
Tourist attractions and accommodation

Warm up

Have you ever felt ill when you were travelling? What was the matter? What happened?

6 Tourist attraction

Health and feeling ill

1 Complete the dialogues with phrases (a–h) below.

Feeling unwell

A: Are you all right?
B: No, actually. (1) ....
A: Yes, you do look pale.
(2) .... ?
B: No, thanks, maybe I'll go home early today.
A: Yes, I think you should.

Fixing an appointment to see a doctor

A: Hello, (3) .... , please.
B: Can I have your name?
A: Yes, it's Raul Ochoa. I'm from Spain. (4) ....
B: Fine. I'm afraid the doctor is busy all morning. Can you come at 3.15 this afternoon?

At the doctor's

A: Hello, I have an appointment with the doctor at 3.15.
B: 3.15, yes. (5) .... , please?
A: OK. (6) .... ?
B: No, I don't think so. But write your home doctor's details here.

Back at work

A: Ah, you're back! Are you better now?
B: Yes, (7) ....
A: Good. (8) .... Welcome back.

a I'm here temporarily, on business
b Do you need my insurance details
c Is there anything I can do?
d We've missed you

e I'm much better, thanks
f I don't feel very well
g I'd like an appointment
h Can you fill in this form

Have a go

Cover the dialogues above and make your own, starting with the words below.

Feeling unwell

Are you all right? ...

Fixing an appointment to see a doctor

Hello, I'd like ...

At the doctor's

Hello, I have ...

Back at work

Ah, you're back ...

2 Now listen and check. ▶▶ 6.1

3 Practise reading the dialogues with a partner.

Listen to this

Are you looking for somewhere different?

Before you listen Have you ever had a holiday in Australia? Would you like to? Why? What do you know about Tasmania?

1 Listen to Gerry talking about Tasmania. Are these sentences true or false? ▶▶|6.2

   1 Tasmania is about the same size as the Republic of Ireland.   T ▢ F ▢

   2 It's very hot and the sun always shines in Tasmania.   T ▢ F ▢

   3 It was a kind of island prison during the days of the British Empire.   T ▢ F ▢

   4 There are lots of sharks off the Tasmanian coast.   T ▢ F ▢

   5 You can walk for days there without seeing another human being.   T ▢ F ▢

2 Listen again and answer these questions. ▶▶|6.2

   1 What are the main industries?
   2 How many people live in Tasmania?
   3 What are the beaches like?
   4 What can you see in the west?
   5 How much of the state is National Park?
   6 How is Tasmania different from Europe?

What do you think? Gerry says Tasmania is mostly a 'wilderness'. Have you ever visited somewhere like that? Would you like to live in a place like that?

Meet Gerry Kregor, an IT consultant from Tasmania who now lives in the UK.

How is Tasmania different from Europe?

The words you need ... to talk about tourist attractions and accommodation

1 Look at the advertisement for a holiday in Australia.

$1,999

See some of the most extraordinary sights in Australia.

Two week package tour to Australia
(Sydney, Melbourne and Tasmania)

- Explore the beautiful Sydney Harbour, the Opera House and enjoy the wonderful and varied cuisine.
- Learn about Australia's rich Aboriginal culture.
- Visit Tasmania and its deserted beaches and fine mountain scenery.
- See fabulous wildlife and spectacular plant life. Experience the marvellous natural environment of Australia.

Enjoy the spectacular city of Sydney and complete wilderness in the same holiday!

NEXT 8 km

Price includes:

- Return flights to Sydney
- Two internal flights
- Five nights in Sydney
- Two nights in Melbourne
- Five nights on the island of Tasmania
- Luxury coach travel to Melbourne and to main attractions

2 Complete the sentences below using one of the seven underlined words in the advertisement.

1 One of the best things was the spectacular .... , especially the lakes and mountains.

2 I like noisy cities and nightlife. I don't like the idea of an empty ....

3 I always take holidays in places famous for food because I like food and want to discover local ....

4 Everyone sees animals on television, but seeing unusual .... for real is a wonderful experience.

5 Travelling to a new country is, more than anything else, a chance to learn about a different ....

6 Some people think tourism is bad for the .... but you can also learn more about this through tourism.

7 I like city breaks to visit the .... in famous cities like Bruges, Venice, Berlin or Lisbon.

3 Match the different types of accommodation in the box with the right description 1–10.

1 A country house with land, animals, crops, etc. which also receives guests.

2 A private house with some rooms for visitors, which also provides meals.

3 A holiday house or apartment where you cook your own meals.

4 A place where you can sleep in your own tent.

5 An exchange of homes so that you can stay in another person's house at the same time as they stay in yours.

6 A large private rural home, usually in the country and often with a swimming pool or near the sea.

7 A large building with a full range of services for its guests.

8 Low cost accommodation with a lot of beds in each room, usually for younger travellers.

9 A home on wheels – sometimes mobile, sometimes fixed – which is parked on a special site with washing facilities, etc.

10 A private home which offers cheaper accommodation than a guest house or hotel and which does not provide an evening meal.

Which of these have you stayed in on holiday?

house swap   campsite   caravan
hotel   farmhouse   villa   bed and
breakfast   guest house   youth hostel
self-catering accommodation

It's time to talk

Work in pairs. Student A should look at page 104, and Student B at page 108.

Remember

Adjectives for describing places
*lovely   beautiful   spectacular   pretty   cosmopolitan   varied   deserted
mountainous   unique   different   fantastic   fabulous   peaceful   lively*

What's the weather like?
It's warm / hot / cold / wet / dry / raining / snowing / cloudy.

On the agenda

Speaking
Making comparisons

Grammar
Adjectives and adverbs:
comparative, superlative
and as … as

Pronunciation
Stress patterns in long
words

Meet Javier Alvarez. He works for Henkel as a project manager.

7 From Mexico to Germany

Warm up

Javier has worked in Mexico, Germany and Spain. Which, for you, would be the most interesting place to work in? Why?

Henkel
A Brand like a Friend

Listen to this

Work is fun

1 We interviewed Javier about the time he spent working in Mexico and Germany. Listen to him talking. Are these sentences true or false? ▶▶|7.1

1 Javier is currently living and working in Germany. **T** ☐ **F** ☐

2 Mexico is the most interesting place Javier has worked. **T** ☐ **F** ☐

3 Mexicans are always late for meetings. **T** ☐ **F** ☐

4 In Mexican business culture, people are open. **T** ☐ **F** ☐

5 Javier thought German food was good. **T** ☐ **F** ☐

2 Listen again and answer these questions. ▶▶|7.1

1 How long did Javier live and work in Mexico?
2 According to Javier, which type of person is often late for a business meeting?
3 How is the Spanish spoken in Spain different from Mexican Spanish?
4 What is Javier's style of management?
5 Why does Javier like Mexican food?

What do you think? Javier talks about stereotypes. What stereotypes are there about people from your country? How true are they?

Check your grammar

Adjectives and adverbs

Read the examples and answer the questions about comparing with adjectives and adverbs.

1 Adjectives
Javier says Mexican Spanish sounds **older** than the Spanish in Spain.
It's the **most interesting** place I have worked in.

When do we use *-er* and *-est* to build comparative and superlative forms with adjectives? When do we use *more* and *most*?

2 Adverbs
In Mexico you can communicate **more easily**, **more freely** with your boss.

Adverbs of place:	near	low	high
Adverbs of time:	soon	late	early
Adverbs of manner:	quick	hard	fast

We can use *more* to make comparatives with most *-ly* adverbs (e.g. *more efficiently*). However, many adverbs with the same form as adjectives form the comparative with *-er* (e.g. *nearer, earlier, faster*).

What are the comparative forms for the irregular adverbs *badly* and *well*?

3 Comparing with *as ... as*

When we compare things, we can also use (*not*) *as ... as* with adjectives and adverbs:

It wasn't **as bad as** I expected. (= It was better than I expected.)
I didn't enjoy the German food **as much as** the Mexican ... (= I enjoyed Mexican food more.)

> ... (*not*) *as* + adjective + *as*
> ... (*not*) *as* + adverb + *as*

Which sentence (a–c) has the same meaning as Javier's comment?

Javier: It wasn't as expensive as I expected.
a It was more expensive than I expected.
b It was cheaper than I expected.
c It was the same as I expected.

Grammar reference page 114

Do it yourself

1 Correct the mistakes in these sentences.

1 They drive a lot more fastly.
2 I don't speak Spanish as good as I want to.
3 I work more effective in the morning.
4 For me, the bus is not so convenient like my car.
5 The importantest thing to remember is not to forget anything!

2 Complete these general comparisons of Mexico and Germany with words from the box.

1 In general, people in Germany drive more .... than they do in Mexico.

2 In Mexico you can get to know people a lot more .... than here.

3 Some people say that status is more .... in Mexican business culture.

4 In Mexico people normally have their evening meal .... than in Germany.

5 In Mexico prices are generally ....

6 Most people I met in Mexico knew Germany .... than I expected.

Listen and check your answers. ▶▶|7.2

lower   later   easily   better   carefully   important

You can't be too careful!

3 Look at the sentences below comparing two job applicants, Petra Nováková and Kurt Stein. Rewrite the sentences about them, using the words given and keeping the original meaning. More than one answer is sometimes possible.

1 Kurt doesn't speak English as fluently as Petra.
(Petra / speak / fluently / Kurt)
2 Kurt is much more interested in working abroad.
(Petra / interested / abroad)
3 Kurt doesn't have as much overseas experience as Petra.
(Petra / experienced / Kurt)
4 Petra worked the hardest in the team-building task.
(Kurt / hard / task)
5 Kurt was quickest in the group at the logical tasks.
(Petra / do / tasks / quickly / Kurt)
6 Petra's social skills are a little better.
(Kurt / social skills / good / Petra's)

Example:

Petra has better organisational skills.
(Kurt / organisational skills / good / Petra's)
Kurt's organisational skills are not as good as Petra's.

Stress patterns in long words

1 A dictionary can be a great help when learning how to pronounce longer words.
Javier uses the words *strategy* and *strategic* during his interview. Look at the dictionary
definitions. They show you how to say the words with the correct word stress.

> **strategy** /'stræt.ə.dʒi/ ⓤⓢ /'stræt̬-/ *noun* [C or U] a detailed
> plan for achieving success in situations such as war,
> politics, business, industry or sport, or the skill of plan-
> ning for such situations: *The president held an
> emergency meeting to discuss military strategy with his
> defence commanders yesterday.*

> **strategic** /strə'tiː.dʒɪk/ *adj* **1** helping to achieve a plan,
> for example in business or politics: *strategic planning*
> ○ *a strategic withdrawal/adv...*

Now listen to the pronunciation and repeat the words. ▶▶|7.3

2 Listen to these examples of important stress patterns in three- and four-syllable words. ▶▶|7.4

Three syllables

1 **●** • •
  strategy

2 • **●** •
  strategic

3 • • **●**
  understand

Four syllables

4 **●** • • •
  motivated

5 • **●** • •
  comparison

6 • • **●** •
  competition

Decide which stress pattern (1–6) each of the following words has.

employer ▨   Mexico ▨   analysis ▨   complicated ▨   languages ▨   absolutely ▨

engineer ▨   another ▨   conversation ▨   educated ▨   competitor ▨   underline ▨

Listen and check your answers. ▶▶|7.5

Test your partner Write down between five and ten words with three or four
syllables that you have studied in earlier units. Use a dictionary to identify
which stress pattern they have. Then test your partner by asking him/her
to pronounce the words. Can he/she pronounce them with the stress on
the correct syllable?

It's time to talk

Work in pairs. One of you will play the role of Student A
and the other Student B. Student A has invited Student B
(an important customer) to dinner. In the restaurant you
discuss your experiences and compare different places
you have visited and things you have done. Student A
should look at page 104, and Student B at page 108.

Remember

We compare things with adjectives and adverbs.
Adjectives: *It's bigger than …, It's the most interesting …*
Adverbs: *I drive more carefully than …*
Adjectives and adverbs with (not) as … as: *I need it as soon as possible.*

On the agenda

Speaking
Presenting an argument

Vocabulary
Trade and the economy

Communicating at work
Emails 1: Formal and informal writing

Meet Zac Goldsmith, editor of *The Ecologist*, a magazine about the environment. We asked Zac what he thinks about globalisation and world trade.

8 Globalisation

Warm up

What do you understand by the word 'globalisation'?
Is it a good thing?

Read on

Can Zac save the planet?

1 We asked Zac Goldsmith about his views on globalisation. Match the headings (1–6) with his answers in paragraphs A–D. There are two headings which do not match an answer.

1	Bad news for the Third World	4	The future could be better
2	Third World debts are reduced	5	Meeting local needs
3	World Bank helps big business	6	Energy needs cost the earth

2 What do the following numbers in the article refer to?

1 100 and 70%   4 580 million
2 $7.2 billion   5 1.6 billion
3 20% and 17   6 six

What do you think? Do you agree with Zac that 'things will change'? Do you share Zac's concerns about globalisation?

Globalisation increases international trade, but Zac Goldsmith thinks it is bad environmentally, socially and politically. He criticises the World Bank, which lends money to developing countries, and is an important part of the globalisation process. 'World Bank loans pay for projects like roads, airports and oil refineries,' says Zac. 'It is mostly American multinationals that build these, so they benefit from the World Bank.'

Indeed, multinational corporations (MNCs) dominate the global economy, with just 100 accounting for 70% of world trade. Zac says that big corporations move in to developing countries to control natural resources such as minerals, wood and oil. 'The developing country has only debts. Ghana, for example, has debts of $7.2 billion.' Meanwhile, the local economy changes: instead of trying to meet local needs, the economy moves towards exports and the global economy. 'This is a disaster for the developing countries,' says Zac.

Zac is also unhappy about globalisation and energy. Twenty-five times more is spent on developing energy from oil, gas and coal in the developing world than is spent on 'clean' energy. The richest 20% of the world's population consumes 17 times more energy than the poorest 20%. Some of the world's largest multinational companies are oil companies. This is not surprising, as people travel much more. In 1996 the world population was 5.7 billion and 580 million travelled abroad, but by 2020, 1.6 billion out of 7.8 billion will travel abroad.

Zac, however, is optimistic. 'Trade will change,' he says. He thinks people will go back to local agriculture, farmers' markets, and more direct contact with producers. Eventually too, climate change will force the move away from oil as a source of energy. 'If everyone lived like the average American,' says Zac, 'we would need six planets to meet the energy needs. Of course things will change: they have to.'

The words you need ... to talk about trade and the economy

1 Match the words (1–9) with the correct definition (a–i).

1	inflation	**a**	money that someone has borrowed
2	imports	**b**	take money from a person or organisation that you will pay back later
3	exports		
4	debt	**c**	the annual rise in prices
5	loan	**d**	purchases from other countries
6	to lend	**e**	money that you owe
7	interest rate	**f**	the cost of borrowing money
8	to borrow	**g**	give money to a person or organisation on condition that you are paid back later
9	trade		
		h	buying and selling products and/or services
		i	sales to other countries

Test your partner   Your partner should close his/her book. Read out the definition and see if your partner can remember the key word.

2 Complete these sentences with the correct word.

1 My company makes products which are *environment / environmental / environmentally* friendly.
2 I think the government has a good *economy / economic / economical* policy.
3 I'm not very interested in *politics / political / politician*.
4 I'd like to work in a *develop / developed / developing* country like Vietnam.
5 I pay a lot of *interest / interests / interesting* on my bank loan.
6 Our business *invests / investors / investments* a lot of money in its employees.
7 My country is an *exports / exporter / exporting* of coffee.
8 Ford is a major *national / multinational / multinationalist* company.

Now listen and check your answers. ▶▶|8.1

Make similar sentences about yourself, your organisation and/or national economy with the words in exercises **1** and **2**.

Inflation or hyperinflation? A housewife using money to light a fire in 1930s Germany.

It's time to talk

What are the advantages and disadvantages of globalisation? Work in groups of four. Two students, Team A, should look at the information on page 104, and the other two, Team B, should look at page 108.

Communicating at work

Emails 1: Formal and informal writing

Who was your last email to and what was it about?

1 Read the two emails below. Is one better than the other? Why? Why not? What do you think makes a good email?

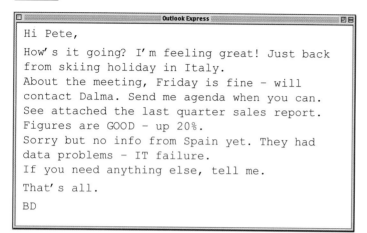

Email 1

> Hi Pete,
>
> How's it going? I'm feeling great! Just back from skiing holiday in Italy.
> About the meeting, Friday is fine – will contact Dalma. Send me agenda when you can.
> See attached the last quarter sales report. Figures are GOOD – up 20%.
> Sorry but no info from Spain yet. They had data problems – IT failure.
> If you need anything else, tell me.
> That's all.
>
> BD

Email 2

> Dear Ms Kyobashi,
>
> I hope all is well with you in Osaka. I am writing regarding the Thailand project which is scheduled to finish next month.
> Elena Sharp has informed me that there have been some delays and that we are running behind schedule. I should be grateful if you would email me to clarify the situation as soon as possible.
> Please do not hesitate to call me if I can be of any assistance.
> I look forward to hearing from you.
>
> Best wishes,
>
> Bob Davidson

Who do you write more formal emails to? Who do you write more informal emails to?

2 Complete 1–6 below by choosing from the formal and informal phrases (a–l).

1 Starting an email
Formal ....
Informal ....

2 Social opening
Formal ....
Informal ....

3 Reason for writing
Formal ....
Informal ....

4 Requesting
Formal ....
Informal ....

5 Offering help
Formal ....
Informal ....

6 Ending
Formal ....
Informal ....

a I should be grateful if you could email me ...
b Hi Pete
c If you need anything else, tell me.
d Send me (...) when you can.
e How's it going?
f About the meeting.
g That's all.
h I am writing regarding the Thailand project.
i Dear Ms Kyobashi
j Please do not hesitate to call me if I can be of any assistance.
k I look forward to hearing from you.
l I hope all is well with you in Osaka.

3 Write two emails.

1 Write an informal email to a colleague who you know well. Start with a social opening – ask how your colleague is. Ask for an opinion on a report you attach to the email.

2 Write a more formal email to a customer. Confirm a meeting and request some product information. Offer to help prepare for the meeting.

> **Remember**
>
> Whether you send a formal or an informal email depends on:
> • who you are sending the email to
> • what it's about
> • your relationship with the person.
>
> Getting the right tone is important in correspondence, so think about all of these before you start to write.

On the agenda

Speaking
News and current affairs

Social phrases
Talking about news

Vocabulary
The news and news media

9 Here is the news

Warm up

How often do you listen to the news?
What are today's big news stories?

Talking about news

1 Complete the dialogues with phrases (a–j) below.

Breaking news

A: Oh no! Have you seen this?
B: (1) .... ?
A: There's been a bad crash.
B: (2) .... Where?

Is it really news?

A: Look at this! Rosenberg beat Juventus!
B: Really? (3) .... ?
A: Three one to Rosenberg.
B: That's a big shock. (4) .... ?

News at work

A: Chris, did you know about Gemma Hudson? (5) .... she's leaving?
B: Really? (6) .... ?
A: She told me. She's leaving next month.
B: Actually (7) .... I didn't think she was very happy here.
A: That's right. I think she wants to move back to her home town.

A newspaper article

A: There was a good article in yesterday's paper.
B: (8) .... ?
A: Problems in schools. (9) .... ?
B: No, I didn't see the paper yesterday.
A: You should read it. I'll get a copy off the web and email it to you.
B: OK, thanks. (10) ....

a Have you heard that
b I'll look forward to reading it
c What was the score?
d How do you know that
e Did you see it
f What's happened
g That's awful
h Who scored?
i I'm not surprised
j What was it about

2 Now listen and check. ▶▶ 9.1

3 Practise reading the dialogues with a partner.

Have a go

Cover the dialogues above and make your own, starting with the words below.

Breaking news

Oh no! Have you seen this?

Is it really news?

Look at this! Rosenberg beat Juventus!

News at work

Chris, did you know about Gemma Hudson?

A newspaper article

There was a good article ...

Listen to this

Finding out what's going on

Before you listen Do you get your news from the TV, the radio, newspapers and magazines, or the internet? Which one do you prefer? Why?

1 Listen to what Elaine says about the news. Are these sentences true or false? ▶▶|9.2

   1 Elaine thinks that newspapers are not very popular in Britain.   T   F

   2 Elaine thinks TV news is very good.   T   F

   3 She thinks the internet is a good way to interact with the news.   T   F

   4 She watches the TV news every night.   T   F

Elaine Williams is a freelance newspaper journalist. She talks about her job, the news media, and how people find out what's going on.

2 Listen again and complete the sentences below.

   1 Elaine thinks the news in some newspapers is better than news on TV because it has more ....

   2 People who watch the news on television like the news presented as ....

   3 TV and radio programmes now get people to take part in debates. They have become more ....

   4 One advantage of the internet is that people are able to do their own ....

   5 Elaine finds out about news through ....

What do you think? Do you agree with what she says?
And do you:
- read news stories on the internet?
- contribute to internet chatlines or discussions?
- email internet news items to friends?

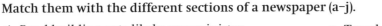

The words you need ... to talk about newspapers and news stories

1 In which part of a newspaper would you find these headlines?
Match them with the different sections of a newspaper (a–j).

   1 Road building cuts likely, says minister   **a** Travel
   2 UN Security Council meets on Middle East   **b** Books
   3 Tesco third quarter results disappoint   **c** Women
   4 Are you saving enough for your pension?   **d** Sport
   5 Skirts go even higher this spring   **e** Cinema
   6 New Flaubert short story discovery   **f** Home news
   7 Star walks out on Spielberg   **g** International news
   8 President calls for medals targets for next Olympics   **h** Personal finance
   9 Go with the jet set to Tahiti this summer   **i** Business news
  10 Work, husband and family – getting the balance right   **j** Fashion

Can you explain the meanings of the headlines?
Can you invent your own headline for each section?

Which paper do you normally read? How often do you read it?
Which section do you usually read first?

I usually read the obituaries first.

2 Complete the following dialogues with a word from the box.

1 A: You know that child that's been lost? He's been found safe and well after a week!

   B: Oh good! That's (1) .... news!

2 A: There was a plane crash in the Pacific Ocean last night. They haven't found any survivors so far.

   B: Oh no! That's (2) ....

3 A: There's only one more day of the world championships and so far we've only won three medals.

   B: Yes, that's rather (3) .... , isn't it?

4 A: It says here that world temperatures are increasing every year because of global warming.

   B: I know. It's very (4) ....

5 A: Scientists are working on a new treatment for skin cancer.

   B: That's (5) .... Show me.

6 A: Look! Here's another article in the newspaper about house prices.

   B: Not *another*! How (6) .... !

7 A: It says here that more people have clean water to drink because of the work of the aid organisations.

   B: That's (7) .... Water is the most important thing in life.

8 A: They're advertising really cheap flights to Italy until the end of the month! Do you want to go?

   B: How (8) .... ! I'd love to.

interesting
boring
disappointing
wonderful
terrible
excellent
worrying
exciting

What sorts of news do you find interesting? And boring?

It's time to talk

Talking about the news is an important skill for socialising at work and outside work.

Work in pairs. Student A should look at page 104, and Student B at page 108.

Remember

We often use the present perfect tense to talk about recent news.

Commenting on the news (TV/radio)
Have you seen/heard the news today?   *Yes, it's amazing / terrible / …*
                                        No, what's happened?

Looking at a newspaper
Have you seen this story about …?   *No, what's it about? What does it say?*

Talking about news
What do you think about … ?

On the agenda

Speaking
Describing work experience

Grammar
Past simple, present perfect simple and present perfect continuous
For, since and *ago*

Pronunciation
Weak forms of *have* and *for* with the present perfect

Henry de Montebello works for Russell Reynolds Associates. Find out what he says about recruiting top people for top companies.

10 Executive search

Warm up

How did you find out about the vacancy for your current job? How do you normally find out about job vacancies? How does your company or organisation recruit its employees?

Listen to this

Finding the right people

1 We talked to Henry de Montebello about his work in executive search consultancy. Listen and choose the correct information to complete these sentences. ▶▶10.1

1 Henry works in: Paris ▮ London ▮ Milan ▮

2 Henry worked in the USA: for 5 ▮ 10 ▮ 15 years ▮

3 He helps companies: train people ▮ set budgets ▮ solve problems ▮

4 The most important thing in his job is: to know his clients' needs well ▮ to have a big network of contacts ▮ to meet financial targets ▮

5 He likes his job because: he can travel ▮ he likes people ▮ the job is different every day ▮

2 Listen again and answer the questions. ▶▶10.1

1 Where did Henry study?

2 What did Henry do immediately after his studies?

3 When did Henry start work with Russell Reynolds Associates in Paris?

4 What do companies focus on more following the big scandals at Enron and WorldCom?

5 What kind of 'people at the top' do companies need, in Henry's opinion?

What do you think? Henry has been with one company for a long time. What about you? How many times would you like to change your organisation during your career? Or would you prefer to stay with one organisation?

Check your grammar

Past simple, present perfect simple and present perfect continuous

1 Match the example sentences (1–3) with the correct tense description (a–c) opposite.

1

I've written the report. │ Here you are!

I've lost my mobile phone. Have you seen it anywhere?
_____
NOW

2

I wrote the report last week.

I went to Italy five years ago on holiday.
_____
NOW

3

I've been writing the report.

There's my phone! I've been looking for it for the last three hours.
_____
NOW

a Past simple – to describe past activities, often with time expressions like *yesterday*, *last night*, etc.

b Present perfect continuous – to focus on recent past activities, which may or may not be finished.

c Present perfect simple – to report news (finished past activities with a result in the present).

2 Complete the grammar definitions below. Which is the present perfect simple and which is the present perfect continuous?

We form the .... with *have* + *been* + the *-ing* form of the verb.

We form the .... with *have* + the past participle.

3 Complete the sentences with *for*, *since* or *ago*. Then answer the question.

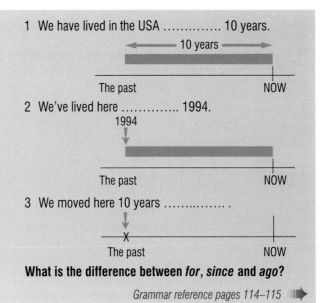

1 We have lived in the USA .... 10 years.

←——— 10 years ———→

The past   NOW

2 We've lived here .... 1994.

1994

The past   NOW

3 We moved here 10 years ....

The past   NOW

What is the difference between *for*, *since* and *ago*?

Grammar reference pages 114–115 ➡

Do it yourself

1 Correct the mistakes in these sentences.

1 Maria lives in London since three years.
2 Since when do you have this problem?
3 I have come here three years ago.
4 When are you arrived? Last night?
5 How long do you have been working for Microsoft?

2 Christopher Gent worked as the Chief Executive of Vodafone, Europe's leading mobile phone services provider. Complete the text below with the correct form of the verb in brackets.

Christopher Gent is one of the most well-known people in the business world today. He (1) .... (enjoy) a long career in business since he (2) .... (join) NatWest Bank in 1967 as a management trainee. He later (3) .... (work) as a computer services manager for Schroders for eight years. After that he (4) .... (take) a senior managing position at Baric in 1979. He (5) .... (move) to Vodafone in 1985 and (6) .... (become) Chief Executive in 1997. At that time BT (7) .... (be) top of the FTSE-500 as the largest company in the UK. However, since 1997 Vodafone (8) .... (establish) itself as a leading mobile phone service provider. More recently, Vodafone (9) .... (try) to expand its activities into the French mobile sector to complete its European coverage. In addition, Vodafone (10) .... (build) the network – it hopes to finish soon – and developing services for the next generation of mobile phones.

3 Complete the sentences with *for*, *since* or *ago*.

1 Christopher Gent has worked in business .... over 25 years.

2 His career began more than three decades .... with NatWest Bank.

3 He worked in banking .... only four years.

4 He was CEO of Vodafone .... six years.

5 A few years .... Vodafone bought its German rival, Mannesman.

6 The mobile phone sector has been experiencing many problems .... the year 2000 but Vodafone remains a market leader.

4 Complete the questions for the sentences in exercise 3.

1 How long ... ? How long has Christopher Gent worked in business?
2 When ... ?
3 How long ... ?
4 How long ... ?
5 When ... ?
6 How long ... ?

Listen and check your answers. ▶▶ 10.2

Weak forms of *have* and *for* with the present perfect

1 In Unit 1, we looked at weak forms in present simple and present continuous questions. Now listen to these questions. Underline the words which we pronounce with weak stress. ▶▶|10.3

How long have you worked in Paris?
How long have you been living here?
How long has he been working in sales?

Practise saying the sentences.

2 Now listen to the answers to the questions. Underline the words which we pronounce with weak stress. ▶▶|10.4

I've worked in Paris for five years.
I've been living here for a few months.
He's been working in sales for the last four months.

Practise saying the sentences.

3 *For* is pronounced in two ways when we use it in the middle of a sentence or phrase. Listen to the examples. ▶▶|10.5

… for five years …
… for a few months …

Why do we link 'for' and 'a' in the second example?

Note that we also pronounce *a*, *an* and *the* with weak stress in combination with *for*.

4 Listen and complete the phrases. ▶▶|10.6

1 for ....
2 for ....
3 for ....
4 for ....
5 for ....
6 for ....

Now listen again and repeat the phrases.

5 Ask your partner questions using the ideas below. Make sure you use weak stress in the questions and your partner uses *for* with weak stress in the answers.

How long have you lived … ?
How long have you been living … ?
How long have you worked … ?
How long have you been working … ?

It's time to talk

Work in pairs. Student A is an executive recruitment consultant.
Student B is applying for the job below.

CHEMCO ENERGY PLC

Chief Executive Officer
£150k p.a. plus benefits
Location: London, UK

The successful candidate will have:
- top level management experience in manufacturing industry
- some knowledge of the chemical and energy sectors
- a drive to succeed in international business
- experience of working in teams.

And will develop:
- a strategic vision for the whole enterprise
- market share in a competitive international environment.

The successful candidate will have:
- an MBA or equivalent and speak English to a high level.

Apply with CV and letter to Executive Recruitment Specialists Ltd (ERS Ltd),
PO Box 145, Mayfair, London W1 1AR.

Closing date for applications: 30 June.

Student A should look at page 105, and Student B at page 109.

Remember
- Use the past simple for finished activities: *Christopher Gent became Chief Executive Officer in 1997.*
- Use the present perfect simple or present perfect continuous to connect the past and now: *Henry has worked / has been working in executive recruitment for some time.*
- Use the present perfect simple for finished activities with a result in the present: *Vodafone has established itself as a leading mobile phone service provider.*

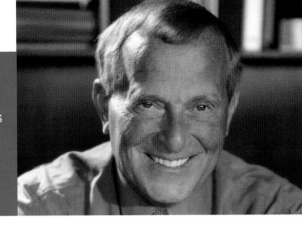

On the agenda

Speaking
Personal finance

Vocabulary
Finance and investments

**Communicating
at work**
Meetings 1: Asking for
and giving opinions

**Philip Cannon is an
independent financial
adviser. We asked him
for some investment
advice.**

11 Making money

Warm up

You have a loan of €20,000 for one year. You can invest it in any way
you want and you can keep any profits you make but you must pay back
the original sum at the end of the year. How will you invest the money?

Read on

Alternative investments

1 We asked Philip Cannon, an independent financial adviser, for advice on some
less common types of investment. Read Philip's advice and answer the questions.

1 Name two of the most frequent ways to invest money.
2 Identify two other ways to make money that Philip recommends.
3 Find two types of investment that Philip does not recommend.

The commonest ways to invest your money are to put
it in the bank to earn a little interest, or to invest in
stocks and shares. But if interest rates are low and the
stock exchange is showing no growth, you might look
for alternatives. What about some of the following?

Buy a second house to let. This can be a good option
in some areas but be sure that you get a rent that pays
not only the mortgage costs, but also the maintenance
of the property, and gives you a profit. If you do your
research well, a second house is often a good asset.
Buy a share in commercial property. A more exciting
option is to buy a share in a commercial property. If it
is in a good location where rents are high and there is
plenty of demand for properties, this can be a good
option.
Support a new business. This is perhaps the most
exciting of all. Many new businesses need capital
and you could be a 'business angel'. If the business
goes well, you can expect a healthy profit from your
investment. Nevertheless, many new businesses fail,
so the risks are high.

Buy art. Can you spot a future Picasso? Buy work by
young artists and hope they become famous. If that
is a risk too far, try established painters and sculptors.
However, be warned. You have to understand not only
art but also art fashions. Not recommended, unless
art really is your passion and you have lots of money!
Invest in furniture or antiques. Like buying art, this is
high risk and depends on changing fashions. You must
know the markets well.
Play the lottery. No. The newspapers love stories about
massive lottery wins, but you are more likely to make
some money from a new business idea than from the
lottery.
Do the football pools. Surprisingly, this is more likely to
bring you some winnings. The prizes are much smaller
than lottery jackpots, but there are more winners.
And you do not have to know anything about football!
Gamble on horse racing. Only bookmakers and very
few professional gamblers make a profit from gambling
on horse racing. An occasional visit to the races can be
good fun, but if you think you'll get rich, this is one to
avoid.

2 Read the text again and answer these questions about investments.

1 If you want to buy a house to let, what do you need to do first?
2 What are the most important considerations in buying commercial property?
3 What is a 'business angel'?
4 What is important to know about buying art?
5 Why is buying furniture or antiques similar to buying art?
6 Why not play the lottery?

What do you think? Have you tried any of these investment methods? Which ones?

The words you need ... to talk about finance and investments

1 Match the words (1–10) with the correct definition (a–j).

1	dividends	**a**	all the wealth that someone (or a company) has
2	investment	**b**	land, houses, buildings
3	bonds	**c**	part ownership of a company that can be bought or sold by members of the public
4	assets		
5	shares	**d**	a regular payment made to investors in a business
6	shareholders	**e**	the cost of borrowing money
7	mortgage	**f**	land or buildings used by businesses
8	property	**g**	people who own shares in a company
9	commercial property	**h**	putting money into something to get more money in the future
10	interest rates	**i**	loan to help buy a property
		j	government or company investments with a fixed interest rate

Test your partner Your partner should close his/her book. Read out the definition and see if your partner can remember the key word(s).

2 Complete the sentences with one of the words (1–10) above.

1 When the stock market is quiet, investors often buy .... as an alternative.

2 Buying a house is attractive, especially when the cost of a .... is low.

3 Mortgages cost little when .... are low.

4 Government .... are a safe but unexciting form of ....

5 A lot of people choose to buy .... in companies.

6 Company .... expect the company to make a profit and pay high ....

7 In a recession, companies are sometimes forced to sell off some of their ....

8 Buying a share in .... can be a good investment in locations where there is demand and rents are high.

The London Stock Exchange

How are the stock markets now? What about the price of property where you live?

It's time to talk

Take a chance! It could be you!
Play *THAT'S REALLY RICH!* –
an investment game for two players.
Student A should look at page 105,
and Student B at page 109.

Communicating at work

Meetings 1: Asking for and giving opinions

Do you take part in meetings in English? If so, what kind of meetings? Will you do this more in the future?

1 Listen to part of the conversation at a meeting between four colleagues in a medium- sized manufacturing company. What are they talking about? ▶▶|11.1

- A new research and development project ☐
- Financial planning and accounts control ☐
- Developing new markets ☐

Which speaker does not make his/her points well? Why not?

2 Listen to the conversation again. Which of these phrases do you hear? ▶▶|11.1

Asking for opinions
What do you think ... ? ☐
What's your opinion on ... ? ☐
What about ... ? ☐
(*Using a name*) Alex? ☐

Agreeing
I agree (with you / that). ☐
Absolutely. ☐
That's true. ☐
You're probably right. ☐
Yes ... ☐

Giving opinions
I think ... ☐
I don't think ... ☐
In my opinion ... ☐
My view is ... ☐

Disagreeing
Actually, I don't agree. ☐
But ... ☐
I'm not sure about that. ☐
I see what you mean but ... ☐
Yes, but ... ☐

3 Use words or phrases from exercise **2** to complete this extract from a conversation at a meeting. There are various possible answers.

A: (1) .... that most people work too many hours.

B: So (2) .... companies should do?

A: (3) .... they should have a 30-hour week maximum.

C: (4) .... It would be impossible. The costs are too high. Thirty hours is far too few.

B: (5) .... the French model? In France most people work 35 hours.

C: (6) .... Most people, in reality, work more than 35 hours.

A: (7) ....

4 Work in groups. Look at the opinions on the following topics. Choose two opinions to discuss. Do people in the group agree or disagree with the opinions? Why?

Work
Working hours 'People work too many hours – there should be more holidays.'
Open plan offices 'Open plan offices are a bad idea. People talk too much, they're too noisy and you can never get any work done.'
Email 'Email is the worst thing to happen to office communication in years. It wastes so much time.'

Outside work
Fashion 'Fashion is bad for us all, but especially women – it makes so many people unhappy.'
Television 'TV is the best form of entertainment and teaches people a lot.'
Modern music 'No one makes good music any more. All the best music was written years ago.'

> **Remember**
>
> Practise using these phrases in your discussions.
>
> *What do you think about ... ?*   *I think ...*
> *Do you agree?*   *Actually, no, I don't think I agree with that.*
> *Yes, sure, you're right.*   *Absolutely. I think Katy's right.*

On the agenda

Speaking
The environment

Social phrases
Getting directions

Vocabulary
Environmental problems

12 Ecotourism

Warm up

Are you good at giving directions?
Are other people? What do some
people do wrong?

Getting directions

1 Complete the dialogues with phrases (a–j) below.

By car

A: Excuse me. (1) .... the
Sculpture Park?
B: Yes, it is. Go straight on to the
roundabout. (2) .... Then
it's about four miles on
the left.
A: So, (3) .... Four miles.
B: Yes, it's easy. You can't go wrong.

Where is it?

A: Hello, I think I'm lost. Can you tell
me where the *Age d'Or* restaurant
is?
B: (4) ....
A: OK, thanks. I'll ask someone else.
B: Just a minute! I can see it,
(5) .... !
A: Oh yes, so it is! Thanks a lot.

Understanding the map

A: Excuse me. (6) .... where we
are?
B: Of course. We're here, next to
King's College. Where do you
want to go?
A: I'm looking for Bank Street.
(7) ....
B: It's not far, (8) .... I'm going
that way.

Getting around a big building

A: Sorry to bother you, (9) .... ,
isn't it?
B: Yes, it is. Where do you want to
be?
A: (10) .... the Brunel Room.
Is it near here?
B: Yes, down this corridor and
through that door, then it's on the
left.

a I'm sorry, I'm not from here	**f** I'll show you
b I'm looking for	**g** it's just over there
c Do you know where it is?	**h** Can you show me
d this is the fifth floor	**i** Turn right
e straight on to the roundabout and right	**j** Is this the right road to

2 Now listen and check. ▶▶ 12.1

3 Practise reading the dialogues with a partner.

Have a go

Cover the dialogues above and make your own,
starting with the words below.

By car

Excuse me. Is this ... ?

Where is it?

Hello, I think I'm lost.

Understanding the map

Excuse me. Can you ... ?

**Getting around a big
building**

Sorry to bother you ...

Listen to this

Tourism and the environment: the Eden Project

Before you listen Is tourism bad for the environment or can it have a positive impact? What is ecotourism?

1 Chris Wait works as a consultant on forestry and environmental projects. Listen to him talking about the Eden Project. Are these sentences true or false? ▶▶|12.2

   1 The biomes contain plants from all over the world.   T   F

   2 The Eden Project is a kind of theme park.   T   F

   3 There is a physical problem because of the number of visitors. T   F

   4 The Eden Project is the vision of a small group of people.   T   F

   5 Cornwall had a lot of economic problems.   T   F

2 Listen again and answer these questions. ▶▶|12.2

   1 What does Chris say is the most important thing about the Eden Project?
   2 What does the Eden Project make people do?
   3 What is the biggest danger in ecotourism?
   4 Name two ways in which the Eden Project has helped the local community.
   5 Who is Tim Smit?

What do you think? Chris says: 'We can have a vision and we can all help to make a difference.' Do you agree? Is this true for you in your work?

Chris Wait is an expert on trees. He talks about the Eden Project in Cornwall, in the south-west of England.

Visitors to the Eden Project can see plants from all over the world in different controlled environments, in biomes.

The words you need ... to talk about the environment

1 Here are some tips about helping the environment.
Match the verb on the left to the correct word(s) on the right.

   1 recycle   **a** electrical appliances
   2 save   **b** public transport
   3 use   **c** glass, metal and paper
   4 switch off   **d** environmental policies at work
   5 share   **e** cars
   6 reduce   **f** traffic congestion
   7 support   **g** the environment
   8 protect   **h** energy

2 Replace the words in *italics* with a word or phrase from the box.

   1 Energy production from burning *oil, coal and gas* increases CO_2 emissions which damage the environment.
   2 Too much *use of power resources* increases *the general rise in temperatures around the world*.
   3 More people work in *agriculture* in developing countries than in developed countries.
   4 All individuals, businesses and organisations should try to reduce *negative impact on the environment*.
   5 *Buildings, transportation and communication systems* projects are important in raising living standards.
   6 It is important to protect *the land, air and water*.

What do you do for the environment?
What more could you do?
Which kind of environmental damage do you think is the worst?

The average British household produces about a tonne of waste every year. How about yours?

pollution   global warming

the natural environment   fossil fuels

energy consumption

infrastructure   farming

Test your partner Say the words in *italics*. Your partner must remember the right words in the box.

It's time to talk

With your partner, decide on ways in which you and your organisation can help to protect the environment.
Decide which things you or your partner do already.

Now decide what you and your partner could do in the future.

	Do already		Will do / won't do	
	YOU	PARTNER	YOU	PARTNER
Use public transport to get to work				
Organise car sharing to work				
Cut the number of spaces in the car park				
Offer free bicycles to all employees who agree to cycle to work				
Recycle all glass, metal and paper				
Fix the number of photocopies employees can make every day				
Switch off electric lights in empty offices				
Switch off unused computers				
Switch off other unused electrical appliances				
Send all correspondence by email				
Your ideas:				

Remember

Getting directions
- *Excuse me, can you tell me how to get to ...?*
- *I'm looking for ...*
- *Straight on / turn left / turn right / it's on the left / right / it's in front of you ...*

The environment
It's good for the environment when you help to:
- *reduce pollution / traffic (congestion) / waste / energy consumption / global warming*
- *save energy*
- *use public transport,* etc.

On the agenda

Speaking
Discussing future plans

Grammar
Future 1: *will*, *going to* and the present continuous

Pronunciation
Contractions with pronouns and auxiliary verbs

We discussed the number of women on the boards of companies with Terje (Norwegian), Ingrid (German) and Pierre (French).

13 Changing culture

Warm up

Only 2% of the board members of Europe's top companies are women. Why do you think this figure is so low?

Listen to this

Guardian Unlimited

ING DIRECT it's your money we're saving
savings account © click here to find out more.

Sign in | Register

Go to: [Guardian Unlimited home] [Go]

GuardianUnlimited Special reports

Home | UK | Business | Online | World dispatch | The Wrap | Weblog | Talk | Search
The Guardian | World | News guide | Arts | Special reports | Columnists | Audio | Help | Quiz

Special report
Gender issues

Norway sets 40% female quota for boardrooms

Companies insist too few qualified women are available to fill posts

Andrew Osborn in Oslo
Thursday August 1, 2002
The Guardian

[Search this site] [Go]

Blazing a trail for women's rights, egalitarian Norway is about to become the first country in the world to insist on female quotas for company boardrooms.

Norway sets female quota for boardrooms

1 Listen to Terje, Ingrid and Pierre discussing a new law in Norway to increase the number of women in boardrooms. Are these sentences true or false? ▶▶|13.1

1 Terje thinks the quota is a good idea.   T ☐ F ☐
2 Norway will introduce the quota system over a period of five years.   T ☐ F ☐
3 Ingrid's company established its own quota for women last year.   T ☐ F ☐
4 According to Pierre, many women already work as top managers in France.   T ☐ F ☐
5 Ingrid agrees with the idea of a quota system.   T ☐ F ☐

2 Listen again and answer these questions. ▶▶|13.1

1 What does Terje see as one advantage of having more women in top management?
2 Why does Terje think the implementation of a quota will take time?
3 According to Pierre, what percentage of women work as managers in the IT sector in France?
4 Why does Pierre think a quota system will create recruitment problems?
5 Why does Ingrid think it will take time to change the position of women at work?

What do you think? Pierre says: 'A quota is not a solution, believe me.' Do you agree? Why? Why not?

Check your grammar

Future 1: *will*, *going to* and the present continuous

We can use *will*, *going to* and the present continuous to speak about the future.

1 Read these sentences and underline the future verb forms.

1 I'll call you at the end of the month.
2 Are you going to push this process in Norway immediately?
3 I'm seeing our directors tomorrow.
4 I'll check and I can get back to you on that.
5 Companies in Norway are going to fix quotas for women in management.
6 We're introducing this change next year.

2 Now match each of these future forms to the correct grammar description (a–c).

will ☐   *going to* ☐   present continuous ☐

a To describe decisions and plans we have already made
b To describe fixed future arrangements, especially for personal travel and meetings
c To describe future actions which we decide to do at the moment of speaking, especially when we promise or offer to do something

Grammar reference pages 115–16 ➡

Do it yourself

1 Correct the mistakes in these sentences.

1 Don't worry. I'll to solve the problem immediately.
2 Sorry, that's my phone ringing. I'm turning it off.
3 I can't come for lunch with you. I'll do some training in the gym.
4 You look stressed. I'm going to help you with that report, if you want.
5 I'm going to fly to Brussels tomorrow at 8.55.

2 Choose *will* or *going to* to complete the dialogues.

1 A: Do you have any plans for tonight?
  B: Yes, *I'm going to watch* / *I'll watch* a video.

2 A: Can you email me the report?
  B: Sorry, I forgot. *I'm going to do* / *I'll do* it immediately.

3 A: Do you want to join us for lunch?
  B: Thanks but *I'm going to work* / *I'll work* through lunch. I've got too much to do.

4 A: There's a problem with the new product.
  B: I know. *I'm going to discuss* / *I'll discuss* it with the person responsible later today.

5 A: Did you send Peter the budget figures?
  B: Sorry, I haven't had time. I promise *I'm going to do* / *I'll do* it before I go home.

6 A: Would you like something to drink?
  B: Yes, thanks. *I'm going to have* / *I'll have* an orange juice, please.

3 Emma calls Mark, a colleague in the company's human resources department, to discuss arrangements for a workshop. Complete the conversation with the correct form of the verb in brackets using *will*, *going to* or the present continuous. In some cases more than one answer is possible.

EMMA: Hi, Mark. It's Emma. Can you give me some more details about the workshop next month?

MARK: OK. (1) .... (I / help) if I can.

EMMA: Well, firstly, according to the schedule, when (2) .... (I / present)?

MARK: Your presentation is on Tuesday 8 September at 10 am. Is that OK?

EMMA: Wednesday at 10 would be better for me.

MARK: Fine. (3) .... (I / change) your time to the Wednesday. OK?

EMMA: Thanks. And what about hotel accommodation?

MARK: It's all arranged. (4) .... (Everyone / stay) in the Manor. It was the cheapest.

EMMA: That's fine. (5) .... (I / tell) Rachel and Sam. They asked me this morning.

MARK: You can also tell them that (6) .... (I / send) everybody an information pack with the hotel details, probably at the end of next week, I'm not sure yet.

EMMA: OK, (7) .... (I / let) them know. In fact, (8) .... (we / meet) later today at 4 so I can tell them then, if I don't forget.

MARK: Right. So, any plans for the rest of the morning?

EMMA: Yes. (9) .... (I / just / finish) a few reports and then it's lunch.

MARK: Sounds good. Thanks for your call. And don't forget to tell Rachel and Sam!

EMMA: Thanks, (10) .... (I / not / forget). Bye.

MARK: Bye.

It was the cheapest.

Listen and check your answers. ▶▶|13.2

Contractions with pronouns and auxiliary verbs

1 Listen and complete the conversation with the missing words. ▶▶|13.3

EMMA: I still (1) .... had the workshop schedule. Did you send it?

MARK: Yes. (2) .... you receive it by email last week?

EMMA: No. I (3) .... have any information and (4) .... a bit stressed.

MARK: (5) .... worry. (6) .... send you another schedule right now.

Why do we generally use contractions rather than long forms in conversation?

2 Contractions

- When speaking we often contract pronouns and auxiliary verbs (*be*, *do*, *have* and modal verbs) into short forms:
  ~~We are~~ We're going to work late tonight.
  ~~She will~~ She'll call you later.
  I ~~do not~~ don't have his telephone number.

- We do not contract the pronoun and auxiliary verb at the end of sentences:
  Are you going to phone him today?
  Yes, I am. [Not ~~Yes, I'm.~~]
  However, we can contract *not* at the end of sentences:
  Can you come to the meeting?
  No, I can't. [Not ~~No, I cannot.~~]

- We sometimes stress the auxiliary verb for emphasis. We do not contract in these cases:
  A: Don't forget her birthday again, please!
  B: I <u>am</u> sorry. I <u>will</u> remember next year.

Contract, where possible, the long forms in the following dialogue.

MARK: Hello, I am calling to check you got the schedule. Have you got it?

EMMA: Yes, I have. It is here in my mailbox but I cannot open it.

MARK: I do not understand.

EMMA: It is very strange. I have never had any problems with emails from you before.

MARK: Did you save the document first?

EMMA: Yes, I did. It did not make any difference. Can you resend it?

MARK: OK, I will send it again straightaway. Please phone me if it does not open.

EMMA: Do not worry. I will!

Listen and check your answers. ▶▶|13.4

Practise reading the dialogue with the contractions.

It's time to talk

Role-play a career development interview between a manager and his/her staff member. Student A should look at page 105, and Student B at page 109.

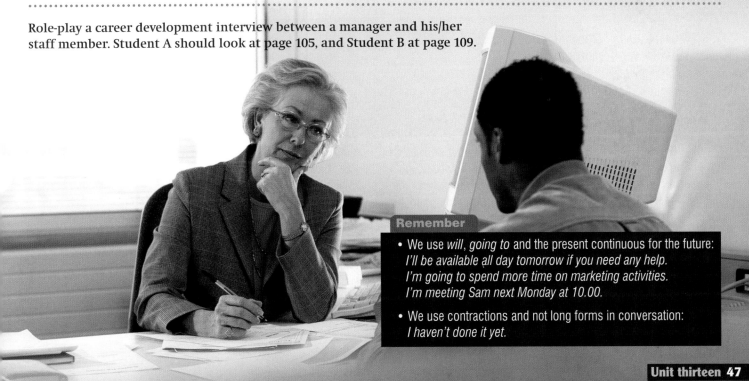

Remember

- We use *will*, *going to* and the present continuous for the future:
  I'll be available all day tomorrow if you need any help.
  I'm going to spend more time on marketing activities.
  I'm meeting Sam next Monday at 10.00.

- We use contractions and not long forms in conversation:
  I haven't done it yet.

On the agenda

Speaking
Customer satisfaction

Vocabulary
Customer service

Communicating at work
Telephoning 2: Making and changing arrangements

Wal*Mart is the USA's biggest supermarket chain and the world's largest private employer. It was started by Sam Walton (1918–92) in 1962.

14 The customer is always right

Warm up

Think of an organisation which has good customer service. What makes its customer service special?

Read on

Ten foot attitude

1 Read these extracts based on Wal*Mart's website about the company and its customer service. Match the headings with the paragraphs. There are two extra headings which you don't need to use.

1 The secret of service success
2 The beginnings of Wal*Mart
3 Giving extra service
4 Customer problems
5 Service to the community
6 Thank you for your business

2 Read the paragraphs again, then answer these questions.

1 What does Wal*Mart call its employees?
2 What examples of good customer service does the website give?
3 What keeps Wal*Mart customers coming back?
4 What is the 'Ten foot attitude'?
5 What does the website say Sam Walton did at university?
6 How does Wal*Mart help the community?

What do you think? Would the 'Ten foot attitude' work in your organisation, or in your country? Would the other details of Wal*Mart customer service work in your organisation and in your country?

At Wal*Mart, we receive letters daily from customers about individual associates who have given extra service. Sometimes the service was as simple as a smile or an associate remembering their name. Other times they write about more special things – for instance, Sheila who jumped in front of a car to stop a little boy from being hit, and Annette who gave up the toy she wanted for her own son so that a customer's son could have it for his birthday.

Sam Walton said to Wal*Mart associates: 'Let's say thank you to customers for coming to our stores. Let's give better service – more than our customers expect.' As Wal*Mart associates we want to show that we are grateful to our customers for shopping in our stores – in every way we can! We believe that doing this is what keeps our customers coming back to Wal*Mart again and again.

One of Wal*Mart's secrets in customer service is our 'Ten foot attitude'. Sam Walton said to associates: 'I want you to promise that whenever you come within ten feet☆ of a customer, you will look him in the eye, greet him and ask him if you can help him. I learned at university always to look ahead and speak to the person coming toward me. If I knew them, I would call them by name, but even if I didn't I would still speak to them. Before long, I probably knew more students than anybody in the university.'

Sam Walton believed that each Wal*Mart store should help the community in ways that its customers want. For example, stores help local schools, hospitals and groups in need. And nationally, Wal*Mart asks its customers to 'buy American', to help protect jobs.

☆ About three metres

The words you need ... to talk about customer service

1 How many times does the word 'service' occur in the text? What words does it go with each time? How many other words can you think of which often go with 'service'?

2 Look at the different types of service (1–6). Match the words in the box with the types of service.

1 great ....

2 poor ....

3 cheap ....

4 expensive ....

5 rapid ....

6 individual ....

Five star service

pricey   low cost   fast   quick
five star   unsatisfactory   exceptional
below standard   personal   costly

3 Complete the sentences about service with words from the box.

1 We are always .... service, 24 hours a day, 365 days a year.

2 We only .... this service to our Gold Card customers.

3 We provide a wide .... of services to our Silver Card customers.

4 We can .... our service to fit your exact needs.

5 We were nearly out of petrol so we stopped at a motorway service ...., filled up the car and had a coffee.

6 There is a small service .... of €20 which you pay if one of our engineers is called out.

7 You can take out a service .... which covers any breakdowns or other problems for two years.

8 The service .... is growing but manufacturing is getting smaller.

9 We always aim to provide the highest .... of service.

standards   sector   range   charge
tailor   offer   agreement   at your   station

Breakdowns are covered

It's time to talk

Think of an example of customer service – good or bad – that you have experienced and answer the questionnaire. Now interview your partner using the questionnaire.

CUSTOMER FEEDBACK – OUR SEARCH FOR EXCELLENCE!

We are committed to offering exceptional customer service. Your feedback is important. Please take a few moments to fill out the questionnaire below.

1 Was your experience with our organisation a positive one?
■ Yes
■ No
Please comment: ....
....

2 How satisfied were you with the overall service provided by our organisation?
■ More than satisfied
■ Satisfied
■ Not satisfied
Please comment: ....
....

3 Were staff:
■ quick to respond?
■ helpful?
■ polite?
■ professional?
Please comment: ....

4 Were you in contact with a particular staff person who was especially helpful to you?
■ Yes
■ No
Please comment: ....
....

5 Do you have any other suggestion(s) or comment(s) to help us improve our service?
Please comment: ....
....
....
....

Communicating at work

Telephoning 2: Making and changing arrangements

How often do you use the phone in English to set up meetings, or to change plans for a meeting?

1 Listen to Chaminda Jay making arrangements for a meeting. Complete the details in his diary. ▶▶|14.1

2 Listen again. Which of these phrases do you hear? ▶▶|14.1

Referring to last contact
We spoke on the phone yesterday. ▢
I sent you an email about our meeting. ▢

Suggesting a meeting
I'd like to have a meeting soon, if possible. ▢
Can we meet next week some time? ▢

Fixing a time
What day would suit you? ▢
When would be a good time to meet? ▢

Confirming
I'll send an email to confirm. ▢
Good, we agreed Thursday at 10. ▢

3 Later Charlotte rings back because she has a problem. What's the problem and what's the solution? Change the diary entry above. ▶▶|14.2

4 Listen again, pausing the recording, and complete the sentences below. ▶▶|14.2

Changing an arrangement

Unfortunately, (1) ....

Explaining the reason

I'm afraid (2) .... all day on Wednesday.

Finding a new time

Could we meet (3) .... instead?

If we say Thursday morning, (4) .... ?

Apologising

I hope (5) ....

5 Role-play a phone call with your partner. Fix a meeting (date, time and place). One of you should then phone back to change the appointment. Now change roles.

MAY

Tuesday 9

Train to London, depart 6.25, arrive 8.18
Conference all day
Hotel: Victoria House, Gray's Inn Road
Leave Thursday evening

Wednesday 10

Charlotte Bennett - where
and when?

Thursday 11

Remember

When making arrangements, it's usually a good idea to:
• repeat the arrangements to confirm key information
• offer to send an email to confirm.

On the agenda

Speaking
Homes

Social phrases
Visiting someone's home for dinner

Vocabulary
Houses and homes

Warm up

What kind of home do you live in?
How much time do you spend on DIY?
Do you like working on your home?

15 An interesting place to live

Visiting someone's home for dinner

1 Complete the dialogues with phrases (a–h) below.

Welcome

A: Hello, nice to see you.
B: Thank you. (1) ....
A: No, not at all. Perfect timing. (2) ....
B: Thank you.

Two small gifts

A: Did you have any problems finding us?
C: No, it was easy. Here, (3) ....
A: Oh, that wasn't necessary – but they really are beautiful. Thank you very much.
C: And (4) ....
A: Oh, that's very kind. In fact, we both love chocolate!

The home

C: What a beautiful house. (5) .... ?
A: Yes, we've been here ten years now. It didn't look like this when we moved in!
C: It's beautiful. And (6) .... photographs too.
A: Yes, Peter loves taking pictures. Do you like photography?

Saying goodbye

B: It's been a wonderful evening. (7) ....
D: Not at all. It was our pleasure.
B: (8) .... Thank you so much.
D: Don't mention it. It was great to see you.

a And the meal was delicious
b you have some lovely
c Thank you for having us
d Have you lived here long
e Let me take your coats
f these. I hope you like chocolates
g we've brought you some flowers
h I'm sorry we're a bit late

Have a go

Cover the dialogues above and make your own, starting with the words below.

Welcome

Hello, nice to see you.

Two small gifts

Did you have any problems finding us?

The home

What a beautiful house.

Saying goodbye

It's been a wonderful evening.

2 Now listen and check. ▶▶15.1

3 Practise reading the dialogues with a partner.

Listen to this

Living in a windmill

Before you listen Would you like to live in a windmill? Why? Why not?

1 Listen to Susanna talking about her home. Are these sentences true or false? ▶▶|15.2

   1 Susanna bought the windmill 20 years ago.   T ☐ F ☐

   2 Susanna made the windmill into a home herself.   T ☐ F ☐

   3 The windmill has five floors.   T ☐ F ☐

   4 The windmill is in a village.   T ☐ F ☐

   5 Her children don't like living in the windmill.   T ☐ F ☐

2 Listen again and complete the sentences in as few words as you can. ▶▶|15.2

   1 Susanna found her home in the ....

   2 The ground floor room is more than ....

   3 The best thing about the house, for Susanna, is ....

   4 Not everyone likes sleeping at the top because ....

   5 Next door to the house they have ....

   6 The main disadvantage of the house is that it's ....

What do you think? Susanna thinks there is a link between her choice of home and her favourite fairy story. What would your perfect house be like? Where would it be? How many rooms would it have? What special features would there be?

Susanna Longley lives in a windmill in the east of England. She talks about her unusual home.

The words you need ... to talk about houses and homes

1 <u>The rooms in your house</u>

How many rooms in a house can you name?
Complete the sentences with one of the rooms (a–k).

   1 We cook in the ....

   2 We have our evening meal in the ....

   3 We sit and watch TV in the ....

   4 I work on my computer in the ....

   5 We hang up our coats in the ....

   6 We keep the washing machine and freezer in the ....

   7 When people come to stay, they sleep in the ....

   8 The children's toys are kept in the ....

   9 I keep my wine in the ....

   10 We keep the car in the ....

   11 When the sun shines, we sit outside on the ....

a garage
b play room
c guest bedroom
d terrace
e kitchen
f lounge / living room / sitting room
g utility room
h study
i dining room
j hall
k cellar

Which is your favourite room at home? Why?

2 Home features

Match these features of a house to the illustrations (a–i).

1 roof
2 shelves
3 staircase
4 pictures
5 garden
6 curtains
7 door
8 floor
9 heating

3 Jobs in the home

How many household jobs can you name?
Complete the sentences explaining different jobs in the home with a word from the list.

1 'I do the ....' means I wash the clothes.

2 'I do the ....' means I wash the dishes.

3 'I do the ....' means I do general cleaning.

4 'I do the ....' means I flatten and press the clothes after they have been washed.

5 ' I .... things ....' means I tidy the house.

6 'I .... the table' means I put things on the table before a meal.

7 'I .... the table' means I take things off the table after a meal.

8 'I .... the bed' means I tidy the bed when I get up.

9 'I .... the dog for a walk' means I go out with the dog for some exercise.

10 'I .... the rubbish' means I place the things we want to throw away in the bin outside the house.

clear
put out
washing
washing-up
lay
make
take
put away
ironing
housework

Which household job do you least like? Which ones do you not mind doing? Who does most of the housework in your household?

It's time to talk

Work in pairs. Student A should look at pages 105–106, and Student B at page 110.

> **Remember**
>
> When you are talking about your home, say:
> • what kind of home it is – *apartment, detached house, cottage in the country*, ...
> • what rooms you have – *kitchen, guest bedroom, play room*, ...
> • what makes it special – *a beautiful view, a big garden, a double garage*, ...

Revision 1 Units 1–15

Grammar

1 Complete these sentences with the correct tenses.

1 I .... (work) for a school management company called Educo Unlimited. The business .... (manage) 24 private schools in Europe and .... (provide) consultancy services to local government.

2 I .... (plan) a trip to Munich for a conference in two months. The conference .... (be) about financial control. Over 400 people .... (come).

3 I .... (just / reverse) out of the car park when I .... (hear) an awful sound. It was the boss's car!

4 Oh, no! I .... (write) this report all morning and my computer .... (just / crash). Why didn't I save the document?

5 I .... (work) here for over 12 months now. I .... (work) on this project for most of this time but finally it .... (almost / finish).

2 Correct the mistakes in these sentences.

1 Seville is more hot than Paris in summer.
2 Bill Gates is the world's richer man.
3 London is not big as Tokyo.
4 The 2002 World Cup was the most bad ever.
5 Wal*Mart has the more big turnover of any retail business in the world.
6 Yesterday I played squash but I played bad.
7 My friend Sam plays squash more good than I do.
8 The weather in northern Spain is not so hot like in the south.

Pronunciation

1 Listen to six exchanges in a conversation. Does the second speaker show interest (✓) or no interest (✗)? ▶▶R1.1

1 ☐ rise/fall ....
2 ☐ rise/fall ....
3 ☐ rise/fall ....
4 ☐ rise/fall ....
5 ☐ rise/fall ....
6 ☐ rise/fall ....

Listen again. Does the intonation rise (↗) or fall (↘)? Write down the words that the second speaker uses. ▶▶R1.1

Now listen to the complete conversation and check your answers. ▶▶R1.2

2 Here are some stressed words taken from a conversation. Can you guess what the missing words in the sentences are?

A: Where .... work?

B: I work .... film company in Bristol.

A: What .... do?

B: .... editor.

A: How long .... working there?

B: .... six years.

A: How long .... lived in Bristol?

B: .... ten years.

Now listen and check. ▶▶R1.3

Business vocabulary

1 Replace the words in *italics* with a word from the box which has a similar meaning.

Volkswagen, which was (1) *started* in 1935 by Ferdinand Porsche, (2) *makes* more cars than any other European automotive company, and has seven (3) *plants* in Germany as well as others in Spain, the Czech Republic, Brazil, Argentina, Canada, the USA and China. The company has a (4) *total sales income* of over €88bn a year. It sells cars (5) *all over the world* and has 50 per cent (6) *of the total car market* in China. The Volkswagen Group is (7) *divided* into four main brands: Volkswagen, Audi, Skoda and SEAT. The company (8) *has a staff of* over 320,000 people, almost half of them in Germany.

market share worldwide organised employs
produces turnover founded factories

2 Match the words (1–9) with the definitions (a–i).

1 shareholders
2 investment
3 loan
4 multinational
5 inflation
6 debt
7 headquarters
8 employees
9 dividend

a liabilities, or what someone owes someone else
b place where a company's senior management is located
c money put into a business in the hope of earning a future profit
d the annual rise in prices
e money borrowed, often from a bank
f people who work for an organisation
g people who have put money into a company and own a part of it
h a regular payment made to investors in a business
i large business with production and sales in different countries

Business communication

Complete this extract from a telephone conversation with phrases from the box.

A: Amtel Communications. Good morning.

B: Hello, I'd (1) .... Mr Kossakowski in the sales office, please.

A: One moment, I'll (2) put ....

*****

C: Sales office. Good morning.

B: Hello, (3) .... to Mr Kossakowski, please?

C: I'm sorry he's not available just now. He's in a meeting. Would you like (4) .... ?

B: Yes, please. It's about our meeting next week. Unfortunately I've (5) ....
(6) .... later in the afternoon?
I hope (7) .... for him.

C: I'll give him the message.

B: Thanks. Could you (8) .... me when he's back? He's got my number.

to leave a message	like to speak to
ask him to phone	could I speak
Could we meet	you through
it's not a problem	got a problem now

Social phrases

Match the sentences (1–10) with the correct responses (a–j).

1 Here, we've brought you some chocolates.
2 Can you tell me where the Rialto is, please?
3 Look at this – another train crash.
4 Are you all right?
5 We'd like a map of the city.
6 It's been a wonderful evening.
7 There's a good story on the BBC web page.
8 I'm back and feeling better!
9 Where do we buy the tickets?
10 Let me take your coats.

a I'm sorry I'm not from here.
b There's a machine over there.
c No, I don't feel very well.
d Not at all. It was our pleasure.
e What's it about?
f Oh, that wasn't necessary. Thank you very much.
g Great! We've missed you.
h Thank you.
i Yes, here you are.
j That's awful. Where?

General vocabulary

Complete the sentences with words from the box.

1 I enjoy learning about a country's history and .... when I'm on holiday. The last holiday I had was visiting National Parks in the States. The .... in Arizona is fantastic.

2 Tonight's .... of *Romeo and Juliet* at the Corn Exchange has been cancelled.

3 We can look at the .... section of the newspaper – it might give us some ideas for our next holiday.

4 Staff are being encouraged to .... as much paper as possible.

5 Look at this place – it's a mess. Do you ever do any .... ? You can start by doing the ....

6 I prefer reading books by .... writers. I don't really enjoy reading the classics.

7 Can you recommend the name of a cheap .... ? We're on a tight budget and can't really afford a ....

8 I've got some .... news. You've won first prize in the competition!

9 Don't forget to .... your computer before you leave the office.

10 I had a really boring weekend – I spent all Saturday putting up some ....

shelves	culture	performance	housework
contemporary	scenery	travel	washing-up
recycle	bed and breakfast	hotel	switch off
wonderful			

On the agenda

Speaking
Describing quantities

Grammar
Quantifiers: *all, every, each, most, much, many, a few, a little, no, any, some*

Pronunciation
Linking

Vanessa Chen works at the Sherwood Taipei Hotel in Taiwan. She talks about her job and the Taiwanese economy.

16 Taiwan – still a tiger

Warm up

Where do most of your organisation's customers come from? How many are from foreign markets? Why do customers use your organisation's products or services?

An IT-based economy

Listen to this

The Taipei Sherwood Hotel – the best in Taipei?

Real competitive advantage

1 We interviewed Vanessa Chen, a service manager responsible for corporate accounts at the Sherwood Taipei Hotel in Taiwan. Are these sentences true or false? ▶▶16.1

1 Most guests at the Sherwood Taipei Hotel are business people.   T ☐   F ☐

2 The hotel has over 400 rooms.   T ☐   F ☐

3 Banking is the most important business activity in Taiwan.   T ☐   F ☐

4 The hotel is very optimistic about future business.   T ☐   F ☐

5 The biggest attraction for guests of the Sherwood Taipei Hotel is its low price.   T ☐   F ☐

2 Listen again and answer the questions. ▶▶16.1

1 What percentage of the hotel's guests come from Japan?

2 Why does the hotel get so many guests from the banking sector?

3 How much of the world's semiconductor production is located in Taiwan?

4 Which is the biggest foreign market for the Taiwanese economy?

5 How does the hotel know what its regular customers like?

What do you think? Vanessa says: 'The real difference in our business, the real competitive advantage, is in the great level of customer service we offer to each customer.' What is the 'real competitive advantage' of your organisation?

Check your grammar

Quantifiers

We can use quantifiers to describe the quantity of something.

All, each, every (total quantity)
Look at the following examples.

Every room has a full internet service.
All guests have a personal profile on the hotel database.
When *each* guest returns to the hotel, we know exactly how to keep him or her happy.

Which of these quantifiers only combine with singular countable nouns?

Most, many, much, a lot of (large quantity)

Choose the correct quantifiers to complete the sentences.
More than one answer is possible in some sentences.

In Taiwan, (1) _most / much / a lot of_ businesses are IT-related.
We do (2) _a lot of / most / much_ conference work and
weddings at weekends.
How (3) _much / many_ work do you do with the corporate
sector?
(4) _Most / Much / A lot of_ families go to other hotels.
Which of these quantifiers combine with <u>both</u> plural countable
<u>and</u> uncountable nouns?

A few, a little (small quantity)

Complete the sentences with _a few_ or _a little_.

You can find (5) .... information about Taiwan on
the hotel website.
We had (6) .... customer complaints last year.
Which of these quantifiers only combines with uncountable
nouns?

No, (not) any (zero quantity)

Complete the sentences with _any_ or _no_.

All my work is with the corporate sector so I don't spend
(7) .... time with tour groups.
We have (8) .... big worries about business in
the future.

> Important note: _some_ and _any_
> We can use _some_ in positive sentences to describe
> unspecified quantities:
> We only offer large discounts to _some_ customers.
> (We don't specify how many customers and the number
> is limited.)
>
> We can use _some_ in requests and offers:
> Could you bring _some_ water, please?
> Would you like _some_ coffee?
>
> We can use _any_ in questions and negatives about quantity:
> Do you have _any_ questions?

Grammar reference page 116 ⏩

Do it yourself

1 Correct the mistakes in these sentences.

1 How much years have you lived here?

2 How many information do you have about Taiwan?

3 We only have a few information about our
customers. We need more for our database.

4 We have much things to talk about.

5 There aren't no tourists here in the winter.

**2 Choose the correct word(s) to complete the sentences
about Taiwan.**

Tourism Taiwan has over 50 international class hotels
with over 17,000 rooms. (1) _All / Each_ major cities and
resorts have hotels that provide excellent service.
Health (2) _Each / All_ Taiwan resident over the age of 70
can enjoy free medical care, as well as subsidised
public transportation and entertainment costs.
Geography Taiwan consists of (3) _many / much_ islands,
including the Penghu Archipelago and Mazu,
Changshu and Quemoy.
Agriculture (4) _Much / Many_ agriculture in Taiwan is
based around rice cultivation (34%), but there is also
(5) _some / a few_ sugar, tea and fruit production.
Education (6) _Most / Some_ high school students (over
95%) who complete their nine years of compulsory
education go on to study in higher education.
Economy The service sector now represents over 50%
of the Taiwanese economy. However, (7) _a few / a little_
traditional industries such as wood and leather remain
important.

**Write similar sentences about your country or
another country you know well.**

**3 Choose the correct quantifiers. In each question,
there are two possible answers.**

1 A: Are there _any / a little / a lot of_ economic sectors
 bigger than IT in the Taiwanese economy?
 B: No. IT is larger than all other manufacturing
 sectors.

2 A: Are _many / all / every_ people in Taiwan Buddhist?
 B: Around 94% are Buddhist, Confucian or Taoist.

3 A: Is there _a lot of / many / much_ rain in the rainy
 season?
 B: Absolutely.

4 A: Does Taiwan invest _much / a lot of / a few_ money
 in conserving the natural environment?
 B: Yes. In fact, Taiwan has six large national parks.

5 A: Are there _many / any / a little_ direct flights to
 China now?
 B: Some. People often travel via Hong Kong or Macau.

Test your partner What does your partner know
about Taiwan? Write down questions based on
information in exercise 2. After answering, your
partner must tell you if your questions are
grammatically correct.

Linking

1 Listen and complete the conversation with the missing words. ▶▶|16.2

A: Shall we .... some lunch? I need something to ....

B: Sorry, I don't have a lot of time. I've .... important report to finish.

A: OK. Don't work too hard. I'll see .... Jo's free .... little lunch.

When we speak naturally, we usually link words together. Listen again and notice how the speakers link the words in the conversation. ▶▶|16.2

Practise the dialogue with your partner using the same pronunciation and at the same speed.

2 When we speak naturally we can link words together in three main ways:

- Final consonants of words link to following words beginning with a vowel.

  Sorry, I don't have a lot of time.

- Final vowel sounds of words link to following vowel sounds with either a /w/ or a /j/ sound.

  /w/
  Shall we go and get some lunch?

  /j/
  I'll see if Jo's free

- Final /r/ is pronounced before following vowel sounds.

  /r/
  for a little lunch.

Mark the linked words in these questions.

1 Did it cost a lot of money?

2 Shall I order a taxi for Anna?

3 Do you need any help?

4 Did you have a nice evening?

5 Could I ask you a few questions?

6 Are you interested in art?

Now listen and check your answers. ▶▶|16.3

Ask your partner the questions. Make sure you link the words correctly.

It's time to talk

You are attending an international trade fair in Taipei. You meet your partner in the lobby of the Sherwood Taipei Hotel, where you are staying, and start talking about your companies. Student A should look at page 106, and Student B at page 110.

Remember

Use quantifiers to describe the number or quantity of people and things:
- How *much* production is based in Europe?
- *Most* production is based in Germany.
- Do you do *any* business in China?
- We have *a few* customers in China and *some* in Japan.
- Do you have *many* competitors in Europe?
- We have *no* real competitors in Europe. *Most* competitors are US companies.

On the agenda

Speaking
Technology

Vocabulary
Technology and
gadgets

**Communicating
at work**
Emails 2: Handling
customer enquiries

A dog is a man's best friend. Find out about Nick Wirth, co-founder of RoboScience, and his robotic dog, RS-01.

17 RoboDog

Warm up

Look at the picture. What is it? Would you like one of these? What do you think it does?

Read on

Barks and bytes

1 Read this text, based on the website of RoboScience, a robotics manufacturer based in the UK. Find at least six things that RS-01 can do.

RoboDog: Product RS-01 – Future Technology

Nick Wirth, a UK inventor and former Benetton Formula One designer, has created a robotic dog that will receive your emails and play football. It will also greet your kids when they come home from school. Nick is a co-founder of RoboScience, a world leader in robotics technology.

The RoboScience RS-01 is a domestic or work-based robot. The idea of the RS-01 concept was that it should be fun to own and be totally adapted to the human environment.

The RS-01's brain is a miniature PC running the standard Windows® operating system – a first for any commercial robot. RS-01 uses wireless networking (Wi-Fi) to link to its owner's PC.

RS-01 has a wide range of 'senses' that allow it to interact safely with the world. It has on-board artificial intelligence and uses information from sensors to balance, to understand its location, and to hear and see.

The RS-01 has a number of operating modes:
1 In autonomous mode, the RS-01 can think and act for itself without the need for human intervention. In this mode, it can make decisions, find its way around a house or office, and do useful tasks. RS-01 is also fun. When required, it can understand and act on up to 60 verbal instructions.
2 In explorer mode, the owner can take control of the RoboDog via voice command or remotely from their PC. An on-board camera allows the owner to log into the robot via the net and drive it around its environment, seeing through its eyes, hearing through its ears and so on.

RS-01 technology is ideally suited to domestic and industrial robots, and high risk commercial and military activities.

Importantly, for dog lovers, Nick promises a doggy personality. Owners can actually programme their RoboDog to wait by the door for when the kids come home and greet them with a somersault. Nick has yet to announce plans for a robotic cat which RoboDog can chase.

2 Read the text again. Are these sentences true or false?

1 RoboScience is a leader in robotics technology.   T ☐ F ☐

2 The RS-01 can only be used for industrial processes.   T ☐ F ☐

3 The RS-01 brain is a RoboScience processor.   T ☐ F ☐

4 It has a single operating mode.   T ☐ F ☐

5 RS-01 is suitable for dangerous work.   T ☐ F ☐

6 RoboScience have said they are now working on a robotic cat.   T ☐ F ☐

What do you think? Do you have a dog? Would you like a RoboDog?

The words you need ... to talk about technology and gadgets

1 Look at the specifications of Robot RS-01 and complete the questions about it.

Domestic Quadruped Robot RS-01 – key specifications	
CPU:	32 bit Pentium style processor
Robot OS:	Windows®
Sensors:	colour CCD camera
	miniature audio microphone
	navigation systems
	temperature sensor
Battery:	26 v
Dimensions:	height 685 mm
	length 820 mm
	width 400 mm
Weight:	approx 12 kg
Colour:	metallic gold or natural carbon fibre black
Price:	available on application to RoboScience

A: What (1) .... is it?
B: Gold or black.
A: How (2) .... is it?
B: It's 685 mm.
A: How (3) .... is it?
B: It's 820 mm.
A: How (4) .... is it?
B: It's 400 mm.
A: How much does it (5) .... ?
B: 12 kg.
A: How much does it (6) .... ?
B: I don't know. You'll have to contact RoboScience.

2 Match the questions (1–6) about the camera in the picture with the answers (a–f).

1 What's this called?

2 What does it do?

3 What memory does it have?

4 Can you explain that to me again?

5 What sort of computer do I need to run this?

6 What batteries does it take?

a You can use a PC Pentium II or higher with Windows XP/98SE/ME/2000.

b It's a Mini PenCam.

c 128 Mbit Flash + 128 Mbit SDRAM.

d Two AAA alkaline batteries.

e Sure, no problem. It has two sorts of memory.

f You can use it as a digital still camera, or a digital camcorder or a PC camera.

It's time to talk

gadget /'gædʒ.ɪt/ *noun* [C] a small device or machine with a particular purpose: *kitchen gadgets* ○ *Have you seen this handy little gadget – it's for separating egg yolks from whites.* **gadgetry** /'gædʒ.ɪ.tri/ *noun* [U] *We've got a juicer, a ...*

What does it do?

Work in pairs. Student A should look at page 106, and Student B at page 110.

Communicating at work

Emails 2: Handling customer enquiries

Do you prefer getting emails or phone calls in English? Why?
How often do you get emails in English at work? When did you last get one?

1 We send emails to customers for different reasons. Match each of the
email types (1–6) with <u>two</u> of the phrases (a–l).

1 giving good news
2 giving bad news
3 giving assurances
4 saying sorry
5 giving reasons
6 expressing urgency

a I am sorry to tell you ...
b We must ...
c The reason for this ...
d I can assure you that ...
e Please accept my apologies for ...
f I am pleased to tell you that ...
g We have good news about ...
h Unfortunately ...
i I would like to apologise for ...
j It is very important that ...
k This is/was due to ...
l We are confident that ...

2 Complete the three emails below with appropriate phrases from above (a–l).

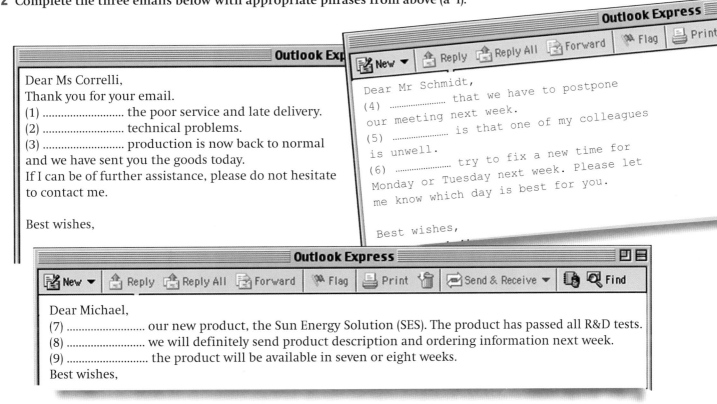

Dear Ms Correlli,
Thank you for your email.
(1) .... the poor service and late delivery.
(2) .... technical problems.
(3) .... production is now back to normal
and we have sent you the goods today.
If I can be of further assistance, please do not hesitate
to contact me.

Best wishes,

Dear Mr Schmidt,
(4) .... that we have to postpone
our meeting next week.
(5) .... is that one of my colleagues
is unwell.
(6) .... try to fix a new time for
Monday or Tuesday next week. Please let
me know which day is best for you.

Best wishes,

Dear Michael,
(7) .... our new product, the Sun Energy Solution (SES). The product has passed all R&D tests.
(8) .... we will definitely send product description and ordering information next week.
(9) .... the product will be available in seven or eight weeks.
Best wishes,

3 Write an email to a customer apologising for a
problem and assuring him/her that the problem
has been or will be solved. Choose from the
reasons and solutions below.

- a late delivery → ready on Monday
- a wrong delivery → we will collect and replace
- a production problem → now resolved

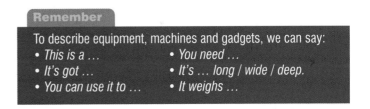

Remember

To describe equipment, machines and gadgets, we can say:
- *This is a ...*
- *It's got ...*
- *You can use it to ...*
- *You need ...*
- *It's ... long / wide / deep.*
- *It weighs ...*

On the agenda

Speaking
Developing a learning action plan

Social phrases
Asking for and giving help

Vocabulary
Learning a language

Warm up

When was the last time you helped someone? What did you do? When was the last time you asked for help? What help did you need?

18 Learning styles

Asking for and giving help

1 Complete the dialogues with phrases (a–h) below.

Technical problems

A: Excuse me. Can you help me? (1) .... ?

B: Let me see. OK, there's a technical problem with the network.

A: (2) .... Can I access the intranet?

B: Yes, you can. But you can't send emails or use the internet just now.

Error _____
Mail could not be sent to account

Explanation _____

Lost or stolen?

A: Oh no! I think I've lost my bag.

B: How? (3) .... ?

A: I put it down here, but now it's gone.

B: Oh dear. (4) .... ?

Using equipment

A: I need to make a photocopy of this. (5) .... ?

B: No problem. Do you know how to use it?

A: (6) .... how to do double-sided?

B: I'm not sure. I'll ask someone to show you.

Getting information

A: I can't remember Phil's phone number. Have you got it?

B: Sorry, I haven't. Cathy will probably know. (7) .... ?

A: No, (8) .... I'll see her at lunch.

B: Are you sure? It's no problem.

A: No, it's OK. I'll see her later.

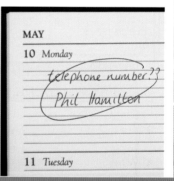

MAY
10 Monday
telephone number??
Phil Hamilton

11 Tuesday

a Can I use this machine?
b it doesn't matter
c Sorry, I don't understand
d Shall I call the police

e Shall I give her a quick call
f Where did you last see it
g What does this mean exactly
h Could you show me

Have a go

Cover the dialogues above and make your own, starting with the words below.

Technical problems

Excuse me. Can you help me?

Lost or stolen?

Oh no! I think ...

Using equipment

I need to make a photocopy of this.

Getting information

I can't remember ...

2 Now listen and check. ▶▶ 18.1

3 Practise reading the dialogues with a partner.

Listen to this

Teaching people how to learn

Before you listen Are you a good learner? Why? Why not?

1 We interviewed Nicholas Bate about part of his job – teaching people how to learn. Listen and tick the points that Nicholas mentions. ▶▶18.2

   Thinking positively
   Using the internet to learn
   Different kinds of learners
   Working with companies
   Studying for long hours
   Teaching memory techniques
   Good teachers

2 Listen again and answer these questions. ▶▶18.2

   1 Nicholas gives two examples of negative thinking about learning which people can have. Can you give one of his examples?
   2 Why does Nicholas ask students to teach others something they are good at?
   3 Nicholas gives two examples of companies with different learning cultures. Can you give one of them?
   4 Why does Nicholas teach people Egyptian hieroglyphs?
   5 Who does Nicholas say should take responsibility for learning?

What do you think? Nicholas says: 'We help learners to understand their own learning style and so learn faster.' Do you think these ideas can help you to learn English faster?

Nicholas Bate of Strategic Edge Ltd talks about teaching people how to learn.

Egyptian hieroglyphs

The words you need ... to talk about learning a language

1 Choose the correct word to complete these sentences.

   1 I need to improve my *knowledge* | *skills* of irregular verbs.
   2 This word is very useful. I will try to *remember* | *remind* it.
   3 I'm going to *remake* | *revise* this language over the weekend.
   4 What's the *mean* | *translation* of 'umsatz'? Is it 'turnover'?
   5 I have quite a good *remember* | *memory* for words.
   6 What does this word *translate* | *mean* exactly?
   7 I *did* | *made* quite a lot of mistakes during the presentation.
   8 I need to *study* | *read* this vocabulary more. It's not clear to me.

Test your partner Read the sentences out but leave a pause instead of the words in *italics*. Your partner has to complete and repeat the sentence.

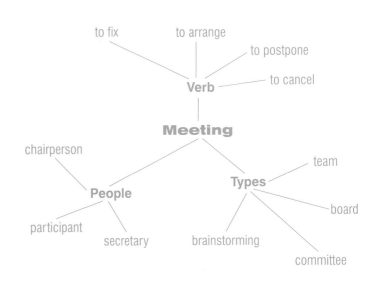

Mind maps can be good for vocabulary learning.

2 Use the words in the box to complete these sentences about vocabulary learning techniques.

1 I .... all new words from English into my own language.

2 Learning a word for me means learning how to say it. .... is very important.

3 I group .... into themes. It makes it easier to learn.

4 I try to learn .... : the noun, the verb, the adjective and the adverb of key words.

5 I use an English–English .... and write down the English definition of new words.

6 I write down typical .... I make. This helps me to make sure I don't repeat them.

7 I .... new words and listen to them every day.

8 When I learn a new word, I always try to learn the .... too, if there is one.

mistakes
word families
opposite
translate
dictionary
Pronunciation
vocabulary
record

Discuss these ideas. Which do you use? Which do you think are a good idea?
What other techniques do you use? Can you add any ideas to this list?

It's time to talk

Nicholas says: 'Learners have to take responsibility for learning ... You have to understand how you learn, and how to stay motivated and to create learning space ... and a personal learning plan.' Create your personal learning plan using the outline here. Complete steps 2 to 4.

LEARNING PLAN

1 How to learn
Be positive, be realistic, be organised.
Create a learning plan.

2 How to stay motivated
2.1 Decide what you want to learn. Set priorities:
1 ....
2 ....
3 ....

2.2 Decide how you learn best. What works best for you? Choose from the following (you may choose more than one):

Visual stimulus   Auditory stimulus   Physical stimulus

Other ideas:
....
....
....

3 How to create learning space in your life
3.1 Time management
When? ....
How much time? ....

3.2 Space management
Where can you learn best? (Order the following 1, 2, 3, etc.)
work ■   home ■   evening class ■
car ■   train ■   plane ■

3.3 How can you organise your learning environment? What equipment do you need? (Choose from the list below.)
pen and paper ■   computer ■   walkman ■
car audio ■   home audio system ■
notebook (for writing things down) ■

4 Other ideas
What else helps you to learn? ....
....
....

Now discuss your learning plan with your partner.
Did you write any of the same things? What things were different?

Remember
- Think about what you learn and how you learn it.
- Think positively about yourself and your learning.
- Plan your learning.
- Learn memory techniques to remember more.

On the agenda

Speaking
Predicting the future

Grammar
Future 2: *will, can, may, might* and the first conditional

Pronunciation
Using sentence stress to speak with emphasis

Meet Richard Scase, author of *Britain in 2010*. He predicts what work and life will be like in British society.

19 Britain at work in 2010

Warm up

Do you agree or disagree with these opinions about the future of work? Tick the ideas you agree with.

	You	Richard
1 The internet will become more important.		
2 Work will be less stressful.		
3 More people will work from home.		
4 People will retire when they are 70 or over.		
5 People will become more interested in politics.		

More people will work from home.

Listen to this

Vision of the future

1 We interviewed Richard Scase about his ideas on Britain in 2010. Listen and tick the ideas above which Richard agrees with. ▶▶ 19.1

2 Listen again and answer these questions. ▶▶ 19.1

1 Where will manufacturing activities in Europe and the USA move to?
2 What does Richard say companies will no longer give people?
3 What problems are there with travelling to work?
4 Richard says: 'And retirement will be different too.' How will retirement be different?
5 According to Richard, what will be the new focus of people's lives in 2010?

What do you think? Do you agree that we will see more of a 'live for today' lifestyle in the future? Why? Why not?

Check your grammar

Future 2: *will, can, may* and *might*

We can use *will, can, may* and *might* to talk about the future. Look at the examples below.

a I think the internet *will be* very important, more important than now.

b Many people from Britain *might* emigrate to France or Spain.

c Retirement *won't* be a passive process any more.

d Working life *may* become much more unstable for many people.

Now answer the following questions.

1 Which sentences describe future events we think are certain?

2 Which sentences describe future events we think are only possible?

The first conditional

We can use first conditional sentences to connect two possible future actions with *will*, *can*, *may* and *might*.

If clause	Main clause
If people get the opportunity,	they *will* choose to work from home.
If this happens,	people *may* adopt a 'live for today' lifestyle.
If you have to write a report,	you *can* do that at home.

We can also start the sentence with the main clause. We do not use a comma in this case, e.g.

People will choose to work from home if they get the opportunity.

Now answer the following questions.

1 What is the difference in meaning between *will*, *can*, *may* and *might* in the examples?

2 Which tense do we normally use in the *if* clause of first conditional sentences?

3 What is the difference in meaning between *if* and *when* in these sentences?
   - **If** people work from home, they'll create far less pollution.
   - **When** people work from home, they'll create much less pollution.

Grammar reference pages 116–17

Do it yourself

1 **Correct the mistakes in these sentences.**

   1 I'm sure we not will have any problems.
   2 I'm not sure where Juan is. He can be in the canteen.
   3 If we take more time, we don't might make so many mistakes.
   4 If you don't send me a new brochure, I don't can place an order.
   5 When I will have time, I promise to send you the report.

2 **Write down your opinions about the future by completing these sentences with *will*, *may* or *might*. (There are no correct answers.)**

   I think ...

   1 the amount of free time that people have .... increase.
   2 internet shopping .... replace traditional shopping.
   3 marriage .... become less popular in the future.
   4 more middle-aged people .... live on their own by the end of this decade.
   5 people .... retire earlier in 20 years' time.
   6 people .... be more interested in politics in the future.

Will work become more stressful?

Now work with a partner and discuss your opinions. Make sure you give a reason for your opinions, as in the example.

Question: Do you think work will become more stressful in the future?

Possible answer: I think work might become much more stressful *because* we'll have to work harder. What do you think?

3 **Complete the following sentences with your own ideas. First, decide whether to use *If* or *When* by circling one of the words. Then decide which modal verb to use – *will*, *can*, *may* or *might* – in the second part of your sentence.**

   1 If / When I retire, ...
      ....

   2 If / When my organisation offers me the chance to work abroad, ...
      ....

   3 If / When I go home this evening, ...
      ....

   4 If / When my company moves to offices 150 kilometres from our current location, ...
      ....

   5 If / When I have to use English for my next meeting at work, ...
      ....

   6 If / When I drive to work tomorrow, ...
      ....

Now work with a partner and discuss your sentences. Check that your sentences are grammatically correct.

Using stress when giving opinions

1 **Listen to two people disagreeing with a proposal about staff cuts. Which words do the speakers place extra stress on in order to express their opinions more strongly?** ▶▶19.2

PROPOSAL: If we cut marketing by ten per cent, we can save a lot of money.
SPEAKER 1: But if we cut marketing by twenty per cent, we can save more money.
SPEAKER 2: But if we cut staff by just one per cent, we can save even more money.

Practise saying the sentences.

Stress: Giving opinions
When we want to express clear opinions, we often speak with more energy and volume to stress the key words which communicate our opinion.

2 **Look at the dialogues about cutting costs in a company. Before you listen, look in particular at Speaker 2's sentences. Underline the words you think Speaker 2 will say with extra stress to communicate a difference in opinion to what Speaker 1 says.**

1
SPEAKER 1: If we increase salaries by ten per cent, staff will be happy.
SPEAKER 2: But if we increase salaries by twenty per cent, staff will be very happy.

2
SPEAKER 1: If we invest less in sales training, we can reduce costs radically.
SPEAKER 2: But if we invest more, we can increase turnover.

3
SPEAKER 1: If we cancel the Christmas party, we can save thousands.
SPEAKER 2: But if we keep the party, staff will be really motivated.

4
SPEAKER 1: If we increase quality, we can increase our prices.
SPEAKER 2: But if we reduce quality just a little, we can save millions.

Listen and check. ▶▶19.3
Practise saying the sentences with the same stress.

3 **Practise using stress when giving opinions. Firstly, on your own, write Speaker 2's disagreement with Speaker 1's opinion in the dialogues. Then role-play the conversations with a partner. Your partner must listen to you and tell you which words in your sentences carry extra stress.**

SPEAKER 1: If we increase our prices by twenty-five per cent, we will increase turnover significantly.
SPEAKER 2: I'm not sure. I think if we ....

SPEAKER 1: If we invest in e-learning software for languages, people will learn faster.
SPEAKER 2: I disagree. I think if we ....

SPEAKER 1: If we reduce management training, managers will still be efficient.
SPEAKER 2: But if we ....

Make proposals for change in your organisation. Your partner has to disagree with you.

It's time to talk

Here are some predictions for the world in 2088 made by experts at the University of Washington. Discuss the ideas with a partner saying how far you agree or disagree with them. What do you think will be the positive or negative results of these predictions, if they come true?

Discuss your own predictions about the future of the world. What will be the results of your predictions, if they come true?

The World of 2088
Education Universities and private industry will be much closer.
Environment We will see forests of genetically-modified trees which grow very fast in order to provide wood for building.
Politics The United States will divide into separate countries.
Health The average age will increase to 200; we will see cures for some major diseases including cancer.
Technology Everybody will be able to create a digital record of their entire life.
Business Advertising will target the individual more and more via the internet.
Society Only the very rich or very poor will have more than two children.
Media Newspapers and television news will continue to focus on war and other 'bad news'.
Space A colony on Mars will be established.

Men will give more time to bringing up children.

Remember

We can build first conditional sentences in four ways:
- with *will*: *If we reduce the number of staff by 10%, we will save a lot of money.*
- with *can*: *If we make all travel economy class, we can save a lot of money.*
- with *may*: *If we stop advertising, we may damage sales.*
- with *might*: *If we cut training, staff might become demotivated.*

We can use *If* to talk about actions in the future which may not happen:
If I see Chris, I'll say hello. (= It's not sure that I will see Chris.)
When I see Chris, I'll say hello. (= It's sure that I will see Chris.)

On the agenda

Speaking
Selling and the sales process

Vocabulary
Sales and selling

Communicating at work
Meetings 2: Leading a meeting

We asked Sylvia Heinzen about finding new clients and selling Jet Membership for Bombardier Flexjet Europe.

20 How the rich travel

Warm up

Would you like to be a salesperson?
Why? Why not?

Read on

Selling jet travel for €8,000 an hour

1 **Look quickly through the text. Then decide which is the best summary.**

   a Learning how to sell
   b Selling jets in America and Germany
   c Selling air travel to special customers

Similar to buying time with telephone cards, Jet Membership customers buy jet flying at a fixed hourly rate to go anywhere, any time. Expensive? Well, a Challenger aircraft costs around €8,000 per hour. But it could be a small price to pay. One client called Sylvia Heinzen during a round of golf to organise an emergency flight to New York. It helped him to win a two million dollar contract.

Sylvia says marketing Bombardier Flexjet is really interesting. 'The clients are special and very rich. Contacting them isn't easy. Mailing doesn't work. Recommendations from existing customers are very important. But we use databases with names of company directors or just very rich people. Then we organise special promotions, maybe golf and a dinner, or a gastronomic evening, where these top people can meet, relax and have a nice time. Of course, we include a short presentation of the company. But it's soft selling.'

Flexjet needs special promotion. As Sylvia says, 'We look after people very well. We had an amazing event in St Moritz. The hotel picked up all the guests from the airport in its 40-year-old Rolls Royce. Then we had a spectacular horse race on a frozen lake. It was fantastic. One client phoned later to say it was the best promotion he'd ever attended. But we have some difficult moments. One guy wanted to get off at 7,000 metres because a fly in the cabin meant he couldn't sleep.'

Selling is never the same for different cultures. Sylvia explains, 'Flexjet had a few problems selling in Germany. We Germans don't like to show we have money. It's not like in, say, America, or even the UK. So it was more difficult to sell this up-market concept in Germany.' But Sylvia has also learned interesting things about herself. 'I learned that I'm not very good at selling. I enjoy market research and promotion. But actually for selling, you need the killer instinct. I don't have it. Direct selling is really not for me!'

2 Read the text again and answer these questions.

  1 What is 'Jet Membership'?
  2 When can the cost of Jet Membership seem like good value?
  3 Name two kinds of promotion that Sylvia organises for possible clients.
  4 What example does Sylvia give of a client who wasn't happy with the Flexjet service?
  5 How did selling Flexjet in Germany compare with America and the UK?
  6 What do you need in order to be good at selling, according to Sylvia?

What do you think? Would you like to sell Jet Membership? Why? Why not?

The words you need ... to talk about sales and selling

1 Match the selling terms (1–9) with the correct definition (a–i).

Selling terms	Definitions
1 up-market	**a** method of selling which uses indirect techniques
2 promotion	**b** exclusive, high quality
3 advertising	**c** any activity that tells people about a product
4 soft selling	**d** telephoning new contacts to tell them about
5 mailing	products or services
6 cold calls	**e** an attempt to say what sales figures will be in the future
7 market research	**f** studies to find out what people want to buy
8 commission	**g** sending information to possible customers by post
9 sales forecast	**h** the business of trying to persuade people to buy
	products or services
	i money paid to sales representatives for sales made

Work with a partner. Ask and answer questions about selling, using some of the vocabulary.
Examples:
What kind of *advertising* does your organisation do?
What do you think of *cold calls* as a *promotion* technique?

Advertising sells

2 Two-part verbs are a difficult but important aspect of English. Choose the correct verb to complete these sentences. (The meaning of each verb is given in brackets.)

Example: We (look)/ *come* / *go after* people very well. (take care of people)

  1 The market is very competitive so we should *keep* / *stay* / *put* prices *down* for another six months. (maintain products at a low price)
  2 I think this new product will help us to *see* / *open* / *break into* China. (enter the Chinese market)
  3 I'm sure that the taxes will *get* / *travel* / *come down* next year. (fall)
  4 This new product will sell well in the summer. Sales will really *put* / *take* / *come off* in August. (increase a lot)
  5 I'd like to *break* / *look* / *see through* your latest brochure. (read it)
  6 We plan to *put* / *set* / *make* prices *up* next year by four per cent. (increase)
  7 We are planning to *give* / *take* / *put away* three cars as a promotion next month. (to offer without payment)
  8 The new XB23 was so popular that it *bought* / *sold* / *went out* in three days! (there are no products left)

Test your partner Say the phrases in brackets above. Your partner must give you the two-part verb that means the same.

It's time to talk

Take it in turns to interview your partner using the quiz on pages 106–7. Then look at the Answer key on page 141 to see if he/she would make a good salesperson.

Communicating at work

Meetings 2: Leading a meeting

Do you have internal meetings in English in your organisation? Do you have meetings in English with customers or other people from outside your organisation? Do you ever chair such meetings?

1 You will hear extracts from two short meetings. Listen to both the extracts and note down the objective and the decision for each meeting. ▶▶|20.1 ▶▶|20.2

2 Listen again to both the extracts. Which of the phrases for Opening and Controlling below do you hear in the first meeting? Write 1 in the box. ▶▶|20.1

Which of the phrases for Controlling and Closing below do you hear in the second meeting? Write 2 in the box. ▶▶|20.2

	Objective	Decision
Meeting 1		
Meeting 2		

Leading a meeting

Opening
Start:	Shall we get started?
Check agenda:	Does everyone have a copy of the agenda
State objective:	Our objective today is to ...
	We need to discuss ...
Begin discussion:	What do you think?

Controlling
Give positive feedback:	Thanks for that.
Clarify:	So you want to ...
	If I understand you correctly, you think ...
Interrupt:	Sorry to interrupt ...
Deal with interuptions:	Can we/you let ... finish?

Closing
Clarify decision:	So we've decided to ...
Check for agreement:	Can we agree to ...?
Give instructions:	Could you ...?
Fix next meeting:	Can we fix a date for the next meeting?
Ask for other points:	Are there any further points?
Close meeting:	I think we can finish there.

3 In the second meeting, why does Julie disagree with Stefan? How well does the chairman handle the situation? ▶▶|20.2

4 In small groups, organise a short meeting using the agenda. You are the management committee which must solve the problem. Take turns to lead the meeting.

Agenda

Meeting to discuss unauthorised use of the internet during working hours

Objective:
To control the use of the internet among company employees.

Information:
A report shows that too many staff use the internet during working time for personal research. The report estimates that employees are much less efficient because of this.

Possible actions:
- Check all websites visited by each member of staff.
- Give internet access to a limited number of staff.
- Send an email to all staff asking them not to use the internet for personal research.
- Include in employment contracts a paragraph that says unauthorised use of the internet can result in suspension or termination of the contract.
- Nothing. Restricting staff freedom may have a negative impact.
- Other actions ...

Remember

Cold calling is a form of *promotional* strategy. All forms of *advertising*, including *mailing*, aim to increase *customer awareness* of products. *Market research* tells companies about what customers want.

Speaking
Cinema and favourite films

Social phrases
Making recommendations and giving advice

Vocabulary
Film and cinema

21 Great cinema

Warm up

What do you recommend to visitors who want to go out for the evening in the place where you live?

Recommendations and advice

1 Complete the dialogues with phrases (a–j) below.

Suggesting entertainment

A: I have to take some clients out tonight. Any ideas?
B: There's a film festival on this week. (1) .... to that.
A: That sounds interesting. I'll do that. Thanks.
B: (2) .... book in advance. It's really popular.
A: OK. Thanks for the tip.

Recommending restaurants

A: I'm eating out tonight. (3) .... a good Indian restaurant?
B: Yes, I can. (4) .... the Bengali Palace on Coney Street.
A: OK, thanks. Any others? What do you think of the Mogul, near the river?
B: (5) .... that one. Sometimes it's almost empty.
A: OK, I'll try the other one. Thanks.

Giving advice about hotels

A: I'm going to Bonn in May. Do you think I need to book a hotel before I go?
B: I think so, yes. (6) .... should book somewhere on the internet.
A: OK, I'll do that.
B: But (7) .... to our travel department first? I'm pretty sure they have some special deals with hotels in Bonn.
A: Good idea. I'll speak to them today. Thanks.

Shopping problems

A: I'm going shopping. (8) .... films on DVD with English and French subtitles?
B: (9) .... is Waterstones. It's a bookshop in the city centre.
A: OK. Anywhere else?
B: I'm not sure. (10) .... the record shops as well. Try HMV or Virgin, for example.
A: OK, thanks. Could you write those down for me, please?

Have a go

a I think the best one is	**e** why don't you talk
b Do you know anywhere which sells	**f** I would take them
	g You might find something in
c It would be a good idea to	**h** Can you recommend
d Probably the best place to look	**i** I think you
	j I'm not sure about

2 Now listen and check. ▶▶ 21.1

3 Practise reading the dialogues with a partner.

Cover the dialogues above and make your own, starting with the words below.

Suggesting entertainment
I have to take some clients ...

Recommending restaurants
I'm eating out tonight ...

Giving advice about hotels
I'm going to Bonn ...

Shopping problems
I'm going shopping ...

Listen to this

Before you listen How often do you go to the cinema? What kinds of film do you like?

The big screen experience

1 Listen to Clare, Anna and Ron talking about films and going to the cinema. Are these sentences true or false? ▶▶|21.2

1	Clare hates most Hollywood films.	T	F
2	Anna likes to watch thrillers.	T	F
3	Ron watches a lot of French and Italian films.	T	F
4	Ron watches more films on video and DVD than at the cinema.	T	F
5	Clare thinks the internet will kill off cinemas.	T	F

2 Listen again. Answer these questions. ▶▶|21.2

   1 Which types of film does Anna hate?
   2 How many times has Ron seen Hitchcock's *North by Northwest*?
   3 Who are Clare's favourite actors?
   4 Why does Ron prefer subtitles to dubbing?
   5 Write down two things that are special about going to the cinema, in Clare's opinion.

What do you think? Do you think the internet will kill off cinemas? Do cinemas have a future?

Clare, Anna and Ron all love going to the movies. They talk about their favourite films.

Ron likes *North by Northwest*.

The words you need ... to talk about film and cinema

1 Match the movie titles with the movie type or genre. Can you add your own titles for each genre?

1	Western	a	Fantasia; Snow White and the Seven Dwarfs
2	Horror	b	Star Wars; Blade Runner
3	Fantasy	c	Saving Private Ryan; Apocalypse Now
4	Cartoon	d	Vertigo; Jaws
5	Action and adventure	e	The Godfather; City of God
6	Comedy	f	Some Like It Hot; Duck Soup
7	Thriller	g	The Magnificent Seven; A Fistful of Dollars
8	Science fiction	h	The Exorcist; Frankenstein
9	Romance	i	Titanic; Casablanca
10	War	j	Lord of the Rings; Harry Potter and the Philosopher's Stone
11	Musical	k	Singing in the Rain; Chicago
12	Crime	l	Indiana Jones and the Last Crusade; Goldfinger

How many of these films do you know? How many don't you know? Are there too many American films in this list?

Can you give a definition for each of these genres?

Which is your favourite movie genre?

2 Complete these comments about films with words from the box.

1 It was a great performance. Jack Nicholson is my
favourite ....

2 She's a real star. I think Meryl Streep is my
favourite ....

3 We had a great evening out. The film was
really ....

4 I saw a good thriller recently. The .... was a bit
complicated but I enjoyed it.

5 Tom Cruise .... the role of a successful New York lawyer
who learns that life is not as simple as he thought.

6 Go and see the latest Spielberg movie. It has a great .... – all
the top names are in it.

7 I went to see *Taxi Driver* with some friends last night. The main
.... is played by Robert De Niro.

8 There's a festival of films .... by Kurosawa on at the local cinema
this week. I've only seen *The Seven Samurai*. I'd like to see some of his others.

9 His new film is .... in Japan in the year 2020.

10 It was a romantic film. It had the usual happy .... but it was quite moving.

11 It was so .... that I had to close my eyes on several occasions. I just couldn't
watch what was happening on the screen.

12 The film was dubbed. I prefer .... so you can hear the original language.

Listen and check your answers. ▶▶|21.3

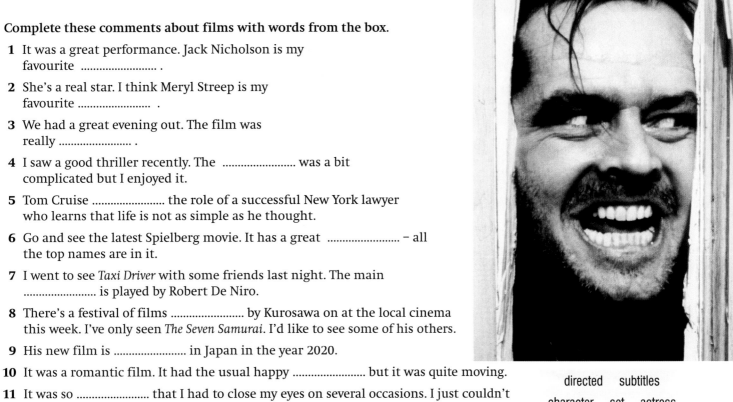

directed	subtitles
character	set actress
plot ending	actor
violent	plays
entertaining	cast

It's time to talk

	You	Partner 1	Partner 2
Types of film I like			
Two films I strongly recommend			
Types of film I don't like and why			
The worst film I have ever seen			
Favourite actors and directors			
Actors and directors I don't like			

1 Complete the table with some short notes about
films. Try to use as much film and cinema vocabulary
presented in the unit as you can.

2 Prepare some questions based on the table to ask two
other people. Use Tapescript 21.2 on pages 129–30 to
help you.

3 Now interview the people and complete the table.

Remember

Asking the right questions is the basis for good conversation.
• *What's the film about?*
• *Who's in it?*
• *What kind of films do you like?*
• *How often do you go to the cinema?*
• *What films can you recommend?*
• *Do you have any favourite actors?*

Jenny Cutler runs a company called Image Counts. We talked to her about how she helps people with their image.

22 Your personal brand image

Warm up

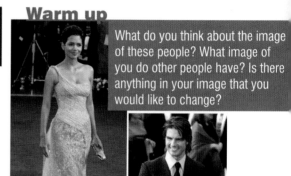

What do you think about the image of these people? What image of you do other people have? Is there anything in your image that you would like to change?

Listen to this

Image Counts

1 We interviewed Jenny Cutler about her consulting company, Image Counts. Listen to her and tick the subjects she talks about. ▶▶|22.1

appearance	clothing
voice	paying restaurant bills
handwriting	shopping
teeth	working internationally
etiquette	shaking hands
small talk	

2 Listen again and answer these questions. ▶▶|22.1

1 Jenny says she helps people in three ways. What are they?
2 Dr Voice is a voice coach. Who are his main clients?
3 In Jenny's opinion, which two things must you not do with a business card?
4 What is the most important thing about body language for her?
5 What are her two golden rules?

What do you think? Jenny says: 'I help people to brand themselves, to market themselves professionally.' Would you like to use an image consultant? Do you think image consultants provide a useful service?

Check your grammar

Must, have to and *need to*

We can use *must, have to* and *need to* talk about things which are necessary or not necessary to do. Look at these examples.

I *must* show you the brochure which has our golden rules. (= I really want to show you the brochure.)

You really *must* listen to people better. (= I strongly recommend you to listen to people better.)

You absolutely *mustn't* write on someone's business card. (= Do not do this.)

You *have to* copy the report to the HR Department. (= It's a rule the HR Department made.)

A director *has to* know how to behave. (= It's a job requirement.)

You *need to* be nice to look at. (= It's important to wear clothes which you look good in.)

You *don't need to* learn everything immediately. (= You can learn some things later.)

Complete the sentences with the words in the box.

> don't need to / needn't   mustn't   have to   need to
>
> don't have to   must

1 We can use .... to give strong advice or to say what we personally think is necessary.

2 We can use .... to talk about rules that somebody else has made. We can also use .... to stress that something is necessary or important.

3 We can use .... or .... to talk about something that is not necessary.

4 We can use .... to give strong advice not to do something or to talk about something we think it is important not to do.

What is the difference between these two sentences?
- He *mustn't* go to the meeting.
- He *doesn't have to* go to the meeting.

What is the past form for both *must* and *have to*?

Grammar reference page 117

Do it yourself

1 Correct the mistakes in these sentences.

1 I really must to stop smoking.
2 Have you to go to the meeting tomorrow?
3 She must not go to the meeting if she doesn't want to.
4 Did you must take a later plane yesterday because of the delay?
5 We have not to work late on Friday after all.

2 An image consultant is discussing work in Japan with a client. Complete these sentences with *must, have to, had to, don't/doesn't have to* **or** *didn't have to.*

1 Don't worry about the language. You .... speak perfect Japanese. Just learn a few phrases.
2 Overall, your presentation wasn't bad, but I think you really .... improve the way you deal with questions afterwards.
3 Don't forget that you will .... buy a new mobile phone in Japan because the technology is totally different from Europe.
4 Most Tokyo restaurants have signs against mobile phone use, so don't forget that you .... turn off your phone before you go in or you'll be very unpopular.
5 Most Japanese businessmen .... wear a suit when they are at work.
6 You can tell your wife that she .... wear a kimono at formal dinners. It's not expected.
7 When I lived in Japan, there were very few regulations. I .... register with the embassy, for example.
8 It took me some time to get to know the culture. I think I .... work at it for a year before I really felt at home.

3 The image consultant is telling a new staff member about rules and regulations at the company. Complete these sentences with *need to, mustn't* **or** *don't have to.*

1 Welcome to the company. First of all, this is the key to the garage. You have your own parking space, so you .... park anywhere else, as other people will get angry if you take their space.
2 You .... be here until 9 o'clock in the morning but you .... make sure you work 37 hours during the week.
3 You .... come in through the car park entrance to the building as it's only for board members. We come in through reception at the front of the building, so you'll .... walk round from the garage.
4 This is your badge. You .... take it off while you're in the building. If you see someone without one, you should ask them who they are.
5 There's a good restaurant on the top floor where you can get lunch, although you .... eat here. You can go out for lunch if you prefer.
6 You have your own office, of course. But you .... have all your meetings there. You can also book a meeting room but you'll .... do that with reception.
7 You have permanent internet access through your PC but you .... use the internet for non-professional things like looking for holidays and so on.
8 We're meeting for a drink after work tonight. You .... come but you'd be very welcome.

Strong and weak stress with modal verbs

1 **Listen to these two sentences.** ▶▶ 22.2
   1 I think you should go to the meeting, not the workshop.
   2 I think you really should go to the meeting, not the workshop.

Why does the speaker use *really* and change the stress in the second sentence?

We can pronounce modal verbs with weak stress and put the main stress on another word which has an important meaning. Or we can put strong stress on *must, mustn't, should* and *can* when the modal verb itself is the main focus of the sentence.

2 **Listen to two speakers talking about their work and giving advice. Mark the modal verbs (in *italics*) with (S) if they have strong stress and (W) if they have weak stress.** ▶▶ 22.3

   1 A: Our organisation *can* help people to develop themselves and their careers. ■
      B: Believe me. Our organisation *can* help people. ■
   2 A: You *shouldn't* use your car. Use a company car. ■
      B: I didn't say it's illegal to use your car but you really *shouldn't*. ■
   3 A: Some people don't want to accept criticism. But they *must* if they want to improve. ■
      B: People *must* accept criticism every day they are with us. ■
   4 A: You *mustn't* forget that there are only three golden rules to learn. ■
      B: I didn't say you shouldn't forget. I said you *mustn't* forget. ■

You shouldn't use your car.
Use a company car.

Work with a partner and practise saying the sentences with the same stress.

3 **Prepare some sentences about making a good impression when you meet visitors to your organisation. Say your sentences to your partner and ask him/her to identify which modal verbs you used and if you used strong or weak stress.**

Example: You should always smile when you meet people for the first time.

It's time to talk

Improving personal image is a key to success in business. Think about your own work environment and write down some things you already have to do to meet your job requirements. Then note down some areas of your own image which you think you need to improve. Talk about these with your partner.

Examples: I don't have to wear a suit but I have to be smart.
I need to improve the way I deal with questions after presentations.

	You	Your partner
Things I already have to do		
Things I need to / must improve		

Compare your ideas about image success with your partner. Ask for advice on those areas which you would like to improve about yourself – dress, voice, personal appearance, etc.

Image success

Personal appearance and dress sense

Business etiquette – titles, business cards and shaking hands

Verbal communication skills – meetings, presentations and telephoning

Non-verbal communication skills – body language and eye contact

Social etiquette – restaurants and social events

Managing relationships with your manager and colleagues successfully

Remember

must: You really *must* improve your image.
mustn't: You *mustn't* use the back entrance. It's for board members only.
have to: You *have to* wear a suit. It's company policy.
don't have to: You *don't have to* arrive until nine o'clock.
need to: If you want to book a meeting room, you'll *need to* talk to reception.
don't need to / needn't: You *don't need to / needn't* go to the meeting tomorrow.

On the agenda

Speaking
Human resources

Vocabulary
Managing people

Communicating at work
Emails 3: Making travel arrangements

Anke Schweikart is an HR manager with Lafarge Zement in Germany. We interviewed her about the business of managing people.

23 Managing people

Warm up

Look at the list of job responsibilities. Which ones does a human resources (HR) manager do?

recruitment   downsizing   pensions planning   product research
marketing   training   negotiating salaries   accounts
negotiating deals with customers

Do you have an HR department in your organisation? What else does it do?

The appraisal process

Read on

We listen to what they say

1 Lafarge Zement is the German subsidiary of a French cement company. We asked Anke Schweikart about her job as human resources manager. Read the text. How many HR activities can you find?

Our HR strategy at Lafarge is to attract the best people, develop their full potential and keep them here. Attract, develop and keep! But HR covers many responsibilities, including recruitment, staff development, negotiating with works councils and unions on working conditions and salaries, pensions planning, company strategy and staff appraisal. There are difficult times too, especially when the economy takes a dip and we have to lay people off. Most companies have to downsize sometimes, and that is always a difficult part of the HR manager's job.

Appraisal is a key HR activity. Appraisal is a system to monitor performance at work by interviewing staff. We listen to what they say about their work and responsibilities, their careers and personal development, and working relationships. We appraise the employee, but the employee also appraises the job and their performance, their role in the company, even their line manager. I think the key to appraisal is two-way communication. The key is to listen to employees. We want them to say what they think.

Lafarge is an international company, so another HR role is expatriation. This is placing employees abroad, usually with a subsidiary. We help people with the decision to go abroad because the move must be good for them, and for us. If expatriation does not work out, this is usually because of relationship problems, especially if the employee's partner is unhappy.

A lot of women work in human resources, probably because it attracts people who like to communicate and love working with people. Women like the personal side of this, and are often good communicators. Women seem to like HR, and also marketing, and other sectors like education, health and social welfare. All these areas are about communication.

I have always worked in HR. Of course, I've learnt something about cement, but to be honest, I find people much more interesting than the chemical formulae for cement! Or the special mix of cement that is best for building bridges! Or even selling cement!

2 Read the text again and answer these questions.

   1 What is a difficult part of the HR manager's job?
   2 What is appraisal?
   3 What does Anke say is the key to good appraisal?
   4 What is expatriation?
   5 Why does expatriation sometimes not work out?
   6 Why do a lot of women work in HR?

What do you think? Do you agree with what Anke says about women at work? Does your human resources department listen to what you say? Do you have staff appraisals?

The words you need ... to talk about managing people

Staff development?

1 Match the terms (1–10) with the words or phrases which have a similar meaning (a–j).

1 personnel	**a** recruitment
2 appraisal	**b** money people get at the end of their working lives
3 staff development	**c** committees of managers and workers
4 salaries	**d** workers' organisations
5 working conditions	**e** human resources
6 works councils	**f** payment for one's main employment
7 trade unions	**g** training employees to learn new skills
8 taking on new employees	**h** monitoring employee performance
9 laying employees off	**i** the work environment
10 pensions	**j** downsizing

Does your organisation have a works council and/or trade unions? Have you taken part in any staff development activities?

Does your organisation have trade unions?

2 Complete the sentences with words from the box.

If the economy is weak and businesses are doing badly, companies may (1) .... workers. There will be an increase in (2) .... Sometimes companies ask older staff to volunteer to stop working: this is called taking (3) .... Other staff may volunteer to leave: this is called taking (4) .... If the economy recovers and businesses are doing well, then companies (5) .... more staff.

Part of HR work is staff (6) .... This helps to improve the (7) .... of the workforce and so helps the organisation. Most good companies spend money on (8) .... their employees.

In Europe there is a long tradition of workers joining (9) .... In the European Union, many large and medium-sized companies have established (10) .... These are committees of workers and managers. They discuss company (11) .... , especially issues which affect employees.

What is the economy of your country like at the moment? Are organisations recruiting staff or laying people off?

early retirement	recruit	policies
works councils	development	
lay off	voluntary redundancy	
training	trade unions	
skills	unemployment	

It's time to talk

Work in pairs and form groups of four. You are going to take part in a meeting to discuss a 'people management' problem. Pair A should look at page 107, and Pair B at page 111. First of all prepare for the meeting with your partner, then have the meeting with the other pair and reach an agreement.

Communicating at work
Emails 3: Making travel arrangements

Do you use email to make travel arrangements?
Does somebody else do this for you?

1 You are fixing a trip to Geneva for yourself and a colleague, Sasha Wang. Match the stages in the process (1–9) with the sentences from your emails (a–i).

1 Agree details of the meeting with your colleague in Geneva
2 Enquire about accommodation in Geneva
3 Book the flights
4 Book the accommodation
5 Inform Sasha of the details
6 Arrange for someone to meet you at Geneva airport
7 Propose a later time for the meeting following a change in Sasha's plans
8 Change to a later flight
9 Inform Sasha of the change of flight

Arrange for someone to meet you at the airport.

a The flight's booked for 0705 on Thursday 18th and we're staying at the Rialto. The meeting is due to start at 10 o'clock.
b I've managed to get a midday flight at no extra charge. Hope it's now OK for you.
c Could you get a driver to pick us up when we arrive? It's flight number BM1047, due in at 9. Thanks.
d Thanks for your speedy reply. I'd like to book two single non-smoking rooms for myself and Ms Sasha Wang for the night of Thursday 18th April.
e Ref. the booking number 2035/C, is it possible to travel later rather than early morning? A flight around 11.30 would be perfect.

f Do you have two single non-smoking rooms for the night of Thursday 18th April? Please let me know the price for this plus breakfast for two.
g Please book two economy class tickets for myself and Ms Sasha Wang to Geneva, departing 0705 on 18th April and returning 1430 on 19th April.
h Sasha and I will see you in your office at 10 on Thursday 18th. OK?
i Sasha can't leave until 10 so I'll have to try and change the flight. Could we start at 2 or 3 instead? Sorry about this.

2 You see the following email from your boss in your inbox.

To:
From: a.bowden@nms.co.uk
Subject: Budapest arrangements

Two things, please. Firstly, can you fix the details for the sales meeting in Budapest? There's a 10.00 flight on 14 March that arrives at about 12.30. Can you book it for me, Ingrid and yourself? Get someone from the Budapest office to pick us up. We need to return on 15 March, around 14.00.
Secondly, I booked three hotel rooms for the wrong night. I asked for 15 March – please change it to 14. Hotel Ibis, same place as last time.
Please tell Ingrid all this.
Thanks,
Anthony

Now write emails to:
• Get There Travel – book the flights
• Janina in the Budapest office – ask to be picked up
• Hotel Ibis – change the reservation
• Your colleague Ingrid – tell her the flight and hotel details

Remember

These are useful phrases for making travel arrangements:
• *Please would you send me … ?*
• *Do you have … ?*
• *Please book …*
• *I'd like to book …*

On the agenda

Speaking
Discussing social problems

Social phrases
Receiving international colleagues

Vocabulary
Social problems and solutions

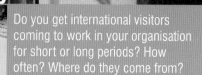

Warm up

Do you get international visitors coming to work in your organisation for short or long periods? How often? Where do they come from?

24 Social issues

Receiving international colleagues

1 Complete the dialogues with phrases (a–j) below.

Welcome

A: Welcome to head office. (1) ....
B: Thanks a lot. I'm really looking forward to working with you.
A: (2) .... ? Was everything OK?
B: Yes, it was fine, thanks. No problems at all.

Security

A: OK, we need to do a couple of things first. (3) ....
B: Fine. Shall I do that now?
A: Yes, please. And (4) ....
B: Do I give it back when I finish in the evening?
A: No, you can keep it until you leave.

VISITOR'S BADGE
Name *Kenji Otsuka*
Company *ITL Press*
Visiting *Joanne Bailey*

Work space

A: So this is your office. (5) ....
B: Not at all. I'm used to it!
A: Fine. And (6) .... It's connected to the internet.
B: Thanks. (7) .... ?
A: Yes, just type 'visitor' for user name and password.
B: And how about the phone?
A: You just (8) ....

Outside work

A: And this is my home number, (9) .... in the evening.
B: Oh, I wouldn't disturb you at home.
A: No, really, feel free. (10) .... or on my mobile.
B: That's very kind. I hope I won't have to.
A: Well, I think that's everything.
B: Thanks. Everything is very clear.

a I hope you don't mind sharing
b Do I need a password
c you can use this computer
d just in case you need anything
e press 1 for an outside line
f You can always reach me at home
g We hope you enjoy your stay
h you have to wear this badge all the time
i You need to fill in your details here
j Did you have a good trip

Have a go

Cover the dialogues above and make your own, starting with the words below.

Welcome	Work space
Welcome to head office ...	So this is your office ...
Security	Outside work
OK, we need to do a couple of things ...	And this is my home number, ...

2 Now listen and check. ▶▶24.1

3 Practise reading the dialogues with a partner.

Listen to this

Rajid | Bill | Mary | Maurice | Joyce

Before you listen

Which of these problems
do you think are the most
and the least important
in your country?

jobs   race   poverty   homes   violence

Social issues in Britain

**Five British people talk about the social issues
they think are important in Britain today.**

1 We asked five British people for their views on the main social
problems in Britain today. Listen to the conversations. Match
each speaker to the problem he/she talks about. ▶▶ 24.2

1 Rajid   **a** Violence
2 Bill   **b** Poverty
3 Mary   **c** Jobs
4 Maurice **d** Race
5 Joyce   **e** Homes

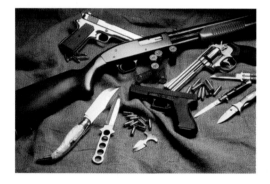

SAY NO TO RACISM

2 Listen again and answer these questions. ▶▶ 24.2

Race
1 In which sport does the speaker say race is a big problem?
2 What does the speaker say is the answer to the problem?

Jobs
3 How many jobless people does the speaker say there were in the eighties?
4 What does the speaker say is the answer to the problem?

Homes
5 How does the speaker describe house prices in Britain?
6 What does the speaker say is the answer to the problem?

Violence
7 When does the speaker say that violence is worst?
8 What does the speaker say is the answer to the problem?

Poverty
9 What causes of child poverty does the speaker talk about?
10 What does the speaker say is the answer to the problem?

What do you think? Do these views
fit with your picture of Britain? Do
you have the same problems in your
country or different ones?

The words you need ... to talk about social problems and solutions

1 **Replace the words in *italics* with a word from the box.**

1 The main problem in this town is *people without work*.
2 When there is not enough work, you get an increase in *theft*, *pickpocketing*, *assault* and *violence*.
3 One of the main social problems in some places is *fighting between different communities*.
4 *People without a house to live in* can be a result of people losing their jobs.
5 It's terrible to see people *asking for money on the streets*.
6 The charity Oxfam fights against *the problem of people living in bad conditions with little or no money*.
7 In many countries there's a big problem of *people stealing automobiles*.
8 The UK has had problems of *violence at football games*.

homelessness
begging
poverty
football hooliganism
car theft
unemployment
street crime
ethnic violence

Test your partner **Say the words in *italics*. Your partner must remember the right words in the box.**

2 **Complete the sentences below with a word from the box.**

1 How can we .... the situation, do you think?

2 I think spending more money on education would make things ....

3 What's the way to resolve this .... , do you think?

4 The government should .... the problem.

5 It could .... the situation worse.

6 It's getting .... because a lot of people can't afford a place to live.

7 Do you think the government can find a .... ?

solution   conflict   worse   make
solve   improve   better

3 **Match the problem on the left to the possible solution on the right.**

1 child poverty
2 vandalism
3 homelessness
4 unemployment
5 ethnic violence
6 car crime

a provide job training
b design better locks and other security features
c encourage mixed race schools
d make the people responsible do community work
e give more help and support to single parents
f build new houses

It's time to talk

Work in pairs. Student A should look at page 107, and Student B at page 111.

Remember

How can we solve the problem?
• *One way to improve the situation could be ...*
• *It could make things better if we ...*
• *I think we have to ...*
• *I think we can find a solution by ...*
• *It would be better to ...*
• *The government should solve the problem.*

On the agenda

Speaking
Discussing possibilities

Grammar
The second conditional

Pronunciation
Silent letters and difficult words

We interviewed Arnauld Schwalm, who works in France as a financial controller. His company, Douwe Egberts, produces and sells coffee.

25 The coffee business

Warm up

A lot of people want companies to do more than make a profit. They want companies to help improve society. Do you work for an ethical organisation? And is it helping to make the world a better place?

Coffee production

Listen to this

Douwe Egberts – coffee producer and seller

1 Listen to Arnauld Schwalm talking about his work in the world of coffee. Are these sentences true or false? ▶▶|25.1

1 Arnauld has little contact with other departments in his company.   T ☐   F ☐
2 The level of global coffee production at the moment is good for Douwe Egberts.   T ☐   F ☐
3 Vietnam is one of the world's top five coffee producers.   T ☐   F ☐
4 Douwe Egberts does very little to help coffee producers in developing countries.   T ☐   F ☐
5 Not many American companies have an ethical policy in developing countries.   T ☐   F ☐

2 Listen again and answer these questions. ▶▶|25.1

1 What is Arnauld's main challenge in his job?
2 According to Arnauld, what would happen if world coffee stocks decreased?
3 Why is Arnauld happy that Vietnam is now a major coffee producer?
4 How would Douwe Egberts help producers if the price of coffee crashed in the future?
5 Why is Arnauld sure some American companies have a real ethical policy and it isn't 'just public relations'?

What do you think? Arnauld says: 'It's an ethical question for companies to think about developing countries. They should do something.' How far do you agree? Why?

Check your grammar

The second conditional
In Unit 19, we looked at first conditional sentences. Here, we move on to the second conditional. We can use second conditional sentences in different ways.

- To think about future events which are the result of impossible present situations:
  I *would try* to improve my golf if I *had* more free time. (= But I don't have more free time.)
- To think about unlikely or imagined future situations and their results:

If world coffee prices *increased* by 20% tomorrow, it *would be* very good for many developing countries. (= The speaker thinks a 20% increase in coffee prices is unlikely.)
- To show disagreement with a proposal or idea during discussion:
  Of course, staff *would be* much more motivated if we *increased* their salaries by 40%. (= The speaker thinks a salary increase of 40% is a bad idea.)

Now answer the following questions.

1 **What is the difference in meaning between these two sentences?**
- If prices *crash* in the future, Douwe Egberts *will continue* to pay a normal price to producers.
- If prices *crashed* in the future, Douwe Egberts *would continue* to pay a normal price to producers.

2 **Which tense do we normally use in the *if* clause of second conditional sentences?**

3 **What is the difference in meaning between *would*, *might* and *could* in the main clause of these second conditional sentences?**
- If I received more detailed forecasts, I *would* be very happy.
- If I received more detailed forecasts, I *could* calculate a more accurate budget.
- If I received more detailed forecasts, I *might* make fewer mistakes.

Grammar reference pages 117–18

Do it yourself

Car pollution

1 Correct the mistakes in these sentences.

  1 If we increase her salary, she would be more motivated.
  2 If we did that, we will meet the target.
  3 If we would change our office around a little, people could work more efficiently.
  4 If we decreased our prices, I think we create a price war.
  5 Do you work on Saturday if we gave you next Monday as a holiday?

2 Here are some ideas on how to make the world a better place. Complete the sentences using the second conditional. Different answers are possible.

Making the world a better place

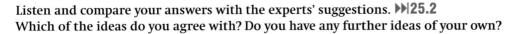

  1 The environmentalist: If we / ban / motor cars / major cities, we / reduce / urban pollution significantly.
  2 The manager: If we / introduce / a 35-hour working week, employees / create / real / work–life balance.
  3 The academic: Companies / be able / find / qualified people more easily / if we / have / better education system.
  4 The police officer: If we / make / criminals wear microchips, we / stop / a lot of crime.

  5 The politician: If we / have to / give 2% of our income / developing countries, we / reduce / poverty significantly.
  6 The company doctor: Our staff / be / much healthier if they / do / 30 minutes of regular exercise every day.
  7 The philosopher: If we / worry / less about money and material possessions, we / be / happier.
  8 The man/woman in the street: If politicians / listen / to the people, the world / be / a much better place.

Listen and compare your answers with the experts' suggestions. ▶▶|25.2
Which of the ideas do you agree with? Do you have any further ideas of your own?

3 In the discussion extracts below, the speakers use both the first and second conditional to propose and discuss solutions to a work problem. Choose the correct form of the verb to complete the sentences.

Making work a better place

1 Staff membership of local fitness club
  A: If we (1) *pay / paid* for staff membership of the local fitness centre, everyone can take some regular exercise.
  B: Yes, but if we (2) *do / did* that, it'd cost a lot of money.
2 Food quality in staff canteen
  A: If we offer better quality food in the canteen, people (3) *will / would* eat more healthily.
  B: Yes, but if we offered better quality food at lunchtime, (4) it *will / would* have little impact on their general diet.

3 Office environment
  A: If we create more open spaces, people (5) *will / would* feel less stressed.
  B: Yes, but if we (6) *create / created* more open spaces, we wouldn't have enough room for all our employees.

Listen and check your answers. ▶▶|25.3

Why do you think the man uses first conditional sentences and the woman uses second conditional sentences?

Silent letters and difficult words

1 With a partner, check that you can pronounce these words correctly.

would	might	climb	who
doubt	know	honest	science

Listen and check the pronunciation. ▶▶ 25.4

2 You can improve your learning by noting down the pronunciation of problem words in different ways. Here are some ideas on how to make notes on the pronunciation of words. Match the ideas (1–5) to the examples.

Techniques for learning pronunciation

would	Sounds like WOOD.
might	Silent 'gh' in single syllable words ending '-ight'.
climb	Sounds like TIME.
who	/huː/
doubt	/daʊt/
know	Sounds like NO.
honest	Don't say the 'h'. Sounds like 'onest'.
science	Don't say the 'c'. The 'i' has a long sound.

1 Crossing out the silent letter(s)
2 Noting down a word with the same sound as the problem word
3 Writing the phonemic transcription from the dictionary entry
4 Noting a pronunciation rule
5 Writing personal notes on how to pronounce words

Which of these techniques do you use? Which do you find the best?

3 Now use these learning techniques – or your own – and write notes for these words.

half	scissors	island	knife	whole	hour
chemist	business	guide	steady	listen	
autumn	lamb	wrong	thought		

Listen and check the pronunciation. Then practise saying the words with a partner. ▶▶ 25.5

Test your partner Check through earlier units of this book and find five or more words you have problems pronouncing. Test your partner and see if he/she can pronounce the words correctly. Then discuss the best ways to learn the correct pronunciation of problem words when learning English.

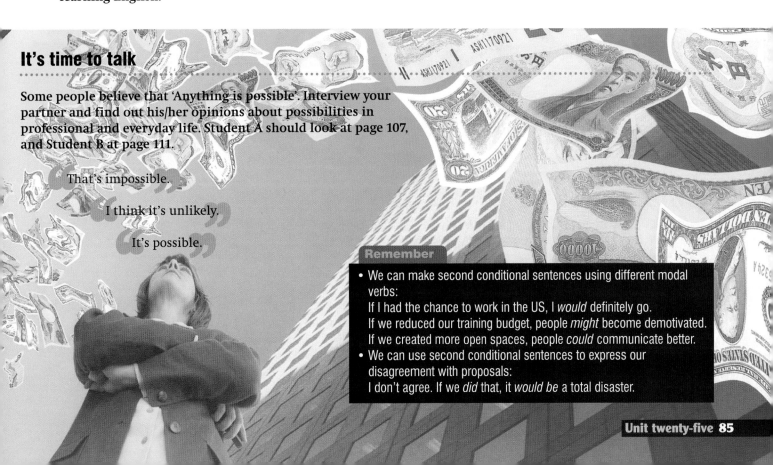

It's time to talk

Some people believe that 'Anything is possible'. Interview your partner and find out his/her opinions about possibilities in professional and everyday life. Student A should look at page 107, and Student B at page 111.

That's impossible.

I think it's unlikely.

It's possible.

Remember

- We can make second conditional sentences using different modal verbs:
  If I had the chance to work in the US, I *would* definitely go.
  If we reduced our training budget, people *might* become demotivated.
  If we created more open spaces, people *could* communicate better.
- We can use second conditional sentences to express our disagreement with proposals:
  I don't agree. If we *did* that, it *would be* a total disaster.

On the agenda

Speaking
Describing products and
their selling points

Vocabulary
Products

**Communicating
at work**
Telephoning 3: Handling
complaints

**Shannon Bentley tells
us about the future of
skiing with Head's new
'Intelligence' skis.**

26 Intelligent skis

Warm up

Do you ski? What are the most important
qualities for a good pair of skis? What do you
think 'Intelligence' skis are?

Read on

Intelligent ski technology

1 Read Shannon Bentley's article about the advantages
of a new and innovative ski from Head. Match the
headings (1–6) with the paragraphs (A–E) in the article.
There is one heading you don't need to use.

1 New 'Intelligence' skis   4 Only for serious skiers
2 From narrow to wide design   5 Chip to fibre in five milliseconds
3 Problems with 'Intelligence' skis   6 Skiing in the past

A Stone-age rock carvings, found above the Arctic Circle in Norway,
show people using skis to hunt animals over 4,500 years ago. Of
course, skis have changed a lot since then, and now technology is
taking skiing one step further.

B Skis used to be narrow and rather stiff. Nowadays, ski design has
changed with manufacturers producing wider and more flexible skis.
These new features are popular with skiers as they make it easier to
turn and increase speed. But wide, flexible skis vibrate more, which is
a disadvantage.

C To solve the problem, the ski company, Head, has designed a new ski
called 'Intelligence', which has a microchip which helps the ski adapt
to different conditions. Also, inside the skis there are microscopic
ceramic fibres, called Intelli-fibres. These run across the ski and can
sense twists and vibrations, which are not good for skiers.

D With 'Intelligence' skis, when a skier hits a problem like ice, the ski
bends, and so do the Intelli-fibres inside. They send an electrical signal
to the computer chip in the ski making the fibres become hard and
stiff. The process happens in five milliseconds using tiny amounts of
electricity and helps skis and skier stay in better contact with the snow.

E Intelligence technology can't change the snow conditions, but it can
improve your skiing. The harder you ski, the more you'll feel the skis
adapt to the speed and terrain, as if they were tailor-made to the snow
conditions. However, it's not a product for amateurs. At $1,200 a pair,
these skis are only for really serious skiers.

2 Read the text again and answer these questions.

   1 What is the advantage of wider and more flexible skis?
   2 What is the main problem with wider and more flexible skis?
   3 What does the microchip in the 'Intelligence' ski help the skis to do?
   4 How do Intelli-fibres work?
   5 Why does Shannon say 'It's not a product for amateurs'?

What do you think? Do you think more technology makes sport more fun? Why? Why not?

The words you need ... to talk about products

1 Look at the underlined words in the phrases (1–8) and match them
with their opposites (a–h).

   1 It's very <u>light</u>.   **a** weak
   2 It's <u>wide</u>.   **b** old fashioned
   3 This is a <u>tailor-made</u> solution.   **c** heavy
   4 It's very <u>well constructed</u>.   **d** standard
   5 It's very <u>tough</u>.   **e** massive
   6 This is a very <u>sophisticated</u> product. **f** simple
   7 <u>State of the art</u>   **g** narrow
   8 The system uses a <u>tiny</u> computer.   **h** badly built

Test your partner Your partner should close his/her book. Read out the
sentences and ask your partner to say the opposite of the underlined words.

2 Replace the words in *italics* in the advertisement below with the words
in the box, keeping the meaning similar.

Find your way **with the Compaq handheld computer with Navigator**

The new Compaq iPAQ 3800 (1) is *perfect for* the international business person who is always on the move. It
(2) *comes with* a top quality diary with computing functions and built-in MP3 player. The GPS navigating system,
when installed, is very (3) *simple to operate* and (4) *allows* you to pinpoint your location anywhere in the world to
within 10 square metres. (5) *It's possible to* be sure that you will make that next meeting on time with turn-by-turn
voice directions. The Compaq iPAQ 3800 (6) *guarantees* stress-free travel and gives you the confidence to relax.

          includes
          enables
          You can
          designed for
          ensures
          user-friendly

Listen and check your answers. ▶▶ 26.1

It's time to talk

Prepare to describe the selling points of one (or more) of the products
from the list below.

A product you bought recently
A product made by your company/organisation
A product bought by your company/organisation
A product you would like to buy if you had enough money

When preparing, make sure you can talk about:
• who the product is designed for
• the main product features, including functionality (what the product does)
• other product features such as cost, weight, size, special functions, etc.

Then work with a partner and take turns describing your products.
The person listening should take notes and ask some follow-up questions
about the product. Then he/she should decide whether or not to buy it.

What is it?   **Cost?**   **Who is it for?**

Colour?

PRODUCT

Special   **Size/weight?**
features/functions?

What does it do?

Communicating at work

Telephoning 3: Handling complaints

Do you ever receive telephone calls from angry customers or colleagues?
What's the best way to deal with angry people?

1 Listen to three phone calls. Match each phone call with one of the
four situations (A–D). You don't need to use one of the situations. ▶▶| 26.2

   A A manager is unhappy about late payment of an invoice ▢

   B A supplier solves a delivery problem ▢

   C Colleagues discuss a project delay ▢

   D A customer complains about an order problem ▢

2 Complete the extracts from the phone calls with the correct phrases.

> We had a lot of problems
>
> Sorry again
>
> get back to you
>
> I really do apologise
>
> Is that OK?

> Let me check
>
> I'm very sorry about that
>
> There was a computer error
>
> We'll talk next week

Call 1

Apologise:	Really. (1) ....
Confirm details of the problem:	(2) .... You said E258, yes?
Promise to investigate and call back:	I'll check with dispatch and (3) .... within the hour. Is that OK?

Call 2

Give the reason for the problem:	(4) .... in the warehouse ... we've dispatched another 5,000 litres today and that will be with you tomorrow morning.
Check customer is happy:	(5) .... ?
Apologise again:	(6) .... for the inconvenience.

Call 3

Apologise strongly:	(7) ....
Give the reason for the problem:	(8) .... last week with the software installation.
Offer a solution:	We'll finish things off by Tuesday next week – so it's only a two-day delay. OK?
Refer to next contact:	Sorry about the delay. (9) .... Have a good weekend.

**Listen to the three phone calls again
and check your answers.** ▶▶| 26.2

3 Work in pairs and practise handling
complaints on the phone. Student A should
look at page 107, and Student B at page 111.

> **Remember**
>
> • Checking reasons for a problem:
>   *Let me check. / I'll get back to you.*
> • Giving reasons:
>   *There was an administrative error / a technical problem. / We've had a lot of
>   problems with ...*
> • Giving assurance:
>   *I'll call you back. / We can organise a new delivery today.*
> • Communication:
>   *Please get back to me if you need anything. / Send me an email to confirm.*

On the agenda

Speaking
Discussing local specialities

Social phrases
In the restaurant

Vocabulary
Food and cooking

27 You are what you eat

Warm up

Can you think of one typical dish from each of these countries?

| Japan | Germany | India | France |
| Mexico | England | China | Italy |

Which is your favourite foreign cuisine?

Food talk

1 Complete the dialogues with phrases (a–i) below.

Understanding the menu

A: Excuse me, can you help me?
(1) .... *coq au vin*?
B: *Coq au vin*? It's chicken cooked in wine, madam.
A: I see. (2) .... ?
B: It's done in a casserole dish in the oven with red wine, onions, bacon, mushrooms and garlic. It's one of the chef's specialities.
A: It sounds delicious. I'll try it.

Complimenting the chef

A: That was very good. You have an excellent chef.
B: Thank you. And we try to cook mainly with local ingredients.
A: That's good. (3) .... ?
B: We have good contacts with all the local farmers.
A: Yes, (4) ....

Explaining the name of a local dish

A: This soup is excellent.
(5) .... ?
B: (6) .... *miso* soup with *wakame*. *Miso* is a kind of bean paste and *wakame* is a kind of green seaweed. We use it a lot in soups.
A: It's very good.
B: Yes, but my wife's is better. She got the recipe from her grandmother.

Describing how something is cooked

A: This fish is delicious. (7) ....
B: (8) .... wine, ginger, garlic and herbs and then cook it in a hot oven.
A: It sounds complicated.
B: No, it's really easy. (9) .... not to overcook it.
A: Well, it's just perfect.

a What's it called	**f** everything tastes very fresh
b What exactly is	
c Where do you get them	**g** How is it cooked
d I'd love to know the recipe	**h** The most important thing is
e I make it with	**i** We call it

2 Now listen and check. ▶▶ 27.1

3 Practise reading the dialogues with a partner.

Have a go

Cover the dialogues above and make your own, starting with the words below.

Understanding the menu
Excuse me, can you help ... ?

Complimenting the chef
That was very good. You have ...

Explaining the name of a local dish
This soup is excellent ...

Describing how something is cooked
This fish is delicious ...

Listen to this

Before you listen Do you like to try lots of local foods when you travel? What do you <u>not</u> like to eat?

How do you like our food?

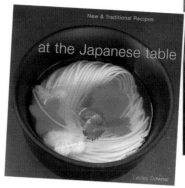

at the Japanese table

New & Traditional Recipes

1 Lesley Downer is a writer and expert on Japanese culture. Listen to her talking about food. Which of these sentences is the best summary of what Lesley says? ▶▶|27.2

- Japanese people eat Japanese food even when they are abroad.
- Food is really important to the Japanese.
- Many Japanese are vegetarian.
- The Japanese like live fish.

Find out the secret of good eating from Lesley Downer. She writes books about food and is an expert on Japanese cooking.

2 Listen again. Answer these questions. ▶▶|27.2
   1 What does Lesley say Japanese food looks like?
   2 Name one of the three most important things about Japanese food.
   3 What did the Japanese student's mother use to do?
   4 What is the first thing the Japanese ask visitors to Japan?
   5 Why do some people get angry about Japanese food?

What do you think? Do you like Japanese food? Do you or could you eat live food? Why? Why not?

The words you need ... to talk about food and cooking

1 Match each of the cooking methods with the right picture (a–j) and the right definition (i–x).

Cooking method
   1 barbecued
   2 roasted
   3 microwaved
   4 poached
   5 baked
   6 steamed
   7 grilled
   8 raw
   9 fried
   10 boiled

Definition
   i food (especially bread or cakes) cooked in an oven
   ii food cooked on a hot metal plate under or over the heat
   iii food cooked in very hot water
   iv food cooked over (not in) very hot water
   v food cooked on hot coals
   vi food (especially eggs) cooked in gently boiling water
   vii food (especially meat) cooked in an oven
   viii food cooked or heated in a special oven using radiation
   ix food cooked in oil or butter in a pan
   x food that is not cooked at all

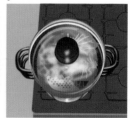

What ways of cooking do you prefer?

2 Complete the sentences below with a word for describing food from the box.

1 These vegetables have been sitting in boiling water for 40 minutes. They are completely ....

2 I love really .... curries – the hotter the better!

3 I'd like my steak very .... , please – don't cook it for more than a few minutes.

4 And I'll have my steak .... , please – not too little and not too well done.

5 The peaches were a bit hard yesterday, but now they are just right – perfectly .... for eating.

6 I didn't enjoy the main dish because I thought the sauce was so .... that you couldn't taste the meat at all.

7 The meat has been cooking in the oven for nearly four hours on a very low heat – no wonder it's incredibly ....

8 It's a sea fish so it has a very nice, slightly .... taste.

9 The cream has gone .... because it's been standing in the sun all day.

10 My favourite course is dessert – I love chocolate and anything ....

11 I'm the opposite. I always prefer something .... to things like puddings and chocolate.

12 There was too much lemon in it – it tasted really ....

rich
tender
off
overcooked
spicy
rare
sweet
medium
ripe
salty
savoury
sour

It's time to talk

Your English client is visiting for a few days and you have invited him/her to one of your favourite local restaurants.

Write down the names of three dishes from your country and show them to your partner. On a separate piece of paper, write down their ingredients, how they are cooked, and some adjectives to describe the dish.

Now role-play a conversation with your partner. He/She will ask you some questions about the dishes you've chosen. Explain what they are.

When you have finished, change roles.

Remember

How is food cooked? How's it done?
It's:
- *grilled on a grill*
- *roasted in the oven*
- *barbecued on a barbecue*
- *boiled in water (in a saucepan)*
- *steamed in a steamer*
- *fried in a frying pan, or simply*
- *prepared and eaten – raw.*

On the agenda

Speaking
Processes

Grammar
The passive

Pronunciation
Corrective stress

Janie O'Connor runs Events Promotions Casting – an entertainment agency with a difference. We talked to her about her job.

28 That's entertainment!

Warm up

Janie helps organisations manage their public relations (PR) with special events. Does your organisation have PR events to launch products, organise promotions or improve its image? Are they good for the organisation's image?

Listen to this

From strongmen to look-alikes

Some of the artists on Janie's books.

1 Listen to Janie O'Connor talking about her company, Events Promotions Casting. Are these sentences true or false? ▶▶|28.1

1 Janie is the managing director of Events Promotions Casting. T ☐ F ☐

2 Janie has worked for the company for ten years. T ☐ F ☐

3 The company is small but hires a lot of freelance people. T ☐ F ☐

4 Janie works with the film industry in India. T ☐ F ☐

5 Kylie Minogue is the most popular look-alike for Events Promotions Casting. T ☐ F ☐

2 Listen again and answer these questions. ▶▶|28.1

1 What kind of corporate events does Events Promotions Casting organise?
2 Which event does Janie describe as the most interesting?
3 How long does a typical event last?
4 What does Janie say is most difficult about working in India?
5 How often is the Frank Sinatra look-alike used?

What do you think? Janie says: 'I love the variety, because every single day is different.' Would you like to work in the entertainment industry?

Is this the real Kylie?

Check your grammar

The passive

Describing processes
We can use the present simple passive to describe work processes. Underline examples of the passive in these sentences.

- Firstly, any possible contract is discussed internally.
- Then performers are contacted.
- If they are available, they're hired immediately.

Now complete the grammar summary by choosing the correct words.

We form the present simple passive using the verb *to be* + the past / present participle. We use the passive / active when we focus on the action more than on the person.

A: Two singers were recruited this morning and the client doesn't like them.
B: Sorry, I recruited them.
A: They were given the wrong music.
B: Andy gave them the wrong music. It wasn't me.

Which speaker uses the passive?

Why does the other speaker choose to use the active?

The passive sentences are about the past. How do we form the past simple passive?

Grammar reference page 118 ▉▶

Do it yourself

1 Correct the mistakes in these sentences.

1 The coffee is normally make by our secretary.
2 The report has prepared by a colleague yesterday.
3 He was asked from his boss to meet a client at the airport.
4 I am fascinating by your ideas.
5 The email was sending yesterday.

2 You have been asked to create a web page showing your company's business process to clients. Complete the steps by describing each process using the present simple passive.

3 Complete this article using the correct form of the present simple passive or past simple passive.

STEP 1:	Firstly, arrange a meeting with the client to identify needs.
STEP 2:	Secondly, contact the freelance people we want to use.
STEP 3:	Thirdly, organise a second meeting to discuss the proposal.
STEP 4:	Then agree a detailed schedule.
STEP 5:	After that negotiate a price.
STEP 6:	Finally, sign the contract.

The Notting Hill Carnival is the biggest street event in Europe and has roots going back hundreds of years. Historically, the Carnival (1) .... (establish) by black slaves. Song, dance and costume (2) .... (use) by the slaves to protest about social conditions and celebrate black culture. The modern London Carnival (3) .... (start) over 30 years ago by the Trinidadian community newly arrived in London. At the beginning it (4) .... also .... (see) as a form of social protest by black people living locally who were facing racism and social inequality. Now it is a fully multicultural event attracting over one million visitors every year. It (5) ...... normally .... (hold) on the last weekend of August with Sunday and Monday as the main days. The Carnival is a festival of music and dance. Music systems (6) .... (turn up) so that dancing can go on all night. The event (7) .... now .... (manage) by London Notting Hill Carnival Ltd. Last year 200 personnel (8) .... (train) in health and safety because of the large crowds. Hundreds of police (9) .... also .... (use) to guarantee the event went smoothly. This year organisers are hoping to build on the success of last year and it (10) .... (expect) that visitor figures will reach 1.5 million.

The biggest street event in Europe

Listen and check your answers. ▶▶ **28.2**

Corrective stress

1 Listen to a journalist who is checking her facts (speaker A) talking to a colleague of Janie's (speaker B). Underline the words B stresses in these sentences. ▶▶ 28.3

> A: So Janie's been with the company for fourteen months, hasn't she?
> B: Actually, it's fourteen years.
>
> A: And she's head of marketing, isn't she?
> B: No, she runs the company.
>
> A: You said Kylie is the number one look-alike, didn't you?
> B: She was, but now it's Sinatra.

Why does speaker B stress these words?

2 When we correct people during a conversation, we can stress the word(s) which communicate the corrected information. Underline the stressed words in speaker B's replies to A's questions.

> A: It's a dating agency you run, isn't it?
> B: No, it's an entertainment agency.
>
> A: Do you do most of your work for private parties?
> B: Not really. Most of our work is corporate.
>
> A: And do you only work in the UK?
> B: We did. Now we work all over the world.
>
> A: You have 500 employees, right?
> B: Actually, we have almost no employees. We use freelance people.

Listen and check your answers. ▶▶ 28.4

3 Write down five similar questions to ask your partner, which you know are wrong. Ask your partner the questions and listen to him/her correct you with the stress on the corrected information.

Example

| You ask: | You live in Italy, don't you? |
| Your partner replies: | No, I live in Germany. (stress on Germany) |

It's time to talk

Prepare a short presentation describing a process in your job or organisation using the present simple passive. Choose one of the ideas below. Draw a flowchart like this one to help you visualise the process when presenting it to a partner.

Ideas
Finding new customers
Preparing financial reports
Handling orders
Recruiting new staff
Developing new products
Preparing a presentation

Finding graduate trainees

Firstly, high potentials are identified by local managers through universities, business and engineering schools

Suitable candidates are sent to an assessment centre

Top performers are interviewed by two HR directors

Five candidates per year are selected

Specialist coaching and training is given to each successful candidate

Candidates are sent to an assessment centre.

> **Remember**
> - We can use the present simple passive to describe processes at work using structuring phrases such as *firstly, secondly, then, next, after that* and *finally*.
> - We use the present simple and past simple passive to focus on the action or the event more than on the person.
> - We use corrective stress when we want to correct people in professional discussion or general conversation.

Speaking
Describing change

Vocabulary
Changes and trends

Communicating at work
Presenting 2: Handling questions effectively

Meet Linda Harvey and Sue Dixon. Find out about their work as life coaches.

29 Life coaching

Warm up

How did you choose your current career? Was it the right decision? Why? Why not?

Read on

Do you need a change?

1 We asked Linda Harvey and Sue Dixon about their work as life coaches. Read the article and decide what the main point is in each paragraph, sentence **a** or **b**.

A **a** Life coaches help people work out their career plans.
   b Life coaches are for people who feel depressed.
B **a** A lot of people are unhappy in their job.
   b There are a lot of benefits from working with a life coach.
C **a** You can meet, phone or email a life coach.
   b Using the services of a life coach is not cheap.
D **a** More people are using life coaches.
   b Stars and ex-politicians are life coaches' main clients.

Many working people today face the problem of falling motivation and a sense that maybe they made the wrong career decision. Some of them go to a life coach for help. Linda Harvey, a life coach based in London, explains her role. 'Lots of people come to me unhappy and depressed about their work, especially around New Year, a typical time to get depressed. My job is to get them to feel positive again. People need to focus on what they want to achieve. Together we work out a clear action plan with exciting work goals which people must agree to one hundred per cent. If you really want change, you need that one hundred per cent!'

People can reinvent themselves with a life coach and find a real purpose at work again. Better working relationships with colleagues and reduced stress are often significant benefits. Sometimes coaching offers that extra kick needed for individuals to change direction completely and go for the exciting career they always wanted. Sue Dixon, who is based in Birmingham, says, 'I think over 70% of people are in jobs they don't want to do.'

'My most important function is to help people to realise where they want to go and then make them think about their own solutions to get there.'
But the advice isn't cheap. Linda and Sue charge clients about £200 a month. This typically includes three long phone calls or meetings, and additional emails or phone calls, as required. Some coaches charge per meeting or phone call, with costs varying from £25 to £75 an hour. Linda and Sue both have a steady client base of about 20 clients and can usually earn around £4,000 a month.

Coaching has grown sharply in Britain over the last few years and continues to rise steadily in popularity. In 1998 there were five members of the ICF (International Coach Federation) in the United Kingdom, but now there are 400. There is no sign that numbers are going to fall. Whilst it's mainly the stars and ex-politicians who use them at the moment, the future for such lifestyle gurus is bright. Sue says: 'A lot of people are more open to it now. In ten years' time it'll be as common to have a life coach as a personal trainer in the gym.'

2 Read the text again and answer these questions.

1 What time of year does Linda Harvey get most of her clients?
2 Name two significant work-related benefits from using a life coach.
3 What does 70% refer to?
4 What does Sue say is her most important role as a life coach?
5 Using information in the text, calculate the average annual salary of a life coach.
6 Which statistic in the text supports Sue's opinion about a positive future for life coaches?

What do you think? Would you like to work as a life coach? Why? Why not? Would you like to have one? Why? Why not?

The words you need ... to talk about changes and trends

1 The words in the table are connected with change. Complete the table with the correct forms of the words. You may need to use a dictionary.

Verb (infinitive)	Past simple	Past participle	Noun	Adjective
				reduced
fall				falling
		grown		growing
rise				

2 The sentences below are all taken from KLM's annual report. Match the two halves of the sentences.

1 The airline industry has seen
2 The number of internet flight reservations
3 There was a sharp fall
4 Unfortunately, revenue
5 One of our key aims is
6 Costs in some areas have
7 We plan to increase flight security
8 Schiphol is a European airport

a in demand for business flights.
b huge changes over recent years.
c grew last year.
d significantly with onboard security.
e for the year dropped substantially.
f to improve the level of passenger comfort.
g with good growth potential.
h risen over the last year.

Now describe two important changes you saw in your organisation last year and two changes you expect next year.

3 We can build sentences which analyse the reasons for change in two ways.

- Start with the change and then explain the reason (a result of / due to), e.g.
  Our low sales last year are a result of / due to bad marketing.
- Start with the reason and then explain the change (lead to / result in), e.g.
  Bad marketing led to / resulted in low sales last year.

Choose the correct phrases to complete this extract from a presentation by a marketing director to her colleagues.

Listen and check your answers. ▶▶ 29.1

It's time to talk

Work with a partner. You are going to describe changes in a graph. Student A should look at page 108, and Student B at page 111.

'As you can see from the graph, the number of customer complaints decreased significantly last year. I think this was mainly (1) *led to / due to* our increased focus on quality. You can see here that quality was much better, up 50% on last year. So we should be happy that the investment in new machinery has (2) *a result of / resulted in* better quality and more satisfied customers. If I can now turn to profits, I'm afraid that the figures are not so good (3) *due to / result in* the higher investment costs we've just discussed. It is also partly (4) *led to / a result of* a slight drop in sales of 3%. We expect things to improve next year. Finally, I would like to say that our new focus on the Central and Eastern European markets will (5) *lead to / due to* a lot of new business next year. So we should go forward with confidence. Thank you.'

Communicating at work

Presenting 2: Handling questions effectively

During or after a presentation, it is sometimes difficult to deal with questions. Why do you think this is?

In this section, we look at some techniques for handling questions effectively.

1 Listen to three extracts from Kurt Van der Meyer's presentation to his colleagues on the status of a project. Circle the correct subject of his colleagues' questions. ▶▶|29.2

Question 1   Budget / Technical specifications
Question 2   Training / Travel
Question 3   Upgrade costs / Staffing costs

Do you think Kurt handles the questions well? Why? Why not?

Any questions?

2 Listen again and complete the sentences Kurt uses when handling questions. ▶▶|29.2

   1 Ask if there are any questions.

     Does .... ?

   2 The audience have no questions. Move on to the next point.

     OK, if there are no more ....

   3 After answering a question, check that the questioner is happy with the answer.

     Does .... ?

   4 Comment on a question from a member of the audience.

     It's ....

   5 The audience seems to have stopped asking questions. Finish now.

     Right, if there are no more ....

3 Work in small groups. Prepare a one-minute presentation on one of the following topics. When you are ready, give your presentation. Invite questions both during and after your talk.

Topic 1: My job
Job title / responsibilities / most interesting thing about the job

Topic 2: A change in my organisation or company
The change / reasons for the change / results

When your partners give their presentations, ask three questions either during or after the presentation. Make a note of how well your partners handle the questions and give some feedback at the end.

Invite questions from your audience.

Remember

When giving a presentation:
- Be proactive and invite questions from your audience.
- Respond positively to any question with a short phrase.
- Check your audience is happy with the answer you give.
- Ask for more questions or move to the next part of the presentation.

On the agenda

Speaking
Discussing work and lifestyle

Social phrases
Saying goodbye

Vocabulary
Continuous learning

Tony Weston is a vegan and he works for the Vegan Society. He talks about his work and his lifestyle.

Warm up

What's the difference between a vegetarian and a vegan? What do you think about their ideas?

30 Work or lifestyle?

Listen to this

Work, belief and lifestyle

1 We interviewed Tony Weston, who works for the Vegan Society of Great Britain. Listen to Tony and answer these questions. ▶▶ 30.1

1 Does Tony buy products tested on animals? Yes ☐ No ☐

2 Does Tony eat Indian curries? Yes ☐ No ☐

3 Does Tony eat multi-vitamin tablets? Yes ☐ No ☐

4 Does Tony enjoy his job? Yes ☐ No ☐

vegan /'viː.gən/ *noun* [C] a person who does not eat or use any animal products, such as meat, fish, eggs, cheese or leather: *Vegans get all the protein they need from nuts, seeds, beans and cereals.* ⊃ Compare **vegetarian. vegan** /'viː.gən/ *adj: a vegan diet* ○ *Sh...*

2 Listen again and answer these questions. ▶▶ 30.1

1 What is Tony in charge of at the Vegan Society?
2 What kind of clothes doesn't Tony wear?
3 What does processed food have too much of?
4 How many people in the UK are vegan?
5 Why does Tony mention 1st November?

3 Listen again to Tony's answer to the interviewer's last question and tick the ideas below which he says are important for him at work. ▶▶ 30.2

1 I do a job which I believe in morally. ☐

2 I do a job which allows me to earn a lot of money. ☐

3 I do a job which helps protect animals. ☐

4 I do a job which helps people to learn. ☐

5 I do a job which enables me to develop as a person. ☐

What do you think? On a scale of 1 (not at all) to 5 (absolutely), how true for you are each of the five sentences in exercise **3**?

The words you need ... for continuous learning

During this course you have used different ways to learn vocabulary. At the end of the course, it's important to review these vocabulary learning methods and develop a personal learning plan for the future.

Learning tips

1 Study the page below from a student's notebook. Match each vocabulary learning method (a–e) with the correct section (1–5).

2 Complete the vocabulary notes using words from the box.

commission   tailor-made   advertise

competitive   tiny   save   narrow   responsibility

Vocabulary learning methods
a Learn key words by avoiding typical mistakes.
b Learn a word and its opposite.
c Learn word families: verb, adjective, noun and adverb.
d Learn words by using an English-English dictionary and then writing your own definitions.
e Learn which verbs and nouns typically go together.

1 ☐ The environment
To recycle glass, metal and paper
To (a) .... energy
To use public transport
To reduce traffic congestion
To protect the environment

2 ☐
Analyse (vb), analytical (adj.),
analysis (noun), analytically (adv.)
Compete (vb), (b) .... (adj.),
competition (noun), competitively (adv.)

3 ☐ Selling
cold calls when you telephone someone you don't know to try and sell them a product or service
(c) .... the money paid to a sales representative for the sales he/she has made
sales forecast an analysis showing what your sales could be in the future
(d) .... to buy space on the TV or in the newspapers to inform the public about your products and services (on TV they're called commercials)

4 ☐
I have ~~responsible for~~ / (e) .... for our corporate brochure.
I'm also in charge of / ~~in charge for~~ web projects.
I'm responsible for / ~~responsibility for~~ 35 people.
My main objective / ~~object~~ is to support the marketing department.

5 ☐
wide - (f) ....
tough - weak
(g) .... - standard
sophisticated - simple
(h) .... - massive

How do you learn vocabulary? Which methods are most effective for you?

It's time to talk

Building vocabulary is only one part of language learning. It is also important to think about creating an action plan to improve your speaking, listening, reading and grammar. Design your action plan for your future learning. Choose the best ideas for you under each heading. Then explain your plan to your partner giving reasons for your choices.

Language learning ideas

Speaking
1 Use the telephone more with English-speaking contacts.
2 Organise English-speaking lunches at work.
3 Stop worrying about the mistakes you make.
4 Record yourself speaking and learn from the playback.
5 *Your own ideas:*
....

Listening
1 Listen to English language radio more.
2 Watch English language TV more.
3 Listen to English language CDs more in the car.
4 Listen to yourself more when you speak English.
5 *Your own ideas:*
....

Reading
1 Read an English newspaper or magazine regularly.
2 Read English books or readers (books written in simplified English).
3 Visit more English language sites on the internet.
4 Read aloud.
5 *Your own ideas:*
....

Grammar
1 Do exercises in a self-study grammar book.
2 Pay attention to the grammar when you read.
3 Learn examples as well as rules by heart.
4 Stop worrying about grammar.
5 *Your own ideas:*
....

Saying goodbye

1 Complete the dialogues with phrases (a–j) below.

Getting away

A: Right, I think I should be going.
B: (1) .... ? It's only half past nine.
A: Sorry, (2) .... I promised I'd get back early tonight.
B: It's a real pity, the party's only just starting.
A: Yes, I'd love to stay but I really have to go. I'll see you next week. Bye.

Getting away quickly

A: OK, have a nice weekend everybody.
B: Oh, (3) .... a quick work question before you go?
A: My train goes in around 20 minutes. (4) .... ?
B: But I just need to run over the agenda for Tuesday morning.
A: Sorry. Can you ask Olivia? I really have to go. Bye.

Give me a call

A: I have to go to a meeting now.
B: OK, but there are a couple more points to discuss.
A: Well, (5) .... .We can talk over some more details then.
B: (6) .... I'll give you a call on Monday morning.
A: Fine. (7) .... Bye.

Until the next time

A: I've just come to say goodbye. I'm leaving now. My train's at five-thirty.
B: OK, well (8) ....
A: Same here. It was great working with you, as always.
B: Yeah, (9) .... And, hopefully, see you next year.
A: Yes, until then, (10) .... Bye.

a	Can we leave it until Monday	
b	call me next week	
c	I really must be going	
d	can I just ask you	
e	it was really good to see you again.	
f	Talk to you then	
g	take care	
h	Already	
i	I will	
j	I enjoyed it too	

2 Now listen and check. ▶▶ 30.3

3 Practise reading the dialogues with a partner.

Cover the dialogues above and make your own, starting with the words below.

Getting away

Right, I think I should be going.

Getting away quickly

OK, have a nice weekend everybody.

Give me a call

I have to go to a meeting ...

Until the next time

I've just come to say goodbye ...

Remember

- Focus on learning the words you need and you will learn faster.
- Set realistic targets for learning new words. Then achieve the target!
- Make English part of your lifestyle – at work and at home.
- Keep enjoying your English!

Revision 2 Units 16–30

Grammar

1 Complete this memo from a HR manager using the words in the box. Sometimes more than one answer is possible.

| each | a little | a few | much | most |
| many | no | some | any |

We need (1) .... people, between three and five sales staff, to work in Russia for (2) .... months. However, although (3) .... of our sales staff are willing to go, we don't have (4) .... staff who can speak Russian to the required level. We have (5) .... time to search for new candidates externally, so those people who are selected will haven to spend (6) .... of their own time learning Russian before they go. This will not cost (7) .... In fact, if (8) .... lesson is taught at our headquarters, we shouldn't spend (9) .... of the training budget.

2 Rewrite these sentences in the passive keeping the original meaning.

Example:
Americans consumed over 1.4 billion kilos of chocolate in 2001.
Over 1.4 billion kilos of chocolate were consumed by Americans in 2001.

American Food Facts

1 Americans eat 11 billion bananas every year.

....

2 Americans consume 20 billion hot dogs every year.

....

3 Nabisco produces six billion Oreos every year. (They . are the best selling candy bar in the world.)

....

4 The Mars M&M factory in Hackettstown, New Jersey, manufactures 100 billion M&Ms a year.

....

5 Frank and Ethel Mars sold Mars's first candy in 1911.

....

3 Complete the conditional sentences with your own ideas.

1 If I take early retirement, ...

2 .... , I'd buy a new car.

3 If I could have dinner with anyone in the world,

....

4 If I could work in another country,

....

5 When I next go on holiday, ...

6 ...., I'd lose my job.

Pronunciation

1 Listen to four short dialogues and write down the missing words. ▶▶ R2.1

1 A: What's her number?
B: It's 0047 51 88 97 83.
A: Did you say .... ?
B: No, ...

2 A: What's his email address?
B: It's marcus.ritter@zurich.ch.
A: Is that .... ?
B: No, ...

3 A: Where do they live?
B: It's 145 Queen Street.
A: .... ?
B: No, ...

4 A: When's the next meeting?
B: It's on the 22nd of September.
A: .... ?
B: No, ...

Listen again. Underline the words which have the most stress in each short dialogue ▶▶ R2.1

2 Listen to these sentences and mark the linked words. ▶▶ R2.2

1 Shall we go and get some lunch?
2 Can I have a cup of coffee?
3 I'm afraid I'm a bit too busy.
4 I've been working here for over a year.
5 Maybe I should take that job after all.
6 How about trying that new Indian restaurant?

Business vocabulary

Unscramble the business word which matches the definition.

1 paplasair ....
Yearly discussion/interview between manager and staff member about performance

2 sponnie ....
Money received by people when they stop working

3 truecir ....
To appoint new members of staff for an organisation

4 donreatiun (2 words) ....
An organisation representing workers' interests

5 feworckor ....
The total number of employees in an organisation

6 gsnwondizi ....
This often means reducing the number of workers in an organisation

Business communication

1 Unscramble the words in brackets to make sentences used when leading a meeting.

1 Start

....?

(get we started shall)

2 Check agenda

.... ?

(the have agenda everyone copy a of does)

3 Say objective

....

(to review our today objective is all our projects)

4 Begin discussion

.... ?

(do think what you)

5 Clarify

....

(I you think understand if you it's good a correctly idea)

6 Handling an interruption

.... ?

(can him finish you let sorry)

7 Fix next meeting

.... ?

(we the date fix a can for meeting next)

8 Ask for other points

.... ?

(there further any are points)

9 Close meeting

....

(I can finish think there we)

2 Complete this email with words from the box.

arrange   take a train   details   flight number
hotel reservation   pick me up   return flight

Dear Jan,

I would like to give you my travel (1) ....
for my visit to Rotterdam. My (2) ....
leaves from Malaga at 10.45 on 21 June and arrives
in Amsterdam at 13.00. The (3) ....
is IB4567. Please can you (4) ....
for someone to (5) .... at the airport or
is it better if I (6) .... ?
Unfortunately, the next day I have to leave early as
the (7) .... is at 7.25 in the
morning from Amsterdam. Would it be better to go
back to Amsterdam on the night of 21 June?
Please can you advise me and if necessary
change my (9) .... ?
Thank you for your help with this.

Best wishes,
Elena Gutierrez

Social phrases

Match the sentences (1-8) with the responses (a-h).

1 Could you show me how to use this?
2 Do you know anywhere which sells Microsoft Word?
3 This is my number. You can always reach me at home.
4 What exactly is 'paella'?
5 Do I need a password?
6 Can I just ask you a question before you go?
7 Can you help me? What does this message mean exactly?
8 I'm entertaining Suzanne and Ryota tonight. Any ideas?

a That's very kind. I hope I won't have to.
b Why don't you try PC World?
c I'd take them to that new Italian restaurant. It's great.
d Sorry, I'm in a hurry. Can we leave it until Monday?
e You had a virus in an email. But don't worry – your software has deleted it.
f I'm not sure. I'll ask someone to show you.
g No, you can get in without one.
h It's a kind of rice dish.

General vocabulary

Complete the sentences with words from the box.

> poverty   thriller   rich   violence   memory
> poached   situation   reduction   rise   subtitles

1   There has been a .... in the number of
people travelling abroad this year.

2   How would you like your eggs? Fried, scrambled or
.... ?

3   I don't really like too much .... food. It
makes me feel sick.

4   I don't like watching dubbed films. .... are
much better.

5   There's too much .... on TV these days.

6   Alfred Hitchcock virtually invented the ....

7   Petra has a terrible .... She never
remembers anything.

8   There's been a .... in interest rates –
they've gone down by 0.25 per cent.

9   This isn't helping. You're only making the
.... worse.

10   Third world .... is probably the biggest
problem we face today.

File cards

2 Power for life
Communicating at work

STUDENT A

1 Phone your partner. You want to speak to him/her. Introduce yourself and leave your name, company or organisation name and number.
2 Phone JayJay Promotions. Ask to speak to Mary Rayner. It is urgent. If she is not available, choose one of the following:
   • ask when she will be back
   • ask for her mobile number
   • leave a message (you want to change an appointment).
3 Phone your partner and ask to speak to Michael Ford. If he is not available, find out when you can speak to him.

6 Tourist attraction
It's time to talk

STUDENT A

You have received this postcard from a friend who is on holiday in Tasmania, Australia. Tell your partner about the holiday your friend describes. Tell him/her about the following:
• accommodation
• things to see
• things to do
• entertainment
• food and drink
• way of travelling
• weather

Fabulous, peaceful island. We've spent most of the time walking in the mountains. Wonderful plant life, birds and all kinds of strange animals, including kangaroos. Weather O.K, but changeable. We're staying in a farmhouse with local people. They're very kind and the food is good, especially the fish. Tomorrow we're going for a few days to the National Park and we're taking the tent to go camping. You'd love it here!

Love,

Sally xxx

Ask your partner about the postcard he/she has received. Now decide with your partner which holiday you would like to go on.

7 From Mexico to Germany
It's time to talk

STUDENT A

Write down three comparative sentences for each idea below. You will use them in your conversation with your partner. Compare:
• different interests you have
• your organisation's products or services and those of your competitors or other similar organisations
• different jobs you have had in your life.

Example

Interests: *I like sport but I don't play as often as I would like.*
Products: *Our products are not as expensive as other brands.*
Jobs: *The worst job I had was in a chocolate factory.*

Now role-play your conversation in the restaurant with your partner. During the conversation you must use the sentences you have written down. Make a note of the sentences you think your partner wrote down. Did you guess correctly?

8 Globalisation
It's time to talk

TEAM A

You are going to argue the case <u>for</u> globalisation in your discussion with Team B. First plan your arguments. You may like to include some of these ideas:
• Trade is good for everyone
• Globalisation means better quality products
• It's interesting to know about other countries
• Everyone can travel and it's easy to have good holidays
• There are more job choices
• English is a world language
• People have more power and more choice about what to buy

Now present your arguments for globalisation in your discussion with Team B.

9 Here is the news
It's time to talk

STUDENT A

1 Imagine you hear this story in a radio report:
   • Government to cut spending on transport
   • Railways: price increases (10–15%) and fewer trains
   • Taxes and road charges will rise to pay for new roads.
   Tell your partner about it. Invent as much detail as you can. Include in your report:
   • what rail passengers think
   • what road users think
   • what the government thinks
   • what railway company managers think.
   Then ask your partner for his/her opinion.
2 Now listen to your partner telling you about another news story.

10 Executive search
It's time to talk

STUDENT A

You are an executive recruitment consultant. Interview Student B for the position of Chief Executive Officer at Chemco Energy PLC.
Ask him/her about the following and make notes:

Company ....

How long / current job ....

Previous job ....

How long / previous job ....

Number of years in management ....

When / leave / school (year)..

Post-school education ....

Level of English / number of years studying ....

Strengths..

Weaknesses ....

Special knowledge / experience...

11 Making money
It's time to talk

STUDENT A

- Look at the choices offered in the next column. Ask your partner to choose one of two investment choices. Then tell your partner the result of his/her investment. You must note down how much money your partner makes or loses with each investment choice.
- After each choice, your partner will offer you a similar choice and tell you the result of your investment.
- After THREE choices each, stop the game. The winner is the investor with the most money.

Each player starts with $50,000.

1 THAT'S REALLY RICH!
Buy a villa by the sea. You take out a mortgage to buy it.
OR
Buy a painting at an auction. It's a Picasso portrait of a woman.
Result
Villa: The villa is too expensive and the mortgage interest rate goes up. You cannot rent the property. You have to sell it but you lose $40,000.
Picasso: Later you decide to sell the Picasso. You sell it at a profit of $80,000.

2 THAT'S REALLY RICH!
Invest in government bonds.
OR
Go horse racing and bet on four horses.
Result
Bonds: Later you sell the bonds. You make a profit of $5,000.
Racing: All the horses win. You make $25,000.

3 THAT'S REALLY RICH!
Buy a lot of gold.
OR
Invest in a new business.
Result
Gold: You sell the gold two years later but with no profit.
Business: The business does well. You make $30,000 in two years.

4 THAT'S REALLY RICH!
Invest in shares on the New York Stock Exchange.
OR
Put money into a high interest bank account.
Result
Shares: After two years the shares have lost value. The companies you invested in failed.
You lose $25,000.
Bank account: After two years you've made $2,000.

13 Changing culture
It's time to talk

STUDENT A

You have a personal development meeting with your manager about future work plans. Discuss the decisions you have made about your development, any arrangements you have already made and any possible problems. Use the correct forms of *will, going to* **and the present continuous during your conversation.**

Decisions made	Reason for decision	How long?
1 Do some training on PowerPoint	Improve presentation skills	1 week
2 Work in Italian subsidiary for one month	Improve Italian for work	4 weeks
3 Participate in marketing project	Learn project management	2 weeks

Arrangements already made
1 Speak to your training manager next Friday at 14.00.
2 Attend a project start-up meeting tomorrow morning at 09.00.

Problems
You need the permission of the personnel director in order to take a five-week holiday. Ask your boss to speak to and (perhaps) persuade the personnel director.

15 An interesting place to live
It's time to talk

STUDENT A

You are going to do a holiday exchange of your home with your partner. This is where you live.
A large twelfth-floor apartment in downtown New York:
- bright and sunny, with good city views to north, south and east
- pre-war art deco style, hardwood floors throughout, high ceilings
- 24-hour doorman, elevator, air conditioning throughout, gym, laundry and storage (but no pets)
- spacious living room with dining area
- four bedrooms
- two bathrooms, one with jacuzzi
- stainless steel kitchen
- private terrace

- modern entertainment system with plasma television and state-of-the-art stereo system
- parking available five minutes away
- close to all the main tourist sites of central New York

Telephone your partner to tell him/her about your home and to get some other information about his/hers. For example about:
- location
- heating
- sports facilities
- parking
- view
- other ideas

16 Taiwan – still a tiger
It's time to talk
STUDENT A

1 Your partner works for Diamond Cross Inc., an American aircraft and ship components manufacturer. Prepare and then ask your partner some questions on the following:
Diamond Cross Inc.
Number of employees ....
Business structure:
• size of aircraft components business.........................
Main markets:
• percentage of products for export ....
• business done in Taiwan ....
Customers:
• sales to British Aerospace ....

2 Your partner will ask you about your company, ChemcoPharma, Geneva, Switzerland.

ChemcoPharma
Products: pharmaceutical products
Total staff: 10,000 worldwide
Head office: Geneva – 5,500 staff
Three subsidiary offices: Düsseldorf, Manchester, Prague
Customers are located in Switzerland, Austria, UK, Germany, France, USA, Japan, China, Taiwan and India
Main export market outside Europe: USA
Exports to Taiwan: 3%

ChemcoPharma – Sales as a proportion of turnover (2004)

17 RoboDog
It's time to talk
STUDENT A
Look at the information about this camera. Your partner will ask you about it. Answer his/her questions.

HP Photosmart R707 Digital Camera
Digital still camera, short video clips

Memory	32MB
Storage	Internal
Burst mode	3 shots at 3 frames per second
Resolution	5.1MP
Colour	Black and white, sepia, full colour
Requirements	USB-compatible PC with Microsoft Windows 98 or above

Your partner has some information about this music player.
Find out these details.

What it is called ....
What it is ....
Memory ....
Capacity ....
Colour ....
Software ....
Playback modes ....

20 How the rich travel
It's time to talk
Sales quiz
Interview your partner using the questions below. Where possible, ask them to give reasons for their answer. Then look at page 141 to find out if they would make a good salesperson.

Are you right for selling?
1 Which would you prefer to have?
   ☐ a safe and secure job
   ☐ lots of money
   ☐ a lot of freedom to do what you want

2 Would you prefer products which ...
   ☐ are new and attractive – really different from the rest?
   ☐ would make you a lot of money?
   ☐ people really need?

3 Do you think making personal deliveries to the customer ...
   ☐ is, unfortunately, a necessary part of customer service?
   ☐ a waste of time – you should be out there selling?
   ☐ a good opportunity to build relationships with the customer?

4 Do you think a 100% money-back guarantee is important because ...
   ☐ the company will pay the customer if he/she is not satisfied?
   ☐ it shows you are sure of the product and so helps to sell it?
   ☐ it gives security to the customer?

5 Do you think a product should be environmentally friendly because ...
   - it shows the company keeps up with modern thinking?
   - environmentally-friendly products are easier to sell?
   - this is what customers want?

6 Do you believe that bonuses to sales representatives should ...
   - be free holidays and free gifts?
   - increase with sales?
   - be part money and part training?

7 In your opinion, are the most important qualities for a salesperson ...
   - a strong personality and good presentational skills?
   - knowing how to make the most money for the minimum effort?
   - long-term planning and market knowledge?

When you have finished, work out your partner's score. Give three points for any third choice; two points for any first choice; one point for any second choice. See the Answer key on page 141.

23 Managing people
It's time to talk

PAIR A

You and your partner are human resources director and managing director of a manufacturing company, Sanchos, with 300 employees. Your company makes fashion clothing.

You are preparing for a works council meeting with some employee representatives.

You have bad news for them. Tell them about:
- the decline in the national economy
- the downturn in the fashion clothing market
- the low prices of imported clothes from competitors.

The company needs to take at least three of the following measures:
- Cut staff training by 50%
- Lay off 35–50 employees
- Cut wages by between 5% and 10%
- Ask 20 employees aged 55 or more to take early retirement
- Sell off the company social club and sports facilities.

24 Social issues
It's time to talk

STUDENT A

Ask your partner to describe each of the following social problems.

homelessness   car crime   begging   vandalism

Match one of the following solutions to each of the social problems your partner has. Do you agree with the solutions?
- Teams with a hooligan problem should get no tickets for their matches.
- The government should give single parent families more money.
- Thieves should meet the people they steal from.
- Taxes should be lower to help companies to create more jobs.

25 The coffee business
It's time to talk

STUDENT A

Here are some hypothetical situations. Ask your partner what he/she would do in these situations.

Professional life

If you were managing director of your organisation, what three things would you change?

If you had to go and work abroad tomorrow for one year, where would you go?

If your boss asked you this afternoon to work every Saturday for the next month, would you agree?

If your organisation decided to move all its staff to another town a long way away, what would you do?

Your own question: ....

Now make questions using first or second conditionals. Your grammar choice will depend on how possible you think the future situation is.

Everyday life

If the birth rate in Europe continues/continued to decrease, do you think ... ?

If the government increases/increased taxes next year, do you think ... ?

If house prices increase/increased a lot next year, do you think ... ?

If more budget airlines start/started up, do you think ... ?

Your own question: ....

Now ask and answer the questions.

26 Intelligent skis
Communicating at work

STUDENT A

Practise making complaints and handling complaints on the phone with your partner.

Problem 1
Take the call
Your name is Peter/Petra Wood. A customer calls you about a contract you had to send to them. Explain that you had some problems with your legal department about the terms and conditions, but you posted it this morning and so your partner will have it in three or four days. Apologise for the delay.

Problem 2
Make the call
Your name is Chris/Christina Anderson and you work in the purchasing department of KLP. Phone Sam Evans of JL Technode. You ordered ten new computers last month but they haven't arrived yet. It is now Thursday and JL Technode promised to deliver them last week. The order number is KL/56382.

Take the call
Sam Evans of JL Technode calls with an explanation of your order delay. Ask for a 5% discount on the price.

29 Life coaching
It's time to talk
STUDENT A

Probe SA is a French company which sells specialised CD systems for cars. The graph shows sales in millions of euros for Probe SA from 1998 to 2003. Look at the graph and then describe the changes to your partner, giving the reasons for the changes.

2 Power for life
Communicating at work
STUDENT B

1 Your partner phones you. Read this out to your partner.
Hello. This is the voicemail of (*your name*). Please leave a message and I will call you back soon.
2 You work for JayJay Promotions. Answer the phone. Mary Rayner is not available. She is away for a week. Offer to take a message.
3 You are the PA to Michael Ford. He is in a meeting and very busy all week. Choose one of the following:
   • Get the caller's number. Promise to ask Michael to call back.
   • Take a message.
   • Ask the caller to ring back later (give a time).

6 Tourist attraction
It's time to talk
STUDENT B

You have received this postcard from a friend who is on holiday in Sydney, Australia. Tell your partner about the holiday your friend describes. Tell him/her about the following:
• accommodation
• things to see
• things to do
• entertainment
• food and drink
• way of travelling
• weather

Fantastic city! Really lively, lots to do. We've been around Sydney Harbour and seen the Opera House. The nightlife is brilliant: lots of clubs, great bars, great food. We've spent loads of money shopping, visited a vineyard, been to the zoo and even found time for sunbathing on the beach. It's really hot, 35°! Tomorrow we're going on a bus trip to see some places where the Aborigines used to live. The hotel's got a sauna, swimming pool and a casino. See you soon!

Bill

Ask your partner about the postcard he/she has received. Now decide with your partner which holiday you would like to go on.

7 From Mexico to Germany
It's time to talk
STUDENT B

Write down three comparative sentences for each idea below. You will use them in your conversation with your partner. Compare:
• other places you have visited or know
• languages you speak
• your organisation and your competitors.

<u>Example</u>
Places: *Sicily is beautiful but it's not as nice as Sardinia.*
Languages: *I don't speak German as well as I speak French.*
Organisations: *We're much bigger than our competitors.*

Now role-play your conversation in the restaurant with your partner. During the conversation you must use the sentences you have written down. Make a note of the sentences you think your partner wrote down. Did you guess correctly?

8 Globalisation
It's time to talk
TEAM B

You are going to argue the case <u>against</u> globalisation in your discussion with Team A. First plan your arguments. You may like to include some of these ideas:
• A lot of people have to work in poor conditions
• The rich are getting richer and the poor are getting poorer
• There are too many people without enough money
• A lot of energy is used (oil, gas, electricity, nuclear power) by a small number of rich countries
• Many people lose their jobs
• Big companies are very powerful and exploit poor countries
• Different countries are becoming more similar

Now present your arguments against globalisation in your discussion with Team A.

9 Here is the news
It's time to talk
STUDENT B

1 Your partner has heard a news story. Ask for information about it. Give him/her your opinion about the story.
2 Now imagine you hear this story in a radio report:
   • Top movie star sues movie magazine
   • Magazine reported star in 'a highly embarrassing situation' in a motor car with a woman not his wife
   • Magazine keeps to its story

Tell your partner about it. Invent as much detail as you can. Include in your report:
• what the magazine said
• what the star said
• what the wife said
• what the other woman said
• what the star's lawyer said.

Then ask your partner for his/her opinion.

10 Executive search

It's time to talk

STUDENT B

You have applied for the position of Chief Executive Officer at Chemco Energy PLC. Prepare some sentences from the notes below to help you in your interview.

Current job: Managing Director, VEBOC Corporation (Very Big Oil Company) (since 2002)

Previous job: Research and Development Manager, Expo Gas Company, Ottawa, Canada (5 years)

Experience in management: Almost 30 years

Education: Left school in 1973; studied chemical engineering at university; MBA in 1990

English: Very good

Strengths: Ambition, confidence

Weaknesses: Sometimes too much focus on small details

Special knowledge/experience: Many years' experience in Canadian business and energy sector; good in teams and team working; leadership skills

11 Making money

It's time to talk

STUDENT B

- Ask your partner to choose a number from 1 to 4.
- Look at the choices offered below. Ask your partner to choose one of two investment choices. Then tell your partner the result of his/her investment. You must note down how much money your partner makes or loses with each investment choice.
- After each choice, your partner will offer you a similar choice and tell you the result of your investment.
- After THREE choices each, stop the game. The winner is the investor with the most money.

Each player starts with $50,000.

1 THAT'S REALLY RICH!
Buy a share in a commercial property. You take out a mortgage to buy it.
OR
Buy some land near a golf course on the coast. You plan to build a small hotel.
Result
Commercial property: the property is a really good one. You sell it three years later for a $50,000 profit.
Land: Some of the land drops into the sea. You lose $40,000.

2 THAT'S REALLY RICH!
Invest in your local football team.
OR
You decide to learn to fly as you plan a new career as a pilot.
Result
Football team: The team does really well. You make a profit of $25,000.
Flying: Flying makes you air sick. You waste $15,000.

3 THAT'S REALLY RICH!
Buy 48 bottles of vintage Bordeaux wine.
OR
Invest in the stock market.
Result
Wine: Your cellar gets flooded, half the wine is spoiled, you drink the rest. You lose £10,000.
Stock market: You sell your shares at a $40,000 profit.

4 THAT'S REALLY RICH!
Buy a second house near the university. You plan to let the house to university students.
OR
Buy a valuable antique clock.
Result
House: Unfortunately the house is destroyed in a fire. You have insurance, but you lose $30,000.
Clock: The clock gets stolen. You did not insure it. You lose $10,000.

13 Changing culture

It's time to talk

STUDENT B

You have a career meeting with an employee about future work plans. Interview your staff member and complete the form below during your meeting.

1 Discuss your employee's decisions about personal development – what he/she is going to do and why.
2 Ask him/her about any arrangements he/she has already made about his/her training.
3 Check the amount of time required for the various plans.
4 Offer to help with any problems.

Personal Development Interview

Employee name: ....

Employee decisions: ....
....

Arrangements made: ....
....

Problems: ....
....

Manager actions: ....
....

Make sure you summarise the information at the end of the interview. Use the correct forms of *will, going to* **and the present continuous during your conversation.**

15 An interesting place to live
It's time to talk

STUDENT B

You are going to do a holiday exchange of your home with your partner. This is where you live.

A comfortable country house near York in the north of England:

- large mid-nineteenth century house with spacious hall, lounge, dining room, four bedrooms and two bathrooms
- central heating throughout
- fully-equipped bar
- games room containing full-sized snooker and billiard table in the basement
- wood-burning fires in reception, dining and living rooms
- marble bathroom
- large garden plus south-facing patio for barbecues, etc.
- small (10 metre) heated indoor swimming pool
- double garage
- 15 minutes' drive from the centre of historic York
- quiet location with good views in three directions

Telephone your partner to tell him/her about your home and to get some other information about his/hers. For example about:

- location
- view
- pets
- entertainment facilities
- parking
- other ideas

16 Taiwan – still a tiger
It's time to talk

STUDENT B

1 **Your partner works for ChemcoPharma, a Swiss drugs company. Prepare and then ask your partner some questions on the following:**

ChemcoPharma

Number of employees worldwide ....

Number of employees in headquarters...

Number of subsidiaries ....

Customers:

- location ....
- main export market ....
- percentage of exports to Taiwan ....

Turnover of each product:

Amsol ....

Amandol ....

Zarcam ....

Others ....

2 **Your partner will ask you about your company, Diamond Cross Inc., Boston, USA.**

Diamond Cross Inc.

Products: components for aircraft and ship engines

Employees: 2,400

Business structure:

- most of your business (around 85%) is for the aircraft industry

Main markets:

- you export about 90% of your products
- you have important customers in Europe and the USA
- 57% of sales are to British Aerospace
- you have a few shipbuilding contracts in Norway and Italy
- you do very little business in big Asian markets: Taiwan, China or Japan

17 RoboDog
It's time to talk

STUDENT B

Your partner has some information about this camera. Find out these details.

What it is called ....

What it is ....

Memory ....

Burst mode ....

Resolution ....

Colour ....

System requirements ....

Now look at the information about this music player. Your partner will ask you about it. Answer his/her questions.

Sony Network Walkman NW-MS90D
Digital music player

Memory	512MB built-in memory
Capacity	340 songs
Colour	Silver
Software included	Sony SonicStage
Playback modes	Random play, one track repeat, all tracks repeat

23 Managing people
It's time to talk

PAIR B

You and your partner work for Sanchos, a fashion clothing manufacturer with 300 employees. You are preparing for a works council meeting. You are representatives of the employees of the company.

You have a meeting with the company's managing director and human resources director. You know that the national economy is doing badly and that the company is not doing well.

This is your position:

- You accept that some employees may lose their jobs (but not many)
- You want them to get good pensions depending on the number of years working for Sanchos
- You cannot accept wage cuts: inflation is already at 5%
- You accept that the company may reduce the training budget
- You want the company to spend less on 'benefits' for managers. These include: first class air travel, free parking, top class hotels and restaurants, company cars.

24 Social issues

It's time to talk

STUDENT B

Ask your partner to describe each of the following social problems.

unemployment   theft   football hooliganism   poverty

Match one of the following solutions to each of the social problems your partner has. Do you agree with the solutions?
- Begging should be illegal.
- Car thieves should go to prison for ten years.
- The government should build more houses in poor areas.
- If children break things their parents should pay.

25 The coffee business

It's time to talk

STUDENT B

Here are some hypothetical situations. Ask your partner what he/she would do in these situations.

Everyday life

If you were leader of your country, what three policies would you introduce?

If you had a million pounds to spend, what would you buy?

If you had ten hours a week for a new hobby, what would you choose?

If you could take a four-week holiday tomorrow anywhere in the world, where would you go?

Your own question: ....

Now make questions using first or second conditionals. Your grammar choice will depend on how possible you think the future situation is.

Professional life

If you get/got an interesting job offer from another company, do you think ... ?

If your organisation changes/changed its structure, do you think ... ?

If several big companies makes/made a loss next year, do you think ... ?

If the stock market falls/fell significantly, do you think ... ?

Your own question: ....

Now ask and answer the questions.

26 Intelligent skis

Communicating at work

STUDENT B

Practise making complaints and handling complaints on the phone with your partner.

Problem 1

Make the call

Your name is Charlie/Charlotte Cooper. You expected to receive the hard copy of a contract last week but nothing has arrived. You need the contract to discuss in a meeting at the beginning of next week. Call Peter/Petra Wood to discuss the problem.

Problem 2

Take the call

Your name is Sam Evans and you work for JL Technode. A customer calls with a complaint about an order. Apologise, take the order number, promise to investigate and call back.

Make the call

Call Chris/Christina Anderson of KLP back and explain the reason for the order delay. Computer components from China were not available and caused the delay. Apologise and promise to send the order on Monday next week.

29 Life coaching

It's time to talk

STUDENT B

COMPIC Computers sells specialised computers to art and design companies. The graph shows the number of computers sold by COMPIC Computers in thousands from 1998 to 2003. Look at the graph and then describe the changes to your partner, giving the reasons for the changes.

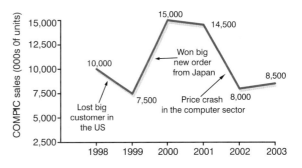

Grammar reference

Index

	page
The present simple and present continuous tenses	112
The past simple and past continuous tenses	113
Comparative and superlative adjectives and adverbs	114
The present perfect simple, present perfect continuous, past simple; *for, since* and *ago*	114
Future 1: *will, going to* and the present continuous	115
Quantifiers: *all, every, each, most, much, many, a few, a little, no, any, some*	116
Future 2: *will, can, may, might* and the first conditional	116
Must, have to and *need to*	117
The second conditional	117
The passive	118
Irregular verbs	119

Grammar reference

The present simple and present continuous tenses (Unit 1)

Present simple

In *English365* Book 2, we look at how we can use the present simple for actions and situations which are not temporary, for example general and personal facts, regular events, likes and dislikes.

Mike lives in Rotterdam and works for the Port Authority.
He speaks five languages.
His partner, Greta, makes films for Dutch television.

Positive	Negative
I /you/we/they work hard.	I/you/we/they do not / don't work hard.
He/she/it works hard.	He/she/it does not / doesn't work hard.

Questions	Short answers
Do I/we/you/they work hard?	Yes, I/we/you/they do. No, I/we/you/they don't.
Does he/she/it work hard?	Yes, he/she/it does. No, he/she/it doesn't.

Time expressions

It's useful to remember how we can use the following time expressions:

Every day/week/month/year
Every year we have a sales conference in Geneva.

Daily/weekly/monthly/yearly
We produce a monthly report.

On + days of the week (plural) for regular events or *every* + day of the week (singular)
On Mondays we have team meetings.
I talk to my colleague in Stuttgart every Friday .

On + date
We have a training day on 30 March. I'm in Milan on 1 April.

In + month of the year/season
We always go on holiday in August.
We go skiing in winter.

At + time/holiday/festival
I start work at 9 o'clock.
I usually visit my parents at Christmas.

The following adverbs and adverbial phrases are commonly used with the present simple tense:

always   almost always   usually   generally   frequently   often
sometimes   occasionally   rarely   hardly ever   never

We usually fly economy class, but we sometimes go business class for long flights.
I hardly ever drive to work. I almost always go by bike.

Present continuous

We can use the present continuous for describing temporary actions and situations which are happening now, for example, current trends and short term events in progress.

It's raining.
I'm working from home today because they're painting my office.
I'm preparing some work for the meeting on Tuesday.
Results are improving and sales are going up.

Positive	Negative
I am / 'm staying here.	I am not / 'm not staying here.
You/we/they are / 're staying here.	You/we/they are not / aren't staying here.
He/she/it is / 's staying here.	He/she/it is not / isn't staying here.

Questions	Short answers
Am I staying here?	Yes, I am.
	No, I'm not.
Are you/we/they staying here?	Yes, you/we/they are.
	No, you/we/they aren't.
Is he/she/it staying here?	Yes, he/she/it is.
	No, he/she/it isn't.

The following adverbs and adverbial phrases are commonly used with the present continuous:

at the moment   this week   this year   currently   at present

At the moment I'm reading a book about the First World War.
We're currently developing a new customer database.
I'm working in a different office this week.

The present continuous is also used to talk about the future (see Unit 13).

Verbs not usually in the continuous form

Some verbs do not usually have a continuous form.

For thinking and feeling	
think	*We think the report is excellent.*
believe	*I believe he's in Japan at the moment.*
know	*They know that she's coming today.*
understand	*I'm sorry, I don't understand.*
remember	*Do you remember that hotel in London?*

For possession	
belong	*This book belongs to Antonia Baena.*
have	*Do you have any red shirts?*
own	*He owns half the island.*

For the senses	
feel	*The office feels very cold today.*
smell	*It smells awful.*
taste	*But it tastes delicious.*
sound	*It sounds OK.*

For wants and likes	
want	*They want a bigger pay rise.*
like	*I like it here.*
love	*I love you more than I can say.*
hate	*She hates the winter.*

need	*I need you so much.*
prefer	*He prefers cross-country to downhill skiing.*
wish	*I wish I could fly.*

For how things look or seem	
look	*It looks absolutely great.*
seem	*It seems OK.*

Others	
matter	*It doesn't matter.*
depend	*It depends on the weather.*
hear	*I hear that you're getting married.*
owe	*He owes me $100.*

The past simple and past continuous tenses (Unit 4)

Past simple

In *English365* Book 2, we look at how we can use the past simple to talk about finished and completed actions.

Sally called a few moments ago. She said Mario came here on Friday and spoke at the conference on Saturday. He flew back to Rome on Monday. She thinks he took the early flight.

Regular verbs
For regular verbs, add *-ed* to the infinitive or *-d* if the infinitive ends with -e.

work + -ed = worked   arrive + -d = arrived   decide + -d = decided

Positive	Negative
I/you/we/they/he/she/it worked hard.	I/you/we/they/he/she/it did not / didn't work hard.

Questions	Short answers
Did I/you/we/they/he/she/it work hard?	Yes, I/you/we/they/he/she/it did. No, I/you/we/they/he/she/it didn't.

Irregular verbs
Some verbs are irregular, e.g. buy → bought, catch → caught. See page 119 for a list of irregular verbs.

Past continuous

We can use the past continuous tense to give background information to main actions, which we can describe with the past simple. The past continuous describes a temporary situation, not a finished action. The focus is on something in progress at some point in the past.

I was driving to work. It was raining. A dog ran into the road but I stopped. I didn't hit the dog.

Positive	Negative
I was working hard.	I was not / wasn't working hard.
You/we/they were working hard.	You/we/they were not / weren't working hard.
He/she/it was working hard.	He/she/it was not / wasn't working hard.

Questions	Short answers
Was I working hard?	Yes, I was.
	No, I wasn't.
Were you/we/they working hard?	Yes, you/we/they were.
	No, you/we/they weren't.
Was he/she/it working hard?	Yes, he/she/it was.
	No, he/she/it wasn't.

The past continuous is often used with the words *when* and *while* to show how an action described in the past happens during an action which is described.

I was working for a language school when I had the idea.
I had a job offer in Poland while I was working at Motorola.

The following adverbs and adverbial phrases are common with the past simple and the past continuous:

ago   for
yesterday   the day before yesterday   last week   last month
last year   this morning (it is now this afternoon)

He went to South America several times last year.
A few years ago I lived in Antwerp, in Belgium.
Elena worked in Bilbao for five years. (= She doesn't work there now.)
Margaret rang this morning. Can you call her back?
I was helping Julia all morning. Now I can do the reports. (= It's now afternoon.)

It's useful to remember how we can use the following time expressions:

Last week/month/year/April/summer, etc.
We met Raul last spring.

We went on holiday in April.	*in* + month
I left the company in 1999.	*in* + year
The course started in the spring.	*in* + season
I was working at home on Tuesday.	*on* + day
I had an appointment with Mrs Chen on 5th March.	*on* + date
I last saw my sister at Christmas.	*at* + holiday /festival
The company closed down at the end of the year.	*at* + time
I was typing the email at 4 o'clock.	*at* + time

Comparative and superlative adjectives and adverbs (Unit 7)

Adjectives

In *English365* Book 2 we look at how we can use comparative and superlative forms to compare people and things.

Paris is bigger than Rome.
Florence is even more beautiful than I expected.
I had the worst holiday ever this year. It was even worse than last year's.

Comparative and superlative adjectives

Rule	Adjective	Comparative	Superlative
One syllable: add *–er/-est*	cheap	cheaper	cheapest
Two syllables ending in 'y': change 'y' to 'i' and add *–er/-est*	tasty	tastier	tastiest
Other two syllable adjectives*: use *more/less* and *most/least*	modern	more/less modern	most/least modern
Three or more syllables: use *more/less* and *most/least*	expensive	more/less expensive	most/least expensive
Learn the irregular adjectives	good bad	better worse	best worst
*Some two syllable adjectives take *–er/-est*	quiet	quieter	quietest
Some can take both forms	polite	politer most/least polite	politest more/less polite

If you are not sure, use a dictionary.

Adverbs

We can use *more* to make comparatives with most *-ly* adverbs, e.g. *more efficiently*. However, many adverbs with the same form as adjectives form the comparative with *-er*, e.g. *nearer, earlier, faster*.

You should drive more carefully.
He's OK but Ben works faster.
She arrived earlier than we expected.

Classification of adverbs

Manner	well	badly	quickly	slowly	carefully
Time	early	late	on time		
Place	here	there	near	far	
Frequency	never	usually	sometimes	frequently	always
Degree	very	extremely	quite	not very	

Comparative and superlative adverbs

We form these in a similar way to adjectives.

The band played even more brilliantly than last time I saw them.
I work most efficiently early in the day.
The prime minister spoke most enthusiastically about her work.

Comparing with *as ... as*

When we compare things, we can also use *(not) as ... as* with adjectives and adverbs:

... (not) as + adjective + as
... (not) as + adverb + as

Vicenza is still as beautiful as it was when I first went there.
I didn't have as much time as I thought I would.
He's not as good as he was.

The past simple, present perfect simple and present perfect continuous; *for*, *since* and *ago* (Unit 10)

Present perfect simple

In *English365* Book 2 we look at how we can use the present perfect simple to report news (finished past activities with a result in the present).

I've spoken to Klara. She's done the work and written a report.

It can also be used to describe an action which started in the past and continues up to the present.

The Economist has been Britain's leading weekly magazine for over 100 years.
Ruth and Patrick have lived in Madrid since 1998.

Positive	Negative
I/you/we/they have / 've finished the report.	I/you/we/they have not / haven't finished the report.
He/she/it has / 's finished the report.	He/she/it has not / hasn't finished the report.

Questions	Short answers
Have I/you/we/they finished the report?	Yes, I/you/we/they have. No, I/you/we/they haven't.
Has he/she/it finished the report?	Yes, he/she/it has. No, he/she/it hasn't.

Present perfect continuous

In *English365* Book 2 we look at how we can use the present perfect continuous to focus on recent past activities over a period of time. They may or may not be finished.

Rachel has been looking for you.
We've been trying to find an agent in Austria.

Positive	Negative
I/you/we/they have been / 've been waiting.	I/you/we/they have not been / haven't been waiting.
He/she/it has been / 's been waiting.	He/she/it has been / hasn't been waiting.
Questions	**Short answers**
Have I/you/we/they been waiting?	Yes, I/you/we/they have.
	No, I/you/we/they haven't.
Has he/she/it been waiting?	Yes, he/she/it has.
	No, he/she/it hasn't.

For, since and ago

- We can use *for* with the past simple, the present perfect and perfect continuous to describe the length of an activity or a period of time.
  I studied Chinese for a year but it was very difficult.
  They've been in the meeting for over five hours now.
  I've been working for a Polish company for ten years.

- *Since* is often used with the present perfect simple or the present perfect continuous to describe a point in time.
  I've worked for the same organisation since I left university.
  I've been answering emails since I arrived at 9 o'clock this morning.

- *Ago* is used with the simple past or the past continuous. It indicates a finished action.
  Warren came to England five years ago. He was thinking of going back to New York a couple of years ago but then he met Anne, and he decided to stay.

- *Yet* is often used with the present perfect simple in questions and negatives to clarify the status of activities.
  Have you finished the report yet?
  No, not yet. / No, I haven't finished it yet. I'm still working on it.

Future 1: *will, going to* and the present continuous (Unit 13)

Will + infinitive without *to*

In *English365* Book 2 we look at how we can use *will* to describe future actions which we decide to do at the moment of speaking, especially when we promise or offer to do something (see Unit 13).

Do you need help? I'll come now.
Let me take that. I'll give it to Magnus.
We'll decide tomorrow.

We can also use it to make predictions about the future (see Unit 19).

I think Real Madrid will win the Champions League this year.
The Republicans will always win elections in Texas.
Do you think Tiger Woods will win the US Open?

In spoken English, *will* is almost always contracted to *'ll* in the positive form and *won't* in the negative, but this can depend on the context.

Positive	Negative
I/you/we/they/he/she/it will / 'll come soon.	I/you/we/they/he/she/it will not / won't come soon.
Questions	**Short answers**
Will I/you/we/they/he/she/it come soon?	Yes, I/you/we/they/he/she/it will.
	No, I/you/we/they/he/she/it will not / won't.

Be + *going to* + infinitive without *to*

We can use *going to* to describe decisions and plans we have already made.

We're going to stay with some friends at the weekend. (= We decided to do this yesterday.)
I'm going to buy a new car. (= I've thought about it and made a decision.)

Positive	Negative
I am / 'm going to come.	I am not / 'm not going to come.
You/we/they are / 're going to come.	You/we/they are not / 're not / aren't going to come.
He/she/it is / 's going to come.	He/she/it is not / 's not / isn't going to come.
Questions	**Short answers**
Am I going to come?	Yes, I am.
	No, I'm not.
Are you/we/they going to come?	Yes, you/we/they are.
	No, you/we/they aren't.
Is he/she/it going to come?	Yes, he/she/it is.
	No, he/she/it isn't.

Present continuous (*be + -ing* form)

We can use the present continuous to describe future fixed arrangements, especially for personal travel and meetings. Often a time phrase is included, such as a date, *next week, for Christmas*, etc.

She's flying to Australia on 30th March.
We're visiting my mother at Christmas.
I can't make 2 o'clock – I'm meeting the marketing manager then.

Positive	Negative
I am / 'm coming soon.	I am not / 'm not coming soon.
You/we/they are / 're coming soon.	You/we/they are not / 're not coming soon.
He/she/it is / 's coming soon.	He/she/it is not / 's not coming soon.
Questions	**Short answers**
Am I coming soon?	Yes, I am.
	No, I'm not.
Are you/we/they coming soon?	Yes, you/we/they are.
	No, you/we/they aren't.
Is he/she/it coming soon?	Yes, he/she/it is.
	No, he/she/it isn't.

The choice of which future form we use often depends on the situation and on the speaker. For example:

Hannah's going to visit us next month. (= It is her intention to come, she plans to come.)
She's coming by train. (= This is a fixed plan, she has told me this, she has a ticket.)
I think she'll stay for a week. (= It's not certain, but in my opinion, she will stay for a week.)

Adverbs used with future verb forms

Some adverbs and adverbial phrases are often used with future verb forms.

tomorrow	*We'll see you tomorrow.*
the day after tomorrow	*Bill's sending the contract the day after tomorrow.*
next week	*We're going to do the work next week.*
next month	*Ali's going to run a marathon next month.*
next year	*House prices will fall next year.*
soon	*There'll be a rise in the stock market soon.*
in a few minutes/hours /days/weeks/years	*Maribel's coming in a few minutes.*

Quantifiers: *all, every, each, most, much, many, a few, a little, no, any, some* (Unit 16)

In *English365* Book 2 we look at how we can use these words to describe the quantity of something.

All, every, each (total quantity)

All, *every* and *each* can be used to talk about the completeness of a group of things. *All* is followed by a plural noun or an uncountable noun. *Every* and *each* are more individual, and are followed by a singular noun and a verb.

All Elixir hotels have restaurants and parking facilities.
All rooms are en suite.
Each/Every room has a television.
Each/Every visitor signs the register in reception.

Most, many, much, a lot of, lots of (large quantity)

We can use *most*, *many*, *much*, *a lot of* and *lots of* to talk about large quantities.

Most + countable or uncountable noun	*Most offices are quite warm.* *Most news is depressing.*
Many + countable noun	*Many people went to the conference.*
Much + uncountable noun	*There was much interest in the event.*
A lot of + plural or uncountable noun	*I met a lot of people.* *I got a lot of information.*
Lots of + plural or uncountable noun	*Lots of things were new to me.* *There was lots of interest.*

A few, a little (small quantity)

We can use *a few* and *a little* to talk about small quantities.

A few + plural noun	*I wrote a lot of letters but only had a few replies.*
A little + uncountable noun	*I need a little help, please.* *Would you like a little milk?*

No, not any, none (zero quantity)

No is used with countable, uncountable or plural nouns. It means the same as *not any*.

We can't have a drink, there's no time.
The hotel's got no rooms free. It's full.
There are no big mountains in England.

None is used after questions about the existence or quantity of something. It indicates non-existence, or zero.

How many people came to the meeting? None. No one came.
Have you got any ideas? None, I'm sorry. I don't understand the subject at all.

Some and *any*

Some + plural and uncountable noun

We can use *some* in positive sentences to describe unspecified quantities.

A woman came in a few minutes ago. I gave her some information about the city.
Some people wanted tickets for the concert.

We can also use *some* when we ask for or offer something.

I'd like some information, please.
Can I get you some coffee?

Any + plural or uncountable noun

Any can be used in questions to ask about the existence of something.

Do you have any maps of the city?
Have you had any news from Tomoko?

Any can be used in negative sentences to talk about non-existence.

My team haven't won any matches all year.
I haven't got any yen. I need to go to the bank.

Future 2: *will, can, may, might* and the first conditional (Unit 19)

Will, can, may and *might*

In *English365* Book 2 we look at how we can use *will*, *can*, *may* and *might* to talk about the future.

Will
We can use *will* to predict things we think are certain or very likely.

Global warming will affect us all.
I think next year business will be better because the economy will improve.

Can
We can use *can* to express the idea of ability.

If you want, you can work at home next week.

May and *might*
We can use *may* or *might* for things we think are possible but not certain.

The economy may improve but there are still a lot of problems.
Yuri might change his job to work in marketing but he's not really sure.

First conditional

We can use first conditional sentences to connect two possible future actions with *will*, *can*, *may* or *might*.

If clause	Main clause
If + present simple	*will/can/may/might* + infinitive
If you come this weekend,	*I'll show you around the city.*
If sales don't increase soon,	*we may have to cut the budget.*
If we don't explain,	*he might not understand.*

We can also start the sentence with the main clause. We do not use a comma in this case.

I'll get you a copy of this if you need one.

We can use *when* instead of *if* when we are sure the action in the *when* clause is sure to happen.

When you come, I'll show you around the city. (= It is certain you will come.)

We can use *unless* instead of *will* when we want to say that the main clause won't happen if a condition is not fulfilled.

Unless you come, you won't see anything of our city. (= This won't happen if you don't come.)

Must, have to and *need to* (Unit 22)

In *English365* Book 2 we look at how we can use *must, have to* and *need to* to talk about things which are necessary or not necessary to do.

Must

We can use *must* to give strong advice or to say what we think is personally necessary or not necessary.

You must stop smoking – it's killing you.
We mustn't make the same mistake again.
Cristina must improve her presentation skills.

Positive	Negative
I/you/we/they/he/she/it must go.	I/you/we/they/he/she/it must not / mustn't go.
Questions	Short answers
Must I/you/we/they/he/she/it go?	Yes, I/you/we/they/he/she/it must.
No, I/you/we/they/he/she/it mustn't.	
Do I/you/we/they have to go?	Yes, I/you/we/they do.
	No, I/you/we/they don't.
Does he/she/it have to go?	Yes, he/she/it does.
	No, he/she/it doesn't.
Past positive	Past negative
I/you/we/they/he/she/it had to go.	I/you/we/they/he/she/it did not / didn't have to go.
Past questions	Short answers
Did I/you/we/they/he/she/it have to go?	Yes, I/you/we/they/he/she/it did.
	No, I/you/we/they/he/she/it didn't.

Have to

We can use *have to* to talk about rules that somebody else has made.

To get this qualification you have to take a three-hour examination.
You have to turn off your mobile when you're filling your car at a petrol station.
Antonia has to go outside when she wants to smoke.

We can use *don't have to* to talk about something that is not necessary.

You don't have to wear a tie to work – only a few men wear them.
Alfonso doesn't have to work on his computer all the time.
Some people don't have to pay for their lunch at work.

Positive	Negative
I/you/we/they have to work hard.	I/you/we/they do not / don't have to work hard.
He/she/it has to work hard.	He/she/it does not / doesn't have to work hard.

Questions	Short answers
Do I/you/we/they have to work hard?	Yes, I /you/we/they do.
	No, I /you/we/they don't.
Does he/she/it have to work hard?	Yes, he/she/it does.
	No, he/she/it doesn't.
Past positive	Past negative
I/you/we/they/he/she/it had to work hard.	I/you/we/they/he/she/it did not / didn't have to work hard.
Past questions	Short answers
Did I/you/we/they/he/she/it have to work hard?	Yes, I/you/we/they/he/she/it did.
	No, I/you/we/they/he/she/it didn't.

Need to

We can use *need to* to stress that something is necessary or important.

I need to get more organised.
Marina needs to tidy her desk before the meeting.
They need to dispatch the orders more quickly.

We can use *don't need to* or *needn't* to talk about something that is not necessary.

We don't need to be there until 11 o'clock.
She doesn't need to worry so much.
Daniel needn't stay for the second half of the meeting.

Positive	Negative
I/you/we/they need to go.	I/you/we/they do not / don't need to go.
He/she/it needs to go.	He/she/it does not / doesn't need to go.
Questions	Short answers
Do I/you/we/they need to go?	Yes, I/you/we/they do.
	No, I/you/we/they don't.
Does he/she/it need to go?	Yes, he/she/it does.
	No, he/she/it doesn't.
Past positive	Past negative
I/you/we/they/he/she/it needed to go.	I/you/we/they/he/she/it did not / didn't need to go.
Past questions	Short answers
Did I/you/we/they/he/she/it need to go?	Yes, I/you/we/they/he/she/it did.
	No, I/you/we/they/he/she/it didn't.

The second conditional (Unit 25)

In *English365* Book 2 we look at how we can use the second conditional in three ways:

- To think about future events which are the result of impossible present situations.
  If I had enough money for a Porsche Carrera, I would buy one tomorrow. (= But I haven't, so I won't.)
- To think about unlikely or imagined future situations and their results.
  If interest rates doubled, many people would be forced to sell their homes. (= The speaker thinks that such a large increase in interest rates is unlikely.)
- To show disagreement with a proposal or idea during discussion.
  If we accepted this proposal, we would risk heavy losses. (= The speaker thinks the proposal is a bad idea.)

The standard form of the second conditional is:

If clause	Main clause
If + past tense	would + infinitive without to
If I lived in Norway,	I would go cross-country skiing.

We can also start the sentence with the main clause. We do not use a comma in this case.

I would earn more if I worked for a different company.

Could

We can use *could* in the *if* clause instead of the past tense, meaning *if possible* (but it's not possible).

If I could speak Spanish, it would be easier to travel around South America. (= But I can't, so travelling around South America is more difficult.)
If you could play golf, we could have a game together. (= But you can't, so we'll have to do something else.)

Could can also indicate a request.

If you could meet me at my hotel, I would be very grateful.

Might

We can use *might* instead of *would* in the main clause, meaning *it is possible that I would.*

If I had more squash lessons, I might get better. (= It's possible that I would get better.)

The passive (Unit 28)

In *English365* Book 2 we look at how we can use the present simple passive to describe work processes.

The machine is switched on here.
The photographs are developed and then they are posted on our website.
The products are tested and then packed into boxes. They are stored in the warehouse.

We also look at how we can use the passive when we want to avoid the subject of the sentence or when it is not important or not known.

Our car was broken into. (= But I don't know who did it.)
The meeting was cancelled. (= It's not important to know who cancelled it.)

A: *They were given the wrong goods.*
B: *Sorry, I won't do it again.* (= Speaker A knows that it was B's fault but politely avoids using his/her name.)

Present simple passive

Positive: subject + *be* + past participle	Negative
The office is cleaned every night.	The office is not / isn't cleaned every night.
The offices are cleaned every night.	The offices are not / aren't cleaned every night.
Questions	Short answers
Is the office cleaned every night?	Yes, it is.
	No, it isn't.
Are the offices cleaned every night?	Yes, they are.
	No, they aren't.

Past simple passive

Positive: subject + *was/were* + past participle	Negative
The meeting was cancelled.	The meeting was not / wasn't cancelled.
The meetings were cancelled.	The meetings were not / weren't cancelled.
Questions	Short answers
Was the meeting cancelled?	Yes, it was.
	No, it wasn't.
Were the meetings cancelled?	Yes, they were.
	No, they weren't.

Irregular verbs

Infinitive	Past simple	Past participle
be	was/were	been
beat	beat	beat
become	became	become
begin	began	begun
bend	bent	bent
bet	bet	bet
blow	blew	blown
break	broke	broken
bring	brought	brought
build	built	built
burn	burnt/burned	burnt/burned
buy	bought	bought
catch	caught	caught
choose	chose	chosen
come	came	come
cost	cost	cost
cut	cut	cut
dig	dug	dug
do	did	done
draw	drew	drawn
dream	dreamt/dreamed	dreamt/dreamed
drink	drank	drunk
drive	drove	driven
eat	ate	eaten
fall	fell	fallen
feed	fed	fed
feel	felt	felt
fight	fought	fought
find	found	found
forget	forgot	forgotten
fly	flew	flown
freeze	froze	frozen
get	got	got
give	gave	given
go	went	gone
grow	grew	grown
have	had	had
hear	heard	heard
hide	hid	hidden
hit	hit	hit
hold	held	held
hurt	hurt	hurt
keep	kept	kept
know	knew	known
lay	laid	laid

Infinitive	Past simple	Past participle
lead	led	led
learn	learnt	learnt
leave	left	left
lend	lent	lent
let	let	let
lie	lay	lain
light	lit	lit
lose	lost	lost
make	made	made
mean	meant	meant
meet	met	met
pay	paid	paid
put	put	put
read	read	read
ride	rode	ridden
ring	rang	rung
rise	rose	risen
run	run	run
say	said	said
see	saw	seen
sell	sold	sold
send	sent	sent
shine	shone	shone
shoot	shot	shot
show	showed	shown
shut	shut	shut
sing	sang	sung
sit	sat	sat
sleep	slept	slept
smell	smelt	smelt
speak	spoke	spoken
spell	spelt	spelt
spend	spent	spent
stand	stood	stood
steal	stole	stolen
swim	swam	swum
take	took	taken
teach	taught	taught
tell	told	told
think	thought	thought
throw	threw	thrown
understand	understood	understood
wake	woke	woken
wear	wore	worn
win	won	won
write	wrote	written

Tapescripts

1 Working internationally

1.1 From Jordan to Switzerland

INTERVIEWER: So, Iyad, what do you do exactly?

IYAD: I work in Zurich for Syngenta as a technical manager. And, basically, my main responsibility is managing new product development. I work closely with people in our research and development department in Zurich to choose new products which I think – I hope – we can sell in my market areas. I like my job because it's very interesting.

INTERVIEWER: And how's business, Iyad? Is business increasing at the moment?

IYAD: Yes, it's very good in my area. Business is really increasing a lot. In Europe, there's a lot of discussion about the environment, it's very political. And so big farming organisations from Spain, from France and Italy, are transferring their business into places like Egypt and Morocco, my area, to grow here. One reason why it makes sense for them to move is because salaries are not so high. But that's business.

INTERVIEWER: Very interesting. And which markets do you work with?

IYAD: The Middle East and North Africa. This means Iran, Iraq, Syria, Lebanon, Jordan, the Gulf countries – that's Saudi, Kuwait, Emirates, Oman and Yemen – and then Egypt, Sudan, Libya, Algeria, Tunisia, Morocco. I really work internationally.

INTERVIEWER: Absolutely. Very international. And do you travel to these countries?

IYAD: Yes, I do. I visit all my sales areas – my countries you can say – once a year for business meetings with local employees and partners who sell our products. So I'm on the road a lot, you can say.

INTERVIEWER: But you live in Zurich now, don't you? Do you enjoy living in Switzerland?

IYAD: Yes, the best thing is the beautiful countryside. I also enjoy living in a country with such a high standard of living. Of course, it's a bit of a change. The Swiss are very precise, you know, about every detail. Time is very important – lunch is always between 12 and 1 – and this can be difficult for me, I'm not so precise. The social life is also very interesting, very different from Jordan. Here people don't mix so much after work. The Swiss like to have a private life alone with the family.

INTERVIEWER: Are you learning Swiss German?

IYAD: Well, I'm learning high German at a local college, which is the written language, for filling in official forms, reading letters, and so on. But the Swiss don't speak that very much – they use Swiss German, which is very different and very difficult for me to understand. You know, there's actually no written grammar. Anyway, I prefer to speak...to work in English because everybody speaks English.

INTERVIEWER: Yes, but you sound happy.

IYAD: Oh, yes. We have a great team which is really international. There's one Swiss, one guy from Russia, South Africa, Romania, Egypt, two guys from the UK and one new guy from Italy.

INTERVIEWER: Really?

IYAD: Yes, so it's very international. Work can sometimes be quite hard, very busy, but the people I work with are fantastic, really nice, that's the best thing, in fact. So I'm very happy, yes!

1.2 Do it yourself

Exercise 3

A: Hi, Marina. Surprise, surprise.

B: Karl! Good to see you. What are you doing here?

A: I'm on my way to Nairobi for a business meeting.

B: Really? I'm going to Paris to meet my brother for the weekend.

A: Oh, does he work in Paris?

B: No. He works in Budapest. Paris is just an easy place for us to meet.

A: OK. How often do you see him?

B: We try to meet twice a year in Paris.

A: Sounds good.

B: It is. Do you know Paris?

A: Not very well. I don't go there very much. Anyway, how's work?

B: Good. I'm working on a new product at the moment. And you?

A: Well, things aren't going well, you know, because it's a very difficult market situation. Oh, I think your plane is boarding.

B: You're right. I've got to go. Bye.

A: Bye. Have a good trip! Really good to see you again.

1.3 Sounds good

Exercise 1

A: <u>Where</u> do you <u>work</u>?

B: I <u>work</u> in <u>Geneva</u>. And <u>you</u>?

A: <u>What</u> do you <u>do</u>?

B: I'm a <u>journalist</u>.

A: <u>Where</u> <u>are</u> you <u>staying</u>?

B: In the <u>Hilton</u>. Where are <u>you</u> staying?

1.4 Sounds good

Exercise 2

A: <u>How</u> <u>often</u> do you <u>travel</u> on <u>business</u>?

B: About <u>once</u> a <u>month</u>. And <u>you</u>?

A: Are you <u>busy</u>?

B: <u>Yes</u>, I'm <u>working</u> on a <u>big</u> <u>project</u> in <u>China</u>.

A: Do you <u>know</u> <u>Madrid</u>?

B: <u>No</u>, I <u>don't</u>. Do <u>you</u>?

A: <u>What</u> are you <u>working</u> on at the <u>moment</u>?

B: A <u>report</u> – the <u>deadline</u> is <u>next</u> <u>week</u>.

A: Did you <u>have</u> a <u>good</u> <u>weekend</u>?

B: <u>Great</u>, <u>thanks</u>. <u>How</u> was <u>yours</u>?

2 Power for life

2.1 Telephoning 1: Getting through / Leaving a message

Call 1

Hello. You've reached the voicemail of Eve Warner. I'm sorry I'm away from my desk at the moment. Please leave a message and I'll call you back as soon as I can. Thank you.

Call 2

A: Hello, Amberside Communications. Matthew speaking, how can I help you?

B: Hello, I'd like to speak to Helen Foster, please. Is she there?

A: I'll put you through to her department. One moment, please.

C: Hello, Product Development.

B: Hello, can I speak to Helen Foster, please?

C: Yes, who's calling?

B: My name's Arne Scholte, from Copenhagen.

Call 3

A: Good morning. John Clayton's office.

B: Hello, can I speak to John Clayton, please?

A: I'm sorry, John's in a meeting at the moment. Can I help you?

B: No, it's OK. Will he be there this afternoon?

A: I'm afraid he's not in the office this afternoon. He has a meeting with a client.

B: Can you tell me when I can call him? Does he have a mobile?

A: Well, he does, but I don't think you'll reach him on that. Would you like to leave a message?

B: Well, no, I need to talk to him personally. Perhaps he could call me. Can I leave you my number?

A: Yes, of course, please do. Who's calling please?

B: Karl Kopmann, I'm calling from Germany.

Call 4

Hello. Thank you for calling Supex Technical Support. We are experiencing high call load at the current time. For web support, please visit our website at www.supex.com/technical. Otherwise, please hold and an operator will be with you as soon as one becomes available.

3 Edinburgh - the festival city

3.1 Arriving in a place you don't know

At left luggage

A: Excuse me, can we leave our bags here?

B: Yes, what have you got?

A: We've got a backpack and a large suitcase.

B: OK. That's £4 for the suitcase and £3 for the backpack. The ticket's valid for 24 hours.

A: Fine, thanks. We'll come and get them around 2 this afternoon.

B: That'll be fine. Have a nice morning.

At the accommodation bureau

A: Hello, we've just arrived and we'd like a bed and breakfast for two or three nights, please.

B: Singles or double?

A: Double, please.

B: OK, Edinburgh's very full but I can phone one in Leith for you.

A: Thank you. How far is it and how do we get there?

B: It's about half an hour by bus.

At tourist information

A: Hello, can you help us? We'd like a map of the city.

B: Yes, here you are.

A: And can you give us some information about the festival?

B: This tells you about the official festival. And this has information about the Fringe – the unofficial festival.

A: Thanks. And one last thing: do you have a bus timetable for Leith?

B: Yes, here you are.

A: Thanks for your help.

Getting there

A: Excuse me, we want to get to Leith. Where does the bus leave from, please?

B: Yes, you want a number 37. The stop is just down the road there.

A: Where do we buy the tickets?

B: You don't need to get a ticket in advance. You can pay on the bus.

A: Thank you.

B: You're welcome.

3.2 The festival city

INTERVIEWER: Joanna, what is the Edinburgh International Festival exactly?

JOANNA: Well, the Edinburgh International Festival is the number one European Arts Festival. So we bring world class dance, opera, theatre and music groups, artists and performers to Edinburgh like the New York City Ballet, the Berlin Philharmonic, the Vienna Philharmonic, theatre companies from Austria, France, a dance company from Japan, and so on. We normally have about 170 different performances over three weeks. All this for the people of Edinburgh and the thousands of visitors who come.

INTERVIEWER How big is the festival?

JOANNA: Well, people now see Edinburgh as 'The Festival City' of the world, because around the International Festival, over August, there's also a Festival Fringe – a big comedy event, there's a book festival, a film festival, a jazz festival, and the Edinburgh Military Tattoo – a big military display in Edinburgh castle. So, it's five weeks of festivals and 450,000 visitors. This generates around £150 million for the city. So you see, we work with two

major objectives, cultural and economic. Festivals are big business.

INTERVIEWER: And what's your role exactly?

JOANNA: Everything from producing tickets to doing the marketing – to sell more of them. I also work with the press, and talk a lot to the sponsors who help to finance the event. My job is to make sure we make money and that we bring in big audiences. And new audiences, young people, and people who don't normally go to see opera or classical music.

INTERVIEWER: Do you think things like opera, classical music, etc. are being enjoyed by more and more people because of your festival?

JOANNA: I think the Edinburgh International Festival is very good for new audiences: it's very open, you can go in jeans and a T-shirt. There's a real buzz about the place. We put shows on at night, 10.30 in the evening, £5 a ticket, so it's cheap, and we get lots of people, all types. We can sell 25 concerts with 2,000 seats at that time of night, no problem. The special thing about our Festival is that it's for everybody. It's very informal. Of course, people jet in from across the world but you can also walk in off the street. It's very easy and very special.

INTERVIEWER: What do you go and see?

JOANNA: My thing is dance. Ballet is my favourite. And, you know, one of the great things about my job is that I actually go and see dance companies during the year to see if we want to bring them to the festival. So it's perfect. Job and hobby together.

4 Changing direction

4.1 Change is fun

INTERVIEWER: Judy, you decided to change your life a couple of years ago. What did you do? And why?

JUDY: Well, I was working for a language school in France when I had the idea. I decided to change my life completely, and so I opened a French *crêperie* called 'Ooh la la' in a place called Kennebunkport, Maine. It's a seaside resort about an hour and 15 minutes north of Boston in the States.

INTERVIEWER: OK. And why did you make the change?

JUDY: Well, the main reason was my two teenage boys. Things were not going well for them at school around this time. I just wanted them to have another experience in life, a real experience. We were living in France at the time and decided to create something for them to have an exciting summer job, and so I thought about the US.

INTERVIEWER: So how did you set up a business in the States? Was it difficult?

JUDY: Well, a *crêperie* seemed good because it didn't need much investment. I wanted to be near Boston, because I have a sister who lives there, and I decided on Kennebunkport because it's just so beautiful. We knew there were a lot of people in summer, and so, after I figured I could make a profit, and the town said we could open a *crêperie*, I set up the place – actually in just 15 days.

INTERVIEWER: Fifteen days? Really, extremely quick!

JUDY: Yes, but I have to say I had a lot of help. I had a good friend in Boston. She was working in the restaurant business and so she came over and she helped design the restaurant and all that. And the place is extremely cute, really it's lovely.

INTERVIEWER: It seems you obviously enjoy running a business.

JUDY: Oh, yeah. It's a lot of fun in the summertime. It's a beautiful place, and in June Kennebunkport is lobster country. People come from all over the world, go out on the lobster boat trip, ride on the ocean, learn about the life cycle of the lobster and things like that. And fish, of course.

INTERVIEWER: Sounds great. And what do the boys think?

JUDY: They love it, they really love it. The *crêperie* is a wonderful experience for them. They meet and talk to people and make a lot of friends. And you know, in the past they were so quiet, but now they're so much stronger and more confident. It was a good decision.

INTERVIEWER: And, finally, the big question, did you make a profit last year?

JUDY: Well, no! This is a special business in that we really only make money in summer – in June, July, August, maybe September and October. If the trees are beautiful, and the weather is good, we have a lot of people. But the rest of the year there's really no money coming in because there aren't enough people. So we don't make any real profit. But it's great fun! Change is fun. Everyone should have a small business. I really recommend it.

4.2 Do it yourself
Exercise 3
INTERVIEWER: How did Nina Simone's career begin?

HILARY: Well, she was working in a nightclub when she had the chance to sign for the Bethlehem record label. She took her opportunity with both hands and her first hit came in 1959.

INTERVIEWER: Was Nina part of the black civil rights movement in the US during the 1960s?

HILARY: Absolutely, yes. When the protest actually started she was already writing songs and so she quickly joined the movement.

INTERVIEWER: Did Nina write any specific songs about the fight for equality?

HILARY: Yes. In fact, *Mississippi Goddam* was a direct response to the killing of four black children.

INTERVIEWER: And did her songs have any impact?

HILARY: Absolutely. At that time people always stopped what they were doing and listened when Nina started to sing.

4.3 Sounds good
Exercise 1
Conversation 1

A: I went on a boat trip on Saturday.

B: Oh.

A: Yes, it was really good. We sailed along the coast. It was really beautiful.

B: Mmm.

A: Yes, and we saw lots of dolphins.

B: Hmm.

A: I think there were at least 20. It was wonderful!

B: OK.

Conversation 2

A: I went on a boat trip on Saturday.

B: How lovely!

A: Yes, it was really good. We sailed along the coast. It was really beautiful.

B: I'm sure it was.

A: Yes, and we saw lots of dolphins.

B: Dolphins! How many?

A: I think there were at least 20. It was wonderful!

B: Sounds fantastic!

4.4 Sounds good
Exercise 2
1 A: United won 5-0 at the weekend.
   B: 5-0?

2 A: I've decided to leave the company.
   B: Why?

3 A: I had a training course on selling last week.
   B: Really?

4 A: A new colleague from Italy started work last week.
   B: Good.

5 A: Business in China is booming.
   B: Great!

5 Job swap

5.1 The words you need
Exercise 2
BEN: I have responsibility for new designs for our corporate brochure. I'm also in charge of specific design projects. I'm responsible for 25 people. My main objective is to support marketing and sales. One of my other key tasks is to make sure we present a clear brand identity to the customer in our brochures. Another important part of my job is to deal with stores which display and sell our products. Sometimes I take care of visitors from our Spanish office because I speak good Spanish. I'm also involved in the social club at work.

5.2 Presenting 1: Welcoming visitors
Exercises 1 and 2
GEMMA: Hello and welcome to everyone. My name's Gemma Wilkins and I work in the HR department – I'm the information officer in the company. I'd like to give you a short introduction to my job and also to explain the programme for the day. To begin then, I want first of all to say just a few words about me. I'm in charge of all external communication. And I'm also your contact person for the day so please ask me if you have any problems. So, that's my job. That's all I want to say about me for now. Right, now I want to go on to the second part – the plan for the day. As you can see from the programme, we have a tour of the production area with Matthew Durston, our production manager, then lunch at 12.30. After lunch we have a video to show you at 2, then a meeting with our marketing manager. For this evening we have booked dinner for eight o'clock at the Hollies, a fantastic restaurant in the town centre. We'll meet at your hotel at 7.15 and walk there. Right, that's all I wanted to say. Does anyone have any questions before the tour? No? OK, thank you for listening. Now I'm going to hand over to Matthew. So, have a good day!

5.3 Presenting 1: Welcoming visitors
Exercise 3
Good morning, everyone. My name's William Brett and I'd like to welcome you to our company, Le Chat Bleu, with a short introduction about my work and the plan for the day. I also have some information about this evening. To begin then, a few words about myself. I'm the human resources manager here at Le Chat Bleu. I'm responsible for recruitment and also for staff training. Right, the important point is the programme for the day. We begin with a visit to our design studio with Simone Laurent. Then Simone will take you for lunch. And after lunch we have a visit to the sports shoe workshops with John Barnes. At about three o'clock we have a project meeting with different colleagues. Then this evening we would like everyone to meet at half past seven in your hotel lobby. We plan to have a short reception and then dinner in a restaurant, Le Clochard. Well, does anyone have any questions? Is everyone happy with this plan? OK, good, then that's all from me. Thank you for listening. I hope you have a good day! Now let me introduce Simone Laurent from our design team – she'll show you the studio.

6 Tourist attraction

6.1 Health and feeling ill
Feeling unwell

A: Are you all right?

B: No, actually. I don't feel very well.

A: Yes, you do look pale. Is there anything I can do?

B: No thanks, maybe I'll go home early today.

A: Yes, I think you should.

Fixing an appointment to see a doctor

A: Hello, I'd like an appointment, please.

B: Can I have your name?

A: Yes, it's Raul Ochoa. I'm from Spain. I'm here temporarily, on business.

B: Fine. I'm afraid the doctor is busy all morning. Can you come at 3.15 this afternoon?

At the doctor's

A: Hello, I have an appointment with the doctor at 3.15.

B: 3.15, yes. Can you fill in this form, please?

A: OK. Do you need my insurance details?

B: No, I don't think so. But write your home doctor's details here.

Back at work

A: Ah, you're back! Are you better now?

B: Yes, I'm much better, thanks.

A: Good. We've missed you. Welcome back.

6.2 Are you looking for somewhere different?

INTERVIEWER: When people think of Australia, they probably think of Sydney, or the Outback, or the Great Barrier Reef, but you're from Tasmania, right?

GERRY: Yeah, I was born in Tasmania. Tasmania is an island off the south coast of Australia. It's approximately the size of the Republic of Ireland. And the weather there is much like the south coast of Ireland, or the north coast of Spain. Not very cold and not very hot either, and it rains a fair bit too.

INTERVIEWER: So what's interesting about Tasmania?

GERRY: Well, it used to be a penal colony, a prison for the British Empire. It was a good prison because it's an island. And anyone who tried to escape got eaten by sharks.

INTERVIEWER: Really? Sharks?

GERRY: Yeah, the sea off Tasmania is full of sharks. So there was no escape. But things have improved since the eighteenth century and Tasmania is famous for better reasons. Really, it's a very beautiful place, with a fantastic natural environment. So tourism is a major industry, along with farming and also food, food products. But tourism is a growing industry.

INTERVIEWER: So what is there for people to see in Tasmania?

GERRY: Well, the landscape is very beautiful. And it's got unique animals and unique plants. There are only half a million people, so it's a large island for a small population. There are long beaches, mostly empty, no people at all. You can have a whole beach to yourself. On the west coast it's very mountainous, mountains all down the west. About a third of the state is National Park and complete wilderness. Tasmania is a World Heritage Area and in many places it's possible to walk for maybe ten days without seeing a road or another human being.

INTERVIEWER: How do you find living in Britain compared with being in Tasmania?

GERRY: I like it here, I get to visit the different cultures of Europe and it's been interesting to learn about British culture. But compared with Tasmania, Britain – even the whole of Europe – it's completely different. In Europe there are so many big cities, so many people, such a high density of population, roads, buildings everywhere. Tasmania is mostly a natural wilderness. You can go for miles and all you hear is insects and birds.

7 From Mexico to Germany

7.1 Work is fun

INTERVIEWER: Javier, you've worked internationally in Mexico and Germany, yes?

JAVIER: Yes, I worked in Mexico, but only for two years. Last year I was based in Germany, which was very interesting, but now I'm back in Spain. So, for work, I spent three years abroad. I think it's good to work in different countries. After this, I think you have a better career and, maybe even, you become a better person.

INTERVIEWER: What was Mexico like? Interesting?

JAVIER: Yes, the most interesting place I've worked. OK, in Mexico, as a manager, you have to push sometimes. Things can move a little more slowly than in Spain, and maybe people are not so motivated as in Germany. I know it's a stereotype, but in Germany they often do things very efficiently. But Mexico is another business culture, quite close to the Spanish in some ways so, for me, it was easier to handle.

INTERVIEWER: Interesting analysis. And what about Mexicans and their famous attitude to time?

JAVIER: It certainly wasn't as bad as I expected. Mexicans aren't always late. That's just a stereotype. It's the same as Germany. It's the same everywhere, in my experience. In business, I think it depends on who is having the meeting. If you have a meeting with top management, people at a higher level often come a little later, they have the right to be late.

INTERVIEWER: I have a question about language. In Mexico, is the Spanish the same as that spoken in Spain?

JAVIER: The languages are very similar but I think Mexican Spanish sounds older than the Spanish in Spain. They use a more historical form, with some words that we don't have here any more, and they also use a lot of American English words in their daily conversation. For example, they use 'highway', and other very common words that you hear every day.

INTERVIEWER: What about the working culture? I guess this was very different in Mexico and Germany?

JAVIER: Yes, the culture is very different. Mexican business culture is more about fun. People are more open. They don't think about hierarchy so much, and, also ... maybe in Mexico you can communicate more easily, more freely with your boss, for example. The door is always open, and so on. My style or strategy of management is to be open and friendly, although lots of very good managers have a different style. It's a strategic question. For me, it creates more possibilities to build relationships with people.

INTERVIEWER: And a final question to compare the food. Which was better, Mexican or German?

JAVIER: The food? Well, I prefer Mexican food. The German food was good but I didn't enjoy it as much as the Mexican, it wasn't as spicy as I normally have. But you know, I like Mexican because it's very close to Spanish food, to what I know, so no comparison, for me, no comparison.

7.2 Do it yourself
Exercise 2

1 In general, people in Germany drive more carefully than they do in Mexico.
2 In Mexico you can get to know people a lot more easily than here.
3 Some people say that status is more important in Mexican business culture.
4 In Mexico people normally have their evening meal later than in Germany.
5 In Mexico prices are generally lower.
6 Most people I met in Mexico knew Germany better than I expected.

7.3 Sounds good
Exercise 1

strategy
strategic

7.4 Sounds good
Exercise 2

1 strategy
2 strategic
3 understand
4 motivated
5 comparison
6 competition

7.5 Sounds good
Exercise 2

1 Mexico / languages
2 employer / another
3 engineer / underline
4 complicated / educated
5 analysis / competitor
6 absolutely / conversation

8 Globalisation

8.1 The words you need
Exercise 2

1 My company makes products which are environmentally friendly.
2 I think the government has a good economic policy.
3 I'm not very interested in politics.
4 I'd like to work in a developing country like Vietnam.
5 I pay a lot of interest on my bank loan.
6 Our business invests a lot of money in its employees.
7 My country is an exporter of coffee.
8 Ford is a major multinational company.

9 Here is the news

9.1 Talking about news

Breaking news

A: Oh no! Have you seen this?
B: What's happened?
A: There's been a bad crash.
B: That's awful. Where?

Is it really news?

A: Look at this! Rosenberg beat Juventus!
B: Really? What was the score?
A: Three one to Rosenberg.
B: That's a big shock. Who scored?

News at work

A: Chris, did you know about Gemma Hudson? Have you heard that she's leaving?
B: Really? How do you know that?
A: She told me. She's leaving next month.
B: Actually, I'm not surprised. I didn't think she was very happy here.
A: That's right. I think she wants to move back to her home town.

A newspaper article

A: There was a good article in yesterday's paper.
B: What was it about?
A: Problems in schools. Did you see it?
B: No, I didn't see the paper yesterday.
A: You should read it. I'll get a copy off the web and email it to you.
B: OK, thanks. I'll look forward to reading it.

9.2 Finding out what's going on

INTERVIEWER: Elaine, you're a print journalist – you write mainly for newspapers – but how do most people get their information about the world in which they live?
ELAINE: I think most people these days – in Britain, anyway – get their information through television. They watch the news on television, but newspapers are still popular in Britain.
INTERVIEWER: But people get news mostly from television?
ELAINE: Yes, I think these days they do. We have 24-hour news coverage. There are many, many channels where you can get news.
INTERVIEWER: How do you compare newspapers and television news?
ELAINE: Well, most of the television news is really terrible. There's no analysis, no detail. If you want to really understand the news, you have to read a good newspaper. In newspapers you get much more analysis. At least, you do in some newspapers.
INTERVIEWER: So you don't like the television, then?
ELAINE: No, not for news. It just tells you a few things and shows lots of pictures, obviously. There's not much information. The news on TV is presented as entertainment. I think that's what most people want. They want the headlines and a few pictures, they don't want lots of details.
INTERVIEWER: What about other technologies?
ELAINE: I think the internet is becoming more important. And it's good because people can interact with the news. For example, they can write opinions to discussion boards, or there are chatlines about the news. And a second good thing is you can send news items to friends. So yes, the internet is good because it's interactive, people get engaged with it.
INTERVIEWER: Has this technology affected other media too?
ELAINE: I'm sure, yes. Radio and television have become more interactive. They actually invite people to take part in debates.
INTERVIEWER: So in a way that's quite good, people can express an opinion, they can participate in news stories?
ELAINE: Yes, and the internet also means many more people write things, they can put their views across in a way they couldn't before. And also, people can find out more from the internet, they do their own research. It's true, yes, people participate more.
INTERVIEWER: So what you are saying is people do have more choice than ever, more variety.
ELAINE: Oh, yes, massive variety. And more pictures. The internet and newspapers all include a lot of pictures but of course the television provides the most: people get an image of the news, something to remember. Not much detail, but they get a picture to remember something.
INTERVIEWER: And finally, how do you get the news, Elaine?
ELAINE: I read the newspapers and listen to the radio! I don't even have a television!

10 Executive search

10.1 Finding the right people

INTERVIEWER: So Henry, tell us something about your life. You live in Paris, don't you?
HENRY: Yes, I was born in France, but I studied – or was educated – in the USA. After that I joined the US Army and actually I was a soldier in Vietnam.
INTERVIEWER: Really? Did that prepare you for a life in business?
HENRY: No, but it made me grow up. When the war was over, I moved to London. I worked for a strategic consultancy business.
INTERVIEWER: So have you always worked in consultancy?
HENRY: Yes, just about. All my working life. But after London I moved to Paris to join Russell Reynolds Associates. That was a long time ago – in 1979.
INTERVIEWER: 1979. And have you been in Paris the whole time?
HENRY: No, I went to the US for ten years and then came back to Paris.
INTERVIEWER: So can you explain your job? What do you do exactly?
HENRY: I'm an executive search consultant.
INTERVIEWER: An executive search consultant. What does that mean exactly? Is it recruitment?
HENRY: Yes, but it's not really recruitment; it's more than just finding someone to sign a contract. It's a consultancy role because we help companies to solve their specific problems. We help them to find the right people to meet very specific company needs – really the job is essentially about solving problems. It's a very strategic function.
INTERVIEWER: Has the job changed much over time?
HENRY: Oh, yes, it's changed a lot. In the last ten years it has become a job that is relationship-driven. The key thing, the most important thing in my job, is to establish partnerships with the client, working together. You have to understand the needs of the client really well. In fact, we've been looking recently at ways to improve this area of the business further.
INTERVIEWER: So what about the big scandals like Enron in 2002, or the accountancy scandal at WorldCom? I mean, do you think companies now want people with good finance skills, in accountancy, for example?
HENRY: Yes, the various scandals had a big impact and companies have changed a lot since Enron. There's now more focus on everyday management skills. But I don't think that it will continue. Really the strategic vision is much more important; the big ideas matter. It's strategic vision that builds companies. Companies need people at the top with vision and leadership.
INTERVIEWER: You obviously like the work?
HENRY: Very much so. I've been enjoying it very much recently, in fact. Executive search is a great job. I love it because every day it's always different, there's always something new from day to day. This makes it really interesting.

10.2 Do it yourself

Exercise 4

1 How long has Christopher Gent worked in business?
2 When did his career begin?
3 How long did he work in banking?
4 How long was he CEO of Vodafone?
5 When did Vodafone buy Mannesman?
6 How long has the mobile phone sector been experiencing problems?

10.3 Sounds good

Exercise 1

How long have you worked in Paris?
How long have you been living here?
How long has he been working in sales?

10.4 Sounds good
Exercise 2
I've worked in Paris for five years.
I've been living here for a few months.
He's been working in sales for the last four months.

10.5 Sounds good
Exercise 3
for five years
for a few months

10.6 Sounds good
Exercise 4
1 for a few months
2 for four weeks
3 for a year
4 for a couple of days
5 for ten hours
6 for the last two weeks

11 Making money
11.1 Meetings 1: Asking for and giving opinions
JON: So, what do you think is the best way for the business to grow in the long term?

ELEANOR: I think we have to export. We have to find new markets.

WAYNE: Actually, I'm not sure about that. Not at the present time. That's only one way. It could be better to find a partner in another country, or different partners. That has cost and marketing advantages. Alex?

ALEX: I disagree. You're both wrong – the discussion is a waste of time. We can't do anything like that. We should forget all about increasing sales at this time.

JON: One moment, Alex. I think it *is* important to talk about these things. It's part of developing a strategy for the future. We have to consider the long term.

ELEANOR: That's true, yes. It's important to look ahead.

ALEX: Well, when the economy is doing badly there's no way you can build up sales in any meaningful way.

WAYNE: But there are plenty of examples of businesses doing well when the competition is having a hard time. Look at Ryanair, for example. Ryanair increased its market share during a downturn for the whole airline industry after September 11th.

ALEX: Yes, but we don't work in the airline business ...

12 Ecotourism
12.1 Getting directions
By car
A: Excuse me. Is this the right road to the Sculpture Park?
B: Yes, it is. Go straight on to the roundabout. Turn right. Then it's about four miles on the left.
A: So, straight on to the roundabout and right. Four miles.
B: Yes, it's easy. You can't go wrong.

Where is it?
A: Hello, I think I'm lost. Can you tell me where the *Age d'Or* restaurant is?
B: I'm sorry, I'm not from here.
A: OK, thanks. I'll ask someone else.
B: Just a minute! I can see it, it's just over there!
A: Oh yes, so it is! Thanks a lot.

Understanding the map
A: Excuse me. Can you show me where we are?
B: Of course. We're here, next to King's College. Where do you want to go?
A: I'm looking for Bank Street. Do you know where it is?
B: It's not far, I'll show you. I'm going that way.

Getting around a big building
A: Sorry to bother you, this is the fifth floor, isn't it?
B: Yes, it is. Where do you want to be?
A: I'm looking for the Brunel Room. Is it near here?
B: Yes, down this corridor and through that door, then it's on the left.

12.2 Tourism and the environment: the Eden Project
INTERVIEWER: Chris, tell us what the Eden Project is about.

CHRIS: Well, it's in Cornwall, in the south-west of England, and basically it's a number of what we call biomes. Biomes are very big structures made of transparent hexagons on a steel framework. And inside these huge biomes we grow different kinds of plant, all kinds of plant from all over the world, from hot regions, mild temperate regions and cold regions. And we control the temperature and the amount of water in the air – the humidity – in each biome so that all these different kinds of plant can grow.

INTERVIEWER: So is it a theme park like Disneyland?

CHRIS: No, not at all. It's much more than that. The most important thing about the Eden Project is that you can learn about the natural environment.

INTERVIEWER: So it has an educational objective.

CHRIS: Absolutely. One of the many good things about the Eden Project is that it makes people think about the relationship between plants and people.

INTERVIEWER: So is it ecotourism?

CHRIS: Definitely, if we mean a form of tourism that increases our understanding of the natural environment. Yes, that's really very true for the Eden Project.

INTERVIEWER: Do you think there are any problems with the concept of ecotourism?

CHRIS: Well, in some ways, yes. At the Eden Project the number of visitors has been extraordinary, so there's the physical problem of traffic, cars, visitor numbers, that can be a problem. But the real danger in ecotourism is if money becomes the priority, the most important thing. If visiting a natural environment, for example rainforests or special habitats like the Galapagos Islands, becomes all about money, that can damage the environment that really we want to protect. Yes, money's the biggest danger.

INTERVIEWER: And what has the Eden Project done for the local community?

CHRIS: Well, there are lots of benefits. It has created jobs, tourism, and brought money to the local community. It has helped to rebuild an area which was badly damaged by industry. It's an educational benefit too as well as a leisure resource. So it's really good for the environment.

INTERVIEWER: Who first thought of the idea?

CHRIS: The Eden Project is the vision of one man, Tim Smit. He thought of the Eden Project. He took a damaged industrial environment in Cornwall with a lot of economic problems. It had an old industry – clay mining – and a lot of people who didn't have jobs. He had a vision, an idea. He wanted to make a difference. The wonderful thing is he achieved that. He made a real difference, not only to this area but to everyone who comes here. I think we can all carry that idea, we can have a vision and we can all help to make a difference.

13 Changing culture
13.1 Norway sets female quota for boardrooms
INTERVIEWER: According to the article in the newspaper, it seems that companies in Norway are going to fix quotas for women in management. They're planning to have 40% women at board level. What do you think about this, as a Norwegian, Terje?

TERJE: Well, I agree with the idea in principle. In a company with only men taking decisions, I think you miss opportunities. Women see things differently. So, for me, more women in top positions means better leadership for companies. And that's why we're introducing this change.

INTERVIEWER: Are you going to push this process in Norway immediately?

TERJE: No, we are going to run this process over a period of two years so that companies can manage things efficiently. They need the time to find enough good women, for one thing.

INTERVIEWER: Ingrid, what do you think?

INGRID: It's interesting. In fact, in my company we've been discussing equality recently and we're going to take some decisions later this month.

INTERVIEWER: Really? Well, I'll call you at the end of the month to find out what you've decided. Pierre, what are your thoughts?

PIERRE: Of course, I agree with the general objective. In France there are also very few women in top management. In the IT business, there are fewer than 10% women. I know Hewlett Packard is led by a woman but this is an exception.

INTERVIEWER: So where's the problem?

PIERRE: In France, we tried quotas with political parties and it didn't work. The parties were happier to pay fines and penalties than to try to have the right quotas. A quota is not a solution, believe me.

INTERVIEWER: Interesting. Is there going to be a penalty system with this, Terje?

TERJE: I'm not sure. I'll check and I can get back to you on that.

INTERVIEWER: Yes, I'd like to know.

INGRID: I think a quota is a good idea, because women can give another point of view at all levels of a company. So it's good to help women to get onto the boards of companies.

PIERRE: But there's another problem. I think 40% is too high. It'll create real recruitment problems for companies. It just isn't possible because we don't have enough women to take this responsibility.

INGRID: There aren't enough women because men normally only recruit men because they know women have other responsibilities with the family. For me, the problem is one of culture and starts in the home.

TERJE: I agree. And I think Scandinavian countries are a little ahead of the rest of Europe. For example, when couples have a child, the man has the same amount of time off as the woman.

INGRID: Yes, the problem is that we need a change in the whole psychology of countries – a big change in culture – to see a long-term change in the position of women at work. You can't change a culture in six months.

13.2 Do it yourself
Exercise 3

EMMA: Hi, Mark. It's Emma. Can you give me some details about the workshop next month?

MARK: OK. I'll help if I can.

EMMA: Well, firstly, according to the schedule, when am I presenting?

MARK: Your presentation is on Tuesday 8 September at 10 am. Is that OK?

EMMA: Wednesday at 10 would be better for me.

MARK: Fine. I'll change your time to the Wednesday. OK?

EMMA: Thanks. And what about hotel accommodation?

MARK: It's all arranged. Everyone is staying in the Manor. It was the cheapest.

EMMA: That's fine. I'll tell Rachel and Sam. They asked me this morning.

MARK: You can also tell them that I'm going to send everybody an information pack with the hotel details, probably at the end of next week, I'm not sure yet.

EMMA: OK, I'll let them know. In fact, we're meeting later today at 4 so I can tell them then, if I don't forget.

MARK: Right. So, any plans for the rest of the morning?

EMMA: Not really. I'm just going to finish a few reports and then it's lunch.

MARK: Sounds good. Thanks for your call. And don't forget to tell Rachel and Sam!

EMMA: Thanks, I won't forget. Bye.

MARK: Bye.

13.3 Sounds good
Exercise 1

EMMA: I still haven't had the workshop schedule. Did you send it?

MARK: Yes. Didn't you receive it by email last week?

EMMA: No. I don't have any information and I'm a bit stressed.

MARK: Don't worry. I'll send you another schedule right now.

13.4 Sounds good
Exercise 2

MARK: Hello, I'm calling to check you got the schedule. Have you got it?

EMMA: Yes, I have. It's here in my mailbox but I can't open it.

MARK: I don't understand.

EMMA: It's very strange. I've never had any problems with emails from you before.

MARK: Did you save the document first?

EMMA: Yes, I did. It didn't make any difference. Can you resend it?

MARK: OK, I'll send it again straightaway. Please phone me if it doesn't open.

EMMA: Don't worry. I will!

14 The customer is always right
14.1 Telephoning 2: Making and changing arrangements
Exercises 1 and 2

CHAMINDA: Hello, I'd like to speak to Charlotte Bennett, please.

CHARLOTTE: Speaking. Hello.

CHAMINDA: Ms Bennett, good morning. My name's Chaminda Jay. I sent you an email about our meeting. Can we meet next week some time?

CHARLOTTE: Yes, that's right. What day would suit you?

CHAMINDA: Wednesday or Thursday, if possible. I'm in London till Thursday evening, so any time really.

CHARLOTTE: Well, we can meet here in my office at Oakwood House at 10 on Wednesday the tenth. Is that OK?

CHAMINDA: 10 am. Fine. Where is that exactly?

CHARLOTTE: Oakwood House is on Smith Square, and Smith Square is easy to get to.

CHAMINDA: That's fine. OK, I'll send an email to confirm, and a few ideas for our meeting.

CHARLOTTE: Very good. Thanks for calling. See you on Wednesday morning at 10.

CHAMINDA: Thanks. Bye.

14.2 Telephoning 2: Making and changing arrangements
Exercises 3 and 4

CHARLOTTE: Hello, is that Mr Jay?

CHAMINDA: Yes, speaking.

CHARLOTTE: Hello, it's Charlotte Bennett here. Thanks for your email, but unfortunately I've got a problem now.

CHAMINDA: Oh, what's that?

CHARLOTTE: I'm afraid I have to be out of the office all day on Wednesday. Could we meet the following day instead?

CHAMINDA: The day after? OK, that's no problem. What time would suit you?

CHARLOTTE: If we say Thursday morning, is that all right with you?

CHAMINDA: Yes, that's fine. 10 o'clock?

CHARLOTTE: A bit later, if you don't mind. Could we make it 12 o'clock?

CHAMINDA: That's OK. Same place?

CHARLOTTE: Yes, same place, Thursday the eleventh at 12 noon. And sorry about the change. I hope it's not a problem for you.

CHAMINDA: Not at all. Have a good week.

CHARLOTTE: OK, thanks very much. I'll email the new details.

CHAMINDA: Thanks. Bye for now.

15 An interesting place to live
15.1 Visiting someone's home for dinner
Welcome

A: Hello, nice to see you.

B: Thank you. I'm sorry we're a bit late.

A: No, not at all. Perfect timing. Let me take your coats.

B: Thank you.

Two small gifts

A: Did you have any problems finding us?

C: No, it was easy. Here, we've brought you some flowers.

A: Oh, that wasn't necessary – but they really are beautiful. Thank you very much.

C: And these. I hope you like chocolates.

A: Oh, that's very kind. In fact, we both love chocolate!

The home

C: What a beautiful house. Have you lived here long?
A: Yes, we've been here ten years now. It didn't look like this when we moved in!
C: It's beautiful. And you have some lovely photographs too.
A: Yes, Peter loves taking pictures. Do you like photography?

Saying goodbye

B: It's been a wonderful evening. Thank you for having us.
D: Not at all. It was our pleasure.
B: And the meal was delicious. Thank you so much.
D: Don't mention it. It was great to see you.

15.2 Living in a windmill

INTERVIEWER: Susanna, how did you find your windmill?
SUSANNA: I saw a photograph of it in the paper, about 15 or 16 years ago.
INTERVIEWER: Was it in a good state? Did you move in straightaway?
SUSANNA: It was possible to live in it but there was a lot of work to do, yes. The staircase was in, which was I suppose an important thing, and the floors were in, but there was no heating and there was no modern kitchen or anything like that. And we had to have new windows put in.
INTERVIEWER: So did you do a lot of work yourself? Are you a DIY person?
SUSANNA: No, no, I can't even put a screw in the walls. We designed it ourselves but we got the builders to do the work.
INTERVIEWER: How many floors does it have? Can you describe it a little?
SUSANNA: It has five floors – ground floor and then first floor, second floor, third floor and fourth floor. And then it has a roof you can get on to. On the ground floor it's a round room and I think it's more than eight metres across. The top floor I think is about four metres across, so the rooms get smaller as you go up. So the walls aren't straight, and it's not just round but it's not straight either. It means we've got problems with hanging pictures, hanging curtains, putting up shelves, everything, it's very difficult.
INTERVIEWER: What's the best thing for you then about your home?
SUSANNA: I like where it is, the location. It's not in a village. It's a really nice spot. And I like it because it's different. We don't have to think a lot about furniture and all that because it already looks completely different.
INTERVIEWER: And what do other people think?
SUSANNA: Well, people like it, but not everyone likes sleeping at the top because the room is round and you can't find the door because the door's in the floor and that sort of thing. And if we have children sleeping over, they wake up in the night wanting to go to the loo, and you shut the door because you're frightened that they'll fall down the stairs, and then they can't get out. It's awful – like Rapunzel. Actually, my favourite fairy story was Rapunzel when I was young.
INTERVIEWER: But do your children like it?
SUSANNA: They love it. I think it was a joy from start to finish for the children.
INTERVIEWER: Do you have much land with the windmill?
SUSANNA: We bought a field next door, so we've got a field and the garden.
INTERVIEWER: And are there any disadvantages?
SUSANNA: The main one is that it's expensive because you have to have everything made to fit it. And the rooms are small because you know, with a round room, once you've put a bed and something else in a round room you've lost huge amounts of space.
INTERVIEWER: But basically it sounds wonderful. Susanna, thank you very much indeed.

Revision 1

R1.1 Pronunciation
Exercise 1

1 A: I saw a film yesterday.
   B: Oh, really?
2 A: There were only three people in the cinema.
   B: Three? Only three?

3 A: It was a really good film as well.
   B: I'm sure.
4 A: It's still on if you want to see it.
   B: Is it?
5 A: Or we could go somewhere else – go to a club?
   B: Oh, right.
6 A: What about the Snowball?
   B: The Snowball? Fine.

R1.2 Pronunciation
Exercise 1

A: I saw a film yesterday.
B: Oh, really?
A: There were only three people in the cinema.
B: Three? Only three?
A: It was a really good film as well.
B: I'm sure.
A: It's still on if you want to see it.
B: Is it?
A: Or we could go somewhere else – go to a club?
B: Oh, right.
A: What about the Snowball?
B: The Snowball? Fine.

R1.3 Pronunciation
Exercise 2

A: Where <u>do you</u> work?
B: I work <u>for</u> a film company in Bristol.
A: What <u>do you</u> do?
B: <u>I'm an</u> editor.
A: How long <u>have you been</u> working there?
B: <u>For about</u> six years.
A: How <u>long have you</u> lived in Bristol?
B: <u>For</u> ten years.

16 Taiwan – still a tiger

16.1 Real competitive advantage

INTERVIEWER: Vanessa, how much of your work in the hotel is with the corporate sector, big companies?
VANESSA: All my work is with the corporate sector. I'm responsible for corporate accounts. So I don't spend any time with tour groups or things like that. I should say that the job is quite important because most of our clients are businesses.
INTERVIEWER: How big is the hotel?
VANESSA: We have 350 rooms including 46 suites.
INTERVIEWER: 350? That's a lot. How many guests are from overseas? Quite a lot, I imagine.
VANESSA: Yes, the overseas market is extremely important to us. So about 30% of our guests come from Japan, 20% from the US and Canada, and just over 8% from Europe. About 40% are from Asia, meaning mostly Hong Kong, Malaysia and the Philippines.
INTERVIEWER: Do you have any guests from Singapore?
VANESSA: We have some people from Singapore, not so many.
INTERVIEWER: And are people mostly on business?
VANESSA: Just over 50% of the guests are corporate, about 30% individuals, and a small part is tour groups. We always have a little tour group business at the hotel. Also we do a few weddings most weeks and a lot of conference work.
INTERVIEWER: What kind of corporate clients do you have?
VANESSA: Well, in Taipei there's a lot of IT. For example, in Taipei there are large subsidiaries of Intel and Hewlett Packard, so a lot of people come from overseas for meetings here. Of course, in Taiwan the economy is very IT-based. But there's also some banking. In fact, in this district there are a lot of banks so the hotel gets lots of – you can say – banking business, because the banks are close.
INTERVIEWER: And how's business nowadays in Taiwan? Is Taiwan still a tiger economy?
VANESSA: Yes, I think so. As I said, the main industry sector here is IT and Taiwan produces 10% of the world's semiconductors. There are a few problems in the world economy but we have no big worries about business in the future. We're always optimistic. China, Japan and Hong Kong are very important economies for

Taiwan. But the US is the biggest market. And with the American economy quite strong and the economy here going well, we're very confident and optimistic about business in the future.

INTERVIEWER: What's the most important attraction of the Sherwood Taipei hotel? Why should I stay there?

VANESSA: Well, firstly, we have the facilities people need, business services, like, for example, every room has a full internet service. And we have a gym, a spa, and an indoor swimming pool. But the real difference in our business – the real competitive advantage – is in the great level of customer service we offer to each customer. We have excellent personnel training. No staff are allowed near guests until they're properly trained. And the other thing we offer is a very personalised service. So, for example, all guests have a personal profile on the hotel database. We keep a record of what people like, so when each guest returns to the hotel we know exactly how to keep him or her happy.

16.2 Sounds good
Exercise 1
A: Shall we go and get some lunch? I need something to eat.
B: Sorry, I don't have a lot of time. I've got an important report to finish.
A: OK. Don't work too hard. I'll see if Jo's free for a little lunch.

16.3 Sounds good
Exercise 2
1   Did it cost a lot of money?
2   Shall I order a taxi for Anna?
3   Do you need any help?
4   Did you have a nice evening?
5   Could I ask you a few questions?
6   Are you interested in art?

18 Learning styles
18.1 Asking for and giving help
Technical problems
A: Excuse me. Can you help me? What does this mean exactly?
B: Let me see. OK, there's a technical problem with the network.
A: Sorry, I don't understand. Can I access the intranet?
B: Yes, you can. But you can't send emails or use the internet just now.

Lost or stolen?
A: Oh no! I think I've lost my bag.
B: How? Where did you last see it?
A: I put it down here, but now it's gone.
B: Oh dear. Shall I call the police?

Using equipment
A: I need to make a photocopy of this. Can I use this machine?
B: No problem. Do you know how to use it?
A: Could you show me how to do double-sided?
B: I'm not sure. I'll ask someone to show you.

Getting information
A: I can't remember Phil's phone number. Have you got it?
B: Sorry, I haven't. Cathy will probably know. Shall I give her a quick call?
A: No, it doesn't matter. I'll see her at lunch.
B: Are you sure? It's no problem.
A: No, it's OK. I'll see her later.

18.2 Teaching people how to learn
INTERVIEWER: Can you say something about how you help or teach people to learn?

NICHOLAS: Sure. We start with people's ideas about learning. Unfortunately, people often have very negative ideas. For example, they say 'I can't speak in front of 20 people,' or British people often say 'I'm no good at languages.' So we need to get people thinking positively about what they can achieve as a start to the learning process.

INTERVIEWER: And after that?

NICHOLAS: Stage two is to concentrate, to understand what you want to learn. And finally, the third stage, we look at the best techniques to learn it. So, those are the three processes, learning ideas, concentrate, and know the best techniques. Then you can become an effective learner.

INTERVIEWER: You talk about learning techniques. What do you mean?

NICHOLAS: People learn in different ways. So you have visual learners, and physical learners, people who want to do and touch things, and you have auditory learners, people who need to hear things, etc. And others. We help learners to understand their own learning style and so learn faster.

INTERVIEWER: How do you do that?

NICHOLAS: One exercise we have is to ask people to teach others something they are good at. This helps people to find out about themselves. So for example, a special skill, say cooking. Some people describe their kitchen and how everything is organised on tables, etc. They are visual thinkers. Others say, 'Right, I've got a carrot and I cut it up ...' That's the physical type. So people learn about themselves with us.

INTERVIEWER: Interesting. And do you work with companies much?

NICHOLAS: Yes, and I find companies have different learning cultures. In Microsoft, people think with pictures. In fact, a lot of IT people are visual learners. Marks & Spencer's culture is more practical, it's about doing things. And companies have different ideas of failure. For some organisations, making mistakes is not an option. But mistakes can be good for learning. People who don't like making mistakes don't make good learners.

INTERVIEWER: Do you think you could help language learners?

NICHOLAS: I think so. Memory is important. So sometimes I teach them something like 50 Egyptian hieroglyphs in an hour with simple memory techniques and positive thinking. People think it's amazing. And why do we do that? It shows people how good their memory can be. Also things like mind maps which I use, these could be really good for vocabulary learning.

INTERVIEWER: But at the end of the day, is learning also about good teachers?

NICHOLAS: Yes and no. I tell my students that learning is not just about good teachers. Teachers help, but learners have to take responsibility for learning. Taking responsibility is really important. You have to understand how you learn, and how to stay motivated and to create learning space in your own life. It's really up to each individual to build a personal learning plan and use it over the long term.

19 Britain at work in 2010
19.1 Vision of the future
INTERVIEWER: Richard, I've read your book with great interest. I'd like to discuss some of the ideas you write about. So, what's the future for Britain in 2010, starting first with the economy?

RICHARD: Well, I think the internet will be very important, more important than now. Through that we'll see many new connections across continents and we'll see lots more global trade. Also, and this is happening already, a lot of manufacturing activities from Britain, Europe and the United States will move to South East Asia, especially China. In Europe and the States, we'll see more focus on design and development, the activities which create real value in products and services.

INTERVIEWER: That's interesting. And what about work – how will our working lives change?

RICHARD: I think we'll see many changes. The first thing to say is that working life may become much more unstable for many people. It's very likely that large companies will no longer give us job security as in the past. If this happens, we'll see a lot more self-employment and people moving between companies to find new opportunities. But with lots more change, working life will become more stressful.

INTERVIEWER: What about home working? Do you think more people are going to work from home in the future?

RICHARD: Well, what we'll see is a redefinition of the workplace. The workplace will still be important, for developing ideas, for building teams, and so on. But if you have to write a report and do all the administration, you can do that at home. And I think this is really important because people travelling to work create big lifestyle problems with heavy traffic and pollution. It makes really good sense for people to stay at home more. Of course, you'll still have some workers, like shop staff and cleaners, who have to go to a workplace from 9 to 5. But I think if people get the opportunity – especially many office staff and managers – they will choose to work from home, perhaps up to 50% of their working time.

INTERVIEWER: We're living longer now. Do you think we'll work later in life?

RICHARD: No, I don't think people will work later in life, definitely not. As now, people will quit their jobs at around 55, as soon as they can. The pressure of work will make people retire – the stress factor again. And in the south of England, if the pension situation doesn't change enormously, we'll see people selling their houses to move to cheaper parts of the country as a way to pay for retirement. In fact, if it becomes easier to buy houses abroad, many people from Britain might actually emigrate to France or Spain. We see it now a little. And retirement will be different too. People will stop work in order to do things, to travel and generally enjoy life more.

INTERVIEWER: In the book you talk a little about enjoyment and pleasure in the future. Is that the future for us all, to enjoy life more?

RICHARD: It's an interesting point about western society. In 2010, in this new global situation, people may feel that they have no strong voice, no impact on politics. If this happens, people may adopt a 'live for today' lifestyle. They won't think about the future, they'll live for the moment. In 2010 the new focus in people's lives will be on personal life, on pleasure and enjoying what they can.

19.2 Sounds good
Exercise 1
SPEAKER 1: But if we cut marketing by <u>twenty</u> per cent, we can save <u>more</u> money.
SPEAKER 2: But if we cut <u>staff</u> by just <u>one</u> per cent, we can save even <u>more</u> money.

19.3 Sounds good
Exercise 2
SPEAKER 1: If we increase salaries by ten per cent, staff will be happy.
SPEAKER 2: But if we increase salaries by <u>twenty</u> per cent, staff will be <u>very</u> happy.
SPEAKER 1: If we invest less in sales training, we can reduce costs radically.
SPEAKER 2: But if we invest <u>more</u>, we can increase <u>turnover</u>.
SPEAKER 1: If we cancel the Christmas party, we can save thousands.
SPEAKER 2: But if we <u>keep</u> the party, staff will be <u>really</u> <u>motivated</u>.
SPEAKER 1: If we increase quality, we can increase our prices.
SPEAKER 2: But if we <u>reduce</u> quality just a <u>little</u>, we can save <u>millions</u>.

20 How the rich travel
20.1 Meetings 2: Leading a meeting
Meeting 1
PAOLO: OK, shall we get started? Does everyone have a copy of the agenda? Yes? Good. Right, we need to discuss where and when we hold the next sales workshop. Stefan? What do you think?
STEFAN: I think we should go to the Athens office. Greece had a very good year and we should show that by travelling there.
PAOLO: OK, thanks for that. So you want to go to Greece. Julie? What's your view?
JULIE: I agree with Stefan. I know it might be expensive but I think our Greek colleagues have something to teach us. They had such a good year.
PAOLO: OK, I agree with you. Good, so we've decided to go to Greece. The next question is when. So can we ...

20.2 Meetings 2: Leading a meeting
Meeting 2
PAOLO: Right, now the last thing we need to decide. We just need a quick decision on which of these two colours to use for the new brochure, the red or the deep blue. Stefan? What are your thoughts?

STEFAN: Definitely the red. We've always had red as a basic colour in our promotional literature and advertising. I think we should stay with that, to be honest. No reason to change something that works. I think ...
JULIE: That's just wrong. You can't say that. The blue design is much ...
PAOLO: Sorry, Julie. Sorry to interrupt. Can we let Stefan finish?
STEFAN: OK, as I was saying, I think we have to focus on maintaining a clear brand image in the market. Our red window is a very well-known logo. I think it confuses our identity if we start changing the colours. Not now – it's not the right time. We should go for red.
PAOLO: Julie?
JULIE: I don't know. Maybe you're right. I just feel that we should be open to change and be ready to do something new in the market, to make people sit up and say 'Wow'! But I can see I'm in a minority here. It was just a feeling. Red is good.
PAOLO: OK. Good. So, we've decided to go for red this time. I think it's a safe and sensible choice. But perhaps we can also all agree to look at this issue further for next year – maybe that's the time to make a change. Can we agree to that?
JULIE: OK.
STEFAN: OK.
PAOLO: Right. Thank you both very much. If there's nothing else, I think we can finish there.

21 Great cinema
21.1 Making recommendations and giving advice
Suggesting entertainment
A: I have to take some clients out tonight. Any ideas?
B: There's a film festival on this week. I would take them to that.
A: That sounds interesting. I'll do that. Thanks.
B: It would be a good idea to book in advance. It's really popular.
A: OK. Thanks for the tip.

Recommending restaurants
A: I'm eating out tonight. Can you recommend a good Indian restaurant?
B: Yes, I can. I think the best one is the Bengali Palace on Coney Street.
A: OK, thanks. Any others? What do you think of the Mogul, near the river?
B: I'm not sure about that one. Sometimes it's almost empty.
A: OK, I'll try the other one. Thanks.

Giving advice about hotels
A: I'm going to Bonn in May. Do you think I need to book a hotel before I go?
B: I think so, yes. I think you should book somewhere on the internet.
A: OK, I'll do that.
B: But why don't you talk to our travel department first? I'm pretty sure they have some special deals with hotels in Bonn.
A: Good idea. I'll speak to them today. Thanks.

Shopping problems
A: I'm going shopping. Do you know anywhere which sells films on DVD with English and French subtitles?
B: Probably the best place to look is Waterstones. It's a bookshop in the city centre.
A: OK. Anywhere else?
B: I'm not sure. You might find something in the record shops as well. Try HMV or Virgin, for example.
A: OK, thanks. Could you write those down for me, please?

21.2 The big screen experience
INTERVIEWER: What kinds of film do you like? Clare?
CLARE: Well, I want to watch films that are entertaining. I need to be entertained. So I quite like most Hollywood films. I hate depressing films.
INTERVIEWER: What about you, Anna?
ANNA: I like to watch thrillers, especially psychological thrillers with a twist in the tail – you know, an ending which is a complete surprise. And things with Jean-Claude Van Damme, action films. And I hate nice films about relationships with happy endings.

INTERVIEWER: What about James Bond? Anna?

ANNA: James Bond? I like to watch them sometimes. I wouldn't go to the cinema to see one. They're a little bit predictable now. The plots are always the same. I suppose I'd watch one on video if I didn't have anything else to do, though.

INTERVIEWER: What about a favourite film of all time? Ron?

RON: For me, it has to be a classic Hitchcock film, maybe *North by Northwest* or *Psycho*.

ANNA: Yes, I like Hitchcock.

RON: I think I've seen *North by Northwest* about 50 times because we've got digital television and they keep showing it. But it's brilliant, great dialogue, and because it's that sort of Technicolor, every frame looks fantastic, the colour is amazing.

INTERVIEWER: Have you got any favourite actors or actresses? Clare?

CLARE: I like watching De Niro. For me, he's maybe the best actor of our generation. And Jack Nicholson, of course, as well. He's really funny.

ANNA: I go more for the director. So I love Tarantino's films, for example.

RON: Do you? I hate all that violence. It's too much. It's not really my idea of entertainment.

ANNA: Yes, but Ron, gangster movies like *The Godfather*, it's classic cinema.

RON: Maybe for you. I prefer quieter films about more ordinary people. I watch a lot of French and Italian films, even though I don't speak French or Italian.

INTERVIEWER: Do you prefer subtitles or if the film is dubbed?

RON: Definitely subtitles.

ANNA: No, dubbed films. In Germany and Italy they do it very well.

RON: I don't like dubbing. I think it changes the feel of a film if you change the actors' voices. Subtitles are far better.

INTERVIEWER: So, how often do you all actually go to the cinema? Ron?

RON: Not much, maybe once a month. I get videos and DVDs now more than I go to the cinema.

INTERVIEWER: Really? And do you think videos or new movies on the internet will kill off cinema in the future?

RON: I'm not sure. Maybe.

CLARE: Oh, come on, Ron. No way. People said the same about television. But cinema is a different experience. I mean, just seeing it on the large screen is great.

INTERVIEWER: Do you think so?

CLARE: Definitely. You can't really compare it.

ANNA: I agree.

CLARE: It's a really different thing. There's something special about watching a film with other people in a sort of community atmosphere. And it's not just seeing the film; it's the going out and meeting your friends for a drink before and afterwards. Cinema is great and it's here to stay!

21.3 The words you need
Exercise 2

1 It was a great performance. Jack Nicholson is my favourite actor.
2 She's a real star. I think Meryl Streep is my favourite actress.
3 We had a great evening out. The film was really entertaining.
4 I saw a good thriller recently. The plot was a bit complicated but I enjoyed it.
5 Tom Cruise plays the role of a successful New York lawyer who learns that life is not as simple as he thought.
6 Go and see the latest Spielberg movie. It has a great cast – all the top names are in it.
7 I went to see *Taxi Driver* with some friends last night. The main character is played by Robert De Niro.
8 There's a festival of films directed by Kurosawa on at the local cinema this week. I've only seen the *Seven Samurai*. I'd like to see some of his others.
9 His new film is set in Japan in the year 2020.
10 It was a romantic film. It had the usual happy ending but it was quite moving.
11 It was so violent that I had to close my eyes on several occasions. I just couldn't watch what was happening on the screen.
12 The film was dubbed. I prefer subtitles so you can hear the original language.

22 Your personal brand image
22.1 Image Counts

INTERVIEWER: Jenny, what is Image Counts and what do you do?

JENNY: Well, I'm an image consultant and I work with people who want to change something about themselves – their image, in fact.

INTERVIEWER: And who are your clients?

JENNY: Well, they're mostly men and a lot of them seem to be 37 or 29 or 49! Many men think, 'I'm nearly 30 – or 40 or 50 – and I haven't got the right job or the right life.' That's when they pick up the phone.

INTERVIEWER: I see. So how do you help people?

JENNY: Well, I help people in three ways: firstly, with their appearance – the way they look; secondly, their voice – the way they talk; and finally, their behaviour – the way they are with other people, in a restaurant, and so on. I help people to brand themselves, to market themselves professionally.

INTERVIEWER: Is the voice important?

JENNY: The voice is very, very important, personally and professionally, and a lot of men do actually have quite a boring voice. I work with two voice coaches. One is called Doctor Voice. He goes all around the world with famous pop groups. OK, you don't have to become a pop star, but an interesting voice helps you in life, and it takes time to improve. You need to be patient.

INTERVIEWER: OK. And what about etiquette?

JENNY: Well, we develop 14 different kinds of etiquette: business etiquette, email etiquette, social etiquette, and so on. You don't need to learn everything immediately – people just choose the key things for them.

INTERVIEWER: And restaurant etiquette?

JENNY: Yes, if a company wants to make someone a director, they often take him or her to a restaurant. A director has to know how to behave and we help clients to pass the test. I had to do a lot of work with a client on this last week, in fact.

INTERVIEWER: Do you go into detail? Do you talk about how to hold a wine glass?

JENNY: Yes, and sometimes we explain that you mustn't butter bread like it's a picnic. And we look at language: things you must and mustn't say.

INTERVIEWER: And clothing?

JENNY: We talk a lot about what people mustn't wear, that's the important thing, to know what they mustn't wear.

INTERVIEWER: Do you brief clients on working internationally?

JENNY: Yes, I have experts for this. Like you absolutely mustn't write on someone's business card and you shouldn't put it in your back pocket, that sort of thing.

INTERVIEWER: What about body language?

JENNY: I think the most important thing to begin with is shaking hands. I always, always teach everybody how to shake hands and almost nobody knows how to do it.

INTERVIEWER: So can you tell us one or two golden rules?

JENNY: Oh, I've got lots! I must show you the brochure which has our golden rules. But first, what's really important ... well, I constantly say to our clients you really must listen to people better, try to listen more than you talk. And another basic one – you need to be nice to look at. That always makes people think 'Ah that's such a nice person.'

22.2 Sounds good
Exercise 1

1 I think you should go to the meeting, not the workshop.
2 I think you really should go to the meeting, not the workshop.

22.3 Sounds good
Exercise 2

1 A: Our organisation can help people to develop themselves and their careers.
  B: Believe me. Our organisation *can* help people.

2 A: You shouldn't use your car. Use a company car.
  B: I didn't say it's illegal to use your car but you really *shouldn't*.
3 A: Some people don't want to accept criticism. But they *must* if they want to improve.
  B: People must accept criticism every day they are with us.
4 A: You mustn't forget that there are only three golden rules to learn.
  B: I didn't say you shouldn't forget. I said you *mustn't* forget.

24 Social issues

24.1 Receiving international colleagues

Welcome
A: Welcome to head office. We hope you enjoy your stay.
B: Thanks a lot. I'm really looking forward to working with you.
A: Did you have a good trip? Was everything OK?
B: Yes, it was fine, thanks. No problems at all.

Security
A: OK, we need to do a couple of things first. You need to fill in your details here.
B: Fine. Shall I do that now?
A: Yes, please. And you have to wear this badge all the time.
B: Do I give it back when I finish in the evening?
A: No, you can keep it until you leave.

Work space
A: So this is your office. I hope you don't mind sharing.
B: Not at all. I'm used to it!
A: Fine. And you can use this computer. It's connected to the internet.
B: Thanks. Do I need a password?
A: Yes, just type 'visitor' for user name and password.
B: And how about the phone?
A: You just press 1 for an outside line.

Outside work
A: And this is my home number, just in case you need anything in the evening.
B: Oh, I wouldn't disturb you at home.
A: No, really, feel free. You can always reach me at home or on my mobile.
B: That's very kind. I hope I won't have to.
A: Well, I think that's everything.
B: Thanks. Everything is very clear.

24.2 Social issues in Britain

Rajid
INTERVIEWER: Rajid, what do you think is the biggest social problem in Britain today?
RAJID: Britain is supposed to be a multi-ethnic society but I think racism is still a huge problem. We just don't get treated the same. It's more difficult for non-whites to get jobs, to do well at school. There's still an incredible amount of racism in football. Politicians talk a lot about racism but they don't do anything about it really.
INTERVIEWER: And what's the answer to the problem?
RAJID: Maybe if we had more jobs and more money in Bradford, things would be better and there would be fewer problems.

Bill
INTERVIEWER: Bill, what, for you, is the biggest social problem in Britain today?
BILL: Well, if you'd asked me that question 20 years ago – in the eighties, say, I would have said unemployment straightaway. We had three million people unemployed then. Today it's much better but jobs are still a big problem. Far too many jobs today are low paid, part-time jobs in service industries – cleaning, hotels, fast food, things like that.
INTERVIEWER: And what's the answer?
BILL: We need better education, a better educated workforce. And more hi-tech industries – that's the way ahead economically.

Mary
INTERVIEWER: Mary, what's your view on the biggest social problem in Britain today?

MARY: The thing I worry about most is homelessness. House prices are so incredibly high. It can be a real problem for young people. If they've got problems at home and have to move away from their family, there's sometimes nowhere for them to go, there's nowhere they can afford, and some of them end up sleeping on the streets, begging. And it can be a real problem for people who lose their jobs too – they often can't pay for their homes and then they have nowhere to go either.
INTERVIEWER: And what do you think the answer to this problem is?
MARY: I think the government has to build houses and flats that ordinary people can afford – a reasonable price or a reasonable rent.

Maurice
INTERVIEWER: Maurice, in your opinion, what's the biggest social problem in Britain today?
MAURICE: Personal safety definitely. It's definitely not safe on the streets at nights, especially at the weekends. There's too much violence, so much aggression sometimes. Every day you read about something in the papers, someone got attacked, and there's more knives and guns. And hooliganism and vandalism – at least where I come from.
INTERVIEWER: And what's the answer to the problem?
MAURICE: I know a lot of people who say the police are the problem but for me the answer is more police, definitely. More police and more black policemen.

Joyce
INTERVIEWER: Joyce, tell me what you think is the biggest social problem in Britain today.
JOYCE: All our problems come from poverty, from social deprivation, people not having enough to live on. We have so many children living in poverty because they're in single parent families, and they're living in poverty because there's so much divorce. And the rich are getting richer and the poor are getting poorer.
INTERVIEWER: And what's the answer?
JOYCE: Britain's a very rich country and we need more equal distribution of the country's wealth. More tax for the rich and more spending on the poor, I think.

25 The coffee business

25.1 Douwe Egberts – coffee producer and seller

INTERVIEWER: So, Arnauld, who do you work for?
ARNAULD: I work for Douwe Egberts in Paris as a financial controller. My main responsibility is to set budgets, to prepare and then update them and to explain results, for the company in general.
INTERVIEWER: Do you have a lot of contact with other departments to get figures?
ARNAULD: Yes, communicating with other departments is important in my job. But the biggest problem or challenge I have is receiving the correct data. I can then set a realistic budget. Business units have to give me figures on their sales for the next three years, to give me a forecast. To be honest, it's very difficult for them to estimate accurately the level of sales. It's not a precise science. If we were able to see into the future, life would be a lot easier.
INTERVIEWER: The market for coffee at the moment – is it tough?
ARNAULD: The global coffee situation is good for us. Production worldwide is still over the level of consumption, so the price of coffee is fairly stable, cheap in fact. That's very good for our company, as we have about 10% oversupply.
INTERVIEWER: What would happen if demand were greater than supply? Or, if world coffee stocks decreased?
ARNAULD: It's clear, if stocks decreased or demand were greater than supply for whatever reason, the price would increase, I don't know how much, but sure, our margin would decrease. It's very difficult to pass on any price increases to the consumer. You have to take care of market share.
INTERVIEWER: What about coffee production, the coffee producers?
ARNAULD: Coffee production depends on the weather. When it's bad, it can cause damage. But that hasn't happened for three or four years. What's new in the market is the arrival of a new producer, Vietnam.
INTERVIEWER: Vietnam – really?

ARNAULD: Yes, and now they've climbed their way up to be one of the five biggest producers of coffee in the world. This is good for us: it guarantees enough production – more producers means more coffee. It's good for us but not for the coffee producers because it won't help the price to go higher. But at Douwe Egberts we also have to take care of the coffee producers. It's an ethical question for companies to think about developing countries. They should do something.

INTERVIEWER: Does Douwe Egberts really take this ethical question seriously?

ARNAULD: Absolutely. They've decided not to communicate this – what they are doing or what they've done – but they do a lot to take care of ... to help producers.

INTERVIEWER: So if the prices totally crashed at some point in the future, would Douwe Egberts help coffee producers by continuing to pay a normal price to producers, to pay above the market price?

ARNAULD: Definitely, yes, we would. We would pay above the market price in some situations. We'd try to support producers through any big crisis. No doubt.

INTERVIEWER: It's good to hear about a company with an ethical attitude.

ARNAULD: Yes, but I think there's a trend. Each big American company is beginning to do something in this area, to be ethical, to be more responsible. Many companies I know have a policy in place.

INTERVIEWER: When you said this, I thought it was just public relations, customer psychology.

ARNAULD: No, it's not 'just public relations' because these companies don't really communicate it. They don't publish information about it or anything. So I really think they just do it out of a feeling of ethical responsibility, which is good.

INTERVIEWER: Absolutely.

25.2 Do it yourself
Exercise 2
1 If we banned motor cars in major cities, we would reduce urban pollution significantly.
2 If we introduced a 35-hour working week, employees could create a real work–life balance.
3 Companies would be able to find qualified people more easily if we had a better education system.
4 If we made criminals wear microchips, we could stop a lot of crime.
5 If we had to give 2% of our income to developing countries, we would reduce poverty significantly.
6 Our staff would be much healthier if they did 30 minutes of regular exercise every day.
7 If we worried less about money and material possessions, we might be happier.
8 If politicians listened to the people, the world would be a much better place.

25.3 Do it yourself
Exercise 3
1 A: If we pay for staff membership of the local fitness centre, everyone can take some regular exercise.
  B: Yes, but if we did that, it'd cost a lot of money.
2 A: If we offer better quality food in the canteen, people will eat more healthily.
  B: Yes, but if we offered better quality food at lunchtime, it would have little impact on their general diet.
3 A: If we create more open spaces, people will feel less stressed.
  B: Yes, but if we created more open spaces, we wouldn't have enough room for all our employees.

25.4 Sounds good
Exercise 1
would
might
climb
who
doubt
know

honest
science

25.5 Sounds good
Exercise 3
half
scissors
island
knife
whole
hour
chemist
business
guide
steady
listen
autumn
lamb
wrong
thought

26 Intelligent skis
26.1 The words you need
Exercise 2
Find your way with the Compaq handheld computer with Navigator. The new Compaq iPAQ 3800 is designed for the international business person who is always on the move. It includes a top quality diary with computing functions and built-in MP3 player. The GPS navigating system, when installed, is very user-friendly, and enables you to pinpoint your location anywhere in the world to within 10 square metres. You can be sure that you will make that next meeting on time with turn-by-turn voice directions. The Compaq iPAQ 3800 ensures stress-free travel and gives you the confidence to relax.

26.2 Telephoning 3: Handling complaints
Call 1
OSCAR: Oscar Hansen.
DANIELA: Oscar. Hi, it's Daniela Beermann.
OSCAR: Hi, Daniela. How are you?
DANIELA: Well, not so good, actually. We've just received the last order of paint from you – order number E258 – and found that it's 5,000 litres short.
OSCAR: Really. I'm very sorry about that. Let me check. You said E258, yes?
DANIELA: That's right. We ordered 15,000 litres at the start of last week and we've just taken delivery of 10,000.
OSCAR: Yes, I have it on screen. You're right. The order was 15,000 litres. I do apologise. I don't really understand why this has happened. I'll check with dispatch and get back to you within the hour. Is that OK? Then we can organise a new delivery as soon as possible.
DANIELA: Fine.
OSCAR: OK, Daniela. Very sorry about this. I'll call you back shortly.
DANIELA: Thanks. Bye.
OSCAR: Bye.

Call 2
DANIELA: Daniela Beermann.
OSCAR: Hi, Daniela. Oscar calling back.
DANIELA: Hi, Oscar. So, any news of what happened?
OSCAR: Yes, it seems there was a computer error in the warehouse which caused the problem. I've asked them to investigate and give me a report. Anyway, we've dispatched another 5,000 litres today and that will be with you tomorrow morning. Is that OK?
DANIELA: Yes, that's fine.
OSCAR: Sorry again for the inconvenience, Daniela.
DANIELA: It's OK. These things can happen. Thanks for sorting it out so quickly.
OSCAR: No problem. Can you send me an email to confirm the arrival of the goods tomorrow?
DANIELA: OK, will do. Thanks, Oscar. Bye.
OSCAR: Thanks, Daniela. Bye.

Call 3

JACK: Hello. Jack Sansom.
ANGELA: Jack. It's Angela. There's a problem.
JACK: What's wrong?
ANGELA: Sam's just told me that there's a delay with the API project. You told me everything would be finished this week.
JACK: Yes, I really do apologise. I know I promised, but the project is very complex. We had a lot of problems last week with the software installation.
ANGELA: But you didn't tell me, Jack.
JACK: I was going to call you this afternoon. But it's not a big problem. We'll finish things off by Tuesday next week – so it's only a two-day delay. OK?
ANGELA: OK, that's not too bad.
JACK: I'll call you on Tuesday afternoon when everything's finished. OK?
ANGELA: Right. That's fine.
JACK: Sorry about the delay. We'll talk next week. Have a good weekend.
ANGELA: OK, you too. Bye.
JACK: Bye.

27 You are what you eat

27.1 Food talk

Understanding the menu
A: Excuse me, can you help me? What exactly is *coq au vin*?
B: *Coq au vin*? It's chicken cooked in wine, madam.
A: I see. How is it cooked?
B: It's done in a casserole dish in the oven with red wine, onions, bacon, mushrooms and garlic. It's one of the chef's specialities.
A: It sounds delicious. I'll try it.

Complimenting the chef
A: That was very good. You have an excellent chef.
B: Thank you. And we try to cook mainly with local ingredients.
A: That's good. Where do you get them?
B: We have good contacts with all the local farmers.
A: Yes, everything tastes very fresh.

Explaining the name of a local dish
A: This soup is excellent. What's it called?
B: We call it *miso* soup with *wakame*. *Miso* is a kind of bean paste and *wakame* is a kind of green seaweed. We use it a lot in soups.
A: It's very good.
B: Yes, but my wife's is better. She got the recipe from her grandmother.

Describing how something is cooked
A: This fish is delicious. I'd love to know the recipe.
B: I make it with wine, ginger, garlic and herbs and then cook it in a hot oven.
A: It sounds complicated.
B: No, it's really easy. The most important thing is not to overcook it.
A: Well, it's just perfect.

27.2 How do you like our food?

INTERVIEWER: Lesley, why do you think food is so important?
LESLEY: I think food is incredibly important in every culture. Very often when Japanese people travel abroad, the very first thing that they think about is the food because Japanese food is incredibly different from western food and lots of Japanese that I know take food with them when they go abroad.
INTERVIEWER: So what's the most important thing about Japanese food?
LESLEY: It's got a fantastic variety of ingredients. The freshness is the most important thing and the presentation – how the food looks on the plate. Japanese food looks like a beautiful picture, it looks just wonderful. So the three things that matter are fresh food, top quality and the presentation. A really special thing in Japan is the Buddhist vegetarian cuisine which is prepared in Buddhist temples and is based on things like tofu and *miso* and lots of soya bean products, all very healthy. Of course it tastes wonderful as well.

INTERVIEWER: Do you think visitors to Japan like Japanese food when they go there, or do they tend to stay with their own western ideas?
LESLEY: These days most people know Japanese food from restaurants. But I must say there are people that don't fancy raw fish, though I have to say they are very silly if they don't try it. It's wonderful. But I know that some Japanese can have problems when they go abroad. I remember a Japanese student in Oxford. He told me that his mum sent him boxes and boxes and boxes of Japanese food. Things like noodles and seaweed. He absolutely couldn't live without them. I think he actually felt sick when he first came to London because he couldn't stand the food and then she started sending him boxes of food. When you talk to Japanese in Japan the very first thing they say is 'How do you like our food?' And if you say you like it very much they are really happy and then you can go on and have the rest of your conversation.
INTERVIEWER: Is there anything you won't eat in Japan – I hear people talk about raw fish, or live fish, whale meat and things like that?
LESLEY: In fact I have – and you won't like me for this – eaten whale because I got so incredibly tired of environmentalist types who whenever the subject of Japan comes up, even at Christmas parties when I'm trying to relax and have a nice time, they start attacking me because Japanese eat whale! So I thought 'I will have some whale.' Now, when people mention whale, I can tell them it tastes really good, rather like tuna, and I enjoyed eating it very much. It makes people really mad with rage! I've never had live food, and there is live food in Japan, there are things like live little fish and live prawns which move around in one's mouth apparently. But I personally don't think I could eat live food, so it's either dead and fresh or it's dead and cooked. Then it's OK!

28 That's entertainment!

28.1 From strongmen to look-alikes

INTERVIEWER: What do you do exactly, Janie?
JANIE: I run – I suppose I'm managing director of an entertainment agency, but it's quite different to most agencies. We use singers, dancers, musicians, models, acrobats, strongmen, jugglers, look-alikes – we do absolutely anything and everything.
INTERVIEWER: So what kinds of event do you organise and for which clients?
JANIE: We mainly do corporate events: product launches and promotions for companies. That means we do the design, the music, the show, everything.
INTERVIEWER: And how old is your company? How many people?
JANIE: Well, I've been working here for 14 years. I started off working from my living room but it was just myself and my assistant Katy then. But we're still a small organisation and we run really on a project basis using freelance people.
INTERVIEWER: So is it a problem to get the right people for each project?
JANIE: Well, firstly, any possible contract is discussed internally. Then, if we think it's interesting, performers are contacted to check their availability. If they're available, they're hired immediately so we can then go ahead with the project. In fact, two singers were recruited this morning for a new project.
INTERVIEWER: OK. So it's very much a virtual organisation with contacts you bring in?
JANIE: Yes, that's right. I mean we've got around 500 people on our books, artists, etc., so it's a huge family here, but, as I said, the actual organisation is very small.
INTERVIEWER: What's the most interesting event you've organised?
JANIE: We did a really interesting project last year. It was a product launch, and we actually organised a fireworks display for the event – we created a really big bang effect for the launch of the product.
INTERVIEWER: How long do these events typically last?
JANIE: Well, that one was a day event, from first thing in the morning until late at night. Most events are one day, in fact. But that one took three months to plan.
INTERVIEWER: OK. And what's the most difficult event you've ever had to organise?

JANIE: Probably the most difficult events are the ones we do in India for the film business just because they work in such a different way to here. Changes are often made at the very last minute in India, people are replaced, new ideas are added, so you have to be extremely patient. And it's so hot – the heat's the hardest thing. One of the most difficult things, I remember, was when I had 50 dancers for a movie scene, with one song, and it took three and a half weeks and we were working 12 to 14 hours a day in heat of well over 40 degrees. That was tough!

INTERVIEWER: Just one last question I have to ask. You mentioned look-alikes. Who's your most popular look-alike?

JANIE: I knew you'd ask that. Well, with look-alikes, it's changing. Britney Spears and Kylie Minogue were always requested by everyone in the past, but at the moment we have a lot of Frank Sinatras. I think our top Frank Sinatra is booked every week at the moment. So old Frank is really making a comeback.

INTERVIEWER: You enjoy the job, I can see, don't you?

JANIE: Oh, absolutely. I love the variety, because every single day is different. There are lots of challenges but lots of fun projects. And I get the chance to travel a lot, which is something I really enjoy doing.

28.2 Do it yourself
Exercise 3

The Notting Hill Carnival is the biggest street event in Europe and has roots going back hundreds of years. Historically, the Carnival was established by black slaves. Song, dance and costume were used by the slaves to protest about social conditions and celebrate black culture. The modern London Carnival was started over 30 years ago by the Trinidadian community newly arrived in London. At the beginning it was also seen as a form of social protest by black people living locally who were facing racism and social inequality. Now it is a fully multicultural event attracting over one million visitors every year. It is normally held on the last weekend of August with Sunday and Monday as the main days. The Carnival is a festival of music and dance. Music systems are turned up so that dancing can go on all night. The event is now managed by London Notting Hill Carnival Ltd. Last year 200 personnel were trained in health and safety because of the large crowds. Hundreds of police were also used to guarantee the event went smoothly. This year organisers are hoping to build on the success of last year and it is expected that visitor figures will reach 1.5 million.

28.3 Sounds good
Exercise 1

A: So Janie's been with the company for fourteen months, hasn't she?
B: Actually, it's fourteen <u>years</u>.

A: And she's head of marketing, isn't she?
B: No, she <u>runs</u> the company.

A: You said Kylie is the number one look-alike, didn't you?
B: She <u>was</u>, but now it's <u>Sinatra</u>.

28.4 Sounds good
Exercise 2

A: It's a dating agency you run, isn't it?
B: No, it's an <u>entertainment</u> agency.

A: Do you do most of your work for private parties?
B: Not really. Most of our work is <u>corporate</u>.

A: And do you only work in the UK?
B: We <u>did</u>. Now we work all over the <u>world</u>.

A: You have 500 employees, right?
B: Actually, we have almost <u>no</u> employees. We use <u>freelance</u> people.

29 Life coaching
29.1 The words you need

As you can see from the graph, the number of customer complaints decreased significantly last year. I think this was mainly due to our increased focus on quality. You can see here that quality was much better, up 50% on last year. So we should be happy that the investment in new machinery has resulted in better quality and more satisfied customers. If I can now turn to profits, I'm afraid that the figures are not so good due to the higher investment costs we've just discussed. It is also partly a result of a slight drop in sales of 3%. We expect things to improve next year. Finally, I would like to say that our new focus on the Central and Eastern European markets will lead to a lot of new business next year. So we should go forward with confidence. Thank you.

29.2 Presenting 2: Handling questions effectively

KURT: OK. So, that's all I want to say about costs. Does anyone have any questions?

COLLEAGUE 1: Just one question. Are we on budget?

KURT: Thanks for that question, Maria. Well, as I said, costs have increased and are a little over budget. This is mainly due to problems with staff, as I explained. But I am sure we will be under budget at the end of the project. Is that OK?

COLLEAGUE 1: Yeah, fine. Thanks.

KURT: Good. OK, if there are no more questions, I'd like to go to the next point. Let's think now about something else that we …

* * *

KURT: OK, so that's all I wanted to tell you about the software part of the project. Are there any questions on that?

COLLEAGUE 2: Yes, I have a question about training. Are we going to have training?

KURT: Well, we've organised training courses for everybody involved so I really don't see any problems here. Does that answer your question?

COLLEAGUE 2: OK. I'd be interested to discuss it more later, if possible.

KURT: Fine, we can talk about training over coffee. Good. Are there any other questions about the software? One thing I forgot to mention …

* * *

KURT: Right. That's all I wanted to say about technical questions. Does anyone have any questions?

COLLEAGUE 3: Well, just a quick question about upgrades. The new system sounds great, and much cheaper than the current one. But when we need to upgrade this new system, costs will rise sharply. Will the budget cover this?

KURT: It's an important question. Thank you. No need to worry. I can tell you that we've already agreed an excellent price for the first upgrade. Is that OK?

COLLEAGUE 3: Well, I think so, yes. Thanks.

KURT: Right, if there are no more questions, I'll finish there. Thank you.

30 Work or lifestyle?
30.1 Work, belief and lifestyle

INTERVIEWER: So, you work for the Vegan Society, Tony. What do you do exactly?

TONY: Well, I'm in charge of media and marketing and that sort of thing. So my job is really to promote our organisation and the ideas of what it is to be a vegan, to help people learn about the philosophy, to help people make new friends. Many things, really.

INTERVIEWER: Can you explain the difference between 'vegetarian' and 'vegan'?

TONY: Yes, vegetarians don't eat meat but will drink milk, eat eggs and so on. A vegan is more strict and won't eat or wear or use anything that comes from an animal. Vegans want to avoid as far as possible all cruelty to animals for food, and for clothing or any other purpose. So I don't wear leather, I don't buy animal-tested products … all that.

INTERVIEWER: What about your diet? What do you eat?

TONY: The same things as everyone else eats. Really normal food you know – pizza and chips, Indian curries, sausages … But I just eat vegan versions of these, often using soya alternatives.

INTERVIEWER: Is it healthy?

TONY: It depends what you eat. Veganism is not always healthy. I think many of us eat too much processed food with too much sugar, salt and processed fats. And then you combine that with a stressful lifestyle. All I can say is that I try to eat healthily and I take multi-vitamin tablets every day to help.

INTERVIEWER: What about the future? Is veganism the lifestyle of the future?

TONY: Well, it's interesting. The number of vegans is growing in the UK – it's about 250,000 now. But it's also international. There are vegan societies from Australia and New Zealand to Sweden, Italy, Spain and Austria. It's global. And it's not only that people want to be kinder to animals. It's also a movement about how we feed the world population efficiently and healthily. If you want to know more, join our celebrations on World Vegan Day on 1st November.

INTERVIEWER: So do you enjoy your job?

TONY: Absolutely. And I enjoy it fundamentally because I'm doing something which I believe in morally. For me, a job must be about more than just making money. So, I'm helping to protect people, animals and the environment – it's the whole picture and one solution for a range of dilemmas that excites me. I'm also helping people to learn, which I enjoy. And for me too, it's an interesting job to work with the media. I learn a lot every day, and that's also important. For me, a job should help you to learn and develop as a person, every day, every minute. A job should be a process of continuous learning.

30.2 Work, belief and lifestyle

INTERVIEWER: So do you enjoy your job?

TONY: Absolutely. And I enjoy it fundamentally because I'm doing something which I believe in morally. For me, a job must be about more than just making money. So, I'm helping to protect people, animals and the environment – it's the whole picture and one solution for a range of dilemmas that excites me. I'm also helping people to learn, which I enjoy. And for me too, it's an interesting job to work with the media. I learn a lot every day, and that's also important. For me, a job should help you to learn and develop as a person, every day, every minute. A job should be a process of continuous learning.

30.3 Saying goodbye

Getting away

A: Right, I think I should be going.

B: Already? It's only half past nine.

A: Sorry, I really must be going. I promised I'd get back early tonight.

B: It's a real pity, the party's only just starting.

A: Yes, I'd love to stay but I really have to go. I'll see you next week. Bye.

Getting away quickly

A: OK, have a nice weekend everybody.

B: Oh, can I just ask you a quick work question before you go?

A: My train goes in around 20 minutes. Can we leave it until Monday?

B: But I just need to run over the agenda for Tuesday morning.

A: Sorry. Can you ask Olivia? I really have to go. Bye.

Give me a call

A: I have to go to a meeting now.

B: OK, but there are a couple more points to discuss.

A: Well, call me next week. We can talk over some more details then.

B: I will. I'll give you a call on Monday morning.

A: Fine. Talk to you then. Bye.

Until the next time

A: I've just come to say goodbye. I'm leaving now. My train's at five-thirty.

B: OK, well it was really good to see you again.

A: Same here. It was great working with you, as always.

B: Yeah, I enjoyed it too. And, hopefully, see you next year.

A: Yes, until then, take care. Bye.

Revision 2

R2.1 Pronunciation

Exercise 1

1 A: What's her number?
  B: It's 0047 51 88 97 83.
  A: Did you say 51 88 57 83?
  B: No, it's 51 88 <u>97</u> 83.

2 A: What's his email address?
  B: It's marcus.ritter@zurich.ch.
  A: Is that M–A–R–K–U–S?
  B: No, it's a <u>C</u>. M–A–R–<u>C</u>–U–S.

3 A: Where do they live?
  B: It's 145 Queen Street.
  A: One hundred and thirty-five?
  B: No, not thirty-five. It's one hundred and <u>forty</u>-five.

4 A: When's the next meeting?
  B: It's on the 22nd of September.
  A: The second?
  B: No, the <u>twenty</u>-second.

R2.2 Pronunciation

Exercise 2

1 Shall we go and get some lunch?
2 Can I have a cup of coffee?
3 I'm afraid I'm a bit too busy.
4 I've been working here for over a year.
5 Maybe I should take that job after all.
6 How about trying that new Indian restaurant?.

Answer key

1 Working internationally

Listen to this
From Jordan to Switzerland
1   1 F   2 T   3 T   4 T   5 F
2   1   Managing new product development
     2   Salaries are lower
     3   Once a year
     4   The countryside
     5   Because everybody speaks English

Check your grammar
Present simple and present continuous
1   (present continuous) b, f   2   (present simple) a, c, d, e

Do it yourself
1   1   He works in Madrid.
     2   Where do you come from originally? Are you German?
     3   Sales are increasing a lot at the moment in China.
     4   I usually go to work by car.
     5   This meal is delicious. The meat tastes really good.
2   1   What do you do?
     2   What are you doing?
     3   Do you specialise in project work?
     4   How often do you come to Zurich?
     5   Where are you staying?
     6   Is your business expanding at the moment?
3   1   are you doing
     2   I'm going
     3   does he work
     4   How often do you see
     5   We try to meet
     6   Do you know
     7   I don't go
     8   I'm working
     9   things aren't going well
    10   your plane is boarding

Sounds good
Strong and weak stress
1   The underlined words carry the main meaning in the sentences. 'You' is stressed where the speaker wants to give emphasis.
2   A: <u>How</u> <u>often</u> do you <u>travel</u> on <u>business</u>?
     B: About <u>once</u> a <u>month</u>. And <u>you</u>?

     A: Are you <u>busy</u>?
     B: <u>Yes</u>, I'm <u>working</u> on a <u>big</u> <u>project</u> in <u>China</u>.

     A: Do you <u>know</u> <u>Madrid</u>?
     B: <u>No</u>, I <u>don't</u>. Do <u>you</u>?

     A: <u>What</u> are you <u>working</u> on at the <u>moment</u>?
     B: A <u>report</u> – the <u>deadline</u> is <u>next</u> <u>week</u>.

     A: Did you <u>have</u> a <u>good</u> <u>weekend</u>?
     B: <u>Great</u>, <u>thanks</u>. <u>How</u> was <u>yours</u>?

2 Power for life

Read on
Total – in the energy business
1   1 B   3 C   4 D   6 A
2   1   The number of barrels of oil we consume every day
     2   The number of cubic metres of gas we consume every year
     3   The year that Total was founded
     4   Total's annual turnover in dollars
     5   Total's profit after tax in dollars
     6   The number of countries in which Total has employees

3   Eight forms of power are mentioned:
     oil, coal, gas, electricity, nuclear, solar, wind, gasoline

The words you need ... to talk about business and business organisation
1   1 Founded   2 sells   3 market leader   4 produces
     5 organised into   6 markets   7 employs   8 worldwide
     9 share   10 turnover
2   1 do   2 global   3 core   4 big   5 sectors   6 card
     7 travel on   8 talk

Telephoning 1: Getting through / Leaving a message
1   Call 1: Leaving a message
     Call 2: Getting through
     Call 3: The person called is not available
     Call 4: Waiting on line
2   1 reached   2 leave a message   3 call you back
     4 to speak to   5 there   6 put you through   7 moment
     8 leave a message   9 need to talk   10 call me
    11 leave you my number   12 experiencing   13 hold
    14 becomes available

3 Edinburgh – the festival city

Arriving in a place you don't know
1 d   2 g   3 h   4 f   5 a   6 e   7 b   8 c

Listen to this
The festival city
1   1 T   2 T   3 F   4 F
2   1   about 170
     2   about 450,000
     3   make money, big audiences
     4   £5
     5   Going to see dance companies

The words you need ... to talk about music, theatre, dance and opera
Going out 1: The performing arts
1 production   2 performance   3 lighting   4 design
5 composition   6 conductor   7 orchestra   8 concert
9 director   10 playwright   11 costume   12 actress
13 Ballet   14 ballerina   15 choreographer   16 contemporary
Going out 2: What you like
From most positive to most negative:
I love ... , I really like ... , I like ... , I quite like ... ,
I'm not very keen on ... , I don't really like ... , I can't stand ... ,
I hate ...

4 Changing direction

Listen to this
Change is fun
1   1   the USA
     2   to give her children a new life
     3   with a friend
     4   like the *crêperie*
     5   didn't make a profit last year
2   1   She has a sister who lives there.
     2   15 days
     3   It's beautiful and because there are lobsters.
     4   They became stronger and more confident.
     5   People only go there in the summer.

Check your grammar

Past simple and past continuous

1 1 I <u>was working</u> (past continuous) for a language school in France when I <u>had</u> the idea. (past simple)
  2 When my son <u>saw</u> it, he <u>was</u> really excited. (past simple x 2)
  3 We <u>were living</u> in France at the time. (past continuous)
  4 After I <u>figured</u> I could make a profit, I <u>set</u> up the place. (past simple x 2)
  5 She <u>was working</u> (past continuous) in the restaurant business and so she <u>came</u> over. (past simple)
  6 Things <u>were not going</u> well for them at school around this time. (past continuous)
  Was is only for first person and third person singular. *Were* is for all others.

2 1 c 2 a 3 b 4 a 5 c 6 b

Do it yourself

1 1 James met Sabine in 1998. He was living in New York at the time.
  2 I wanted to work in marketing. So I joined a marketing company.
  3 I was listening to the radio when you called.
  4 I saw Jess a minute ago. She was talking to Sam.
  5 Why didn't you answer the phone when I called?

2 1 d 2 c 3 b 4 e 5 a

3 1 did ... begin 2 was working 3 had 4 took 5 came
  6 Was 7 was already writing 8 joined 9 Did ... write
  10 was 11 did ... have 12 stopped 13 were doing
  14 listened 15 started

Sounds good

Using intonation to show interest

1 In the first exchange, the listener sounds uninterested because his intonation is unenthusiastic. In the second exchange, the listener is more enthusiastic, and uses varied and more dynamic intonation and a wider variety of responses to indicate interest.

2 1 Type 2 2 Type 3 3 Type 1 4 Type 1 5 Type 1

5 Job swap

Read on

Job swapping

1 1 Job swapping is when two people change jobs for a day or more and learn from the experience.
  2 Sonia is a team coordinator. Her duties include organising meetings, travel and documentation.
  Ben is a design director. His duties include designing corporate brochures and other documents for outside the organisation.
  3 They were both generally very positive about the experience.

2 1 He has to work on a lot of different things, with a variety of tasks.
  2 She could do other things and had more creativity than she thought.
  3 She'll try to contribute more ideas during team meetings in future.
  4 He knew her job was very different from his.
  5 He couldn't print some documents.
  6 It showed him that organisational skills are essential to achieve targets. He learned more about dealing with pressure.

The words you need ... to talk about jobs and personal development

1 1 build 2 contribute 3 work 4 achieve 5 cope
  6 develop 7 improve

2 1 responsibility for 2 in charge of 3 responsible for
  4 objective 5 tasks 6 deal with 7 take care of
  8 involved in

Presenting 1: Welcoming visitors

1 Name: Wilkins
  Job: Information officer
  Morning tour: Production area
  Lunch: 12.30
  Evening programme: Restaurant

2 1 h 2 g 3 i 4 f 5 e 6 a 7 c 8 b 9 d

6 Tourist attraction

Health and feeling ill

1 f 2 c 3 g 4 a 5 h 6 b 7 e 8 d

Listen to this

Are you looking for somewhere different?

1 1 T 2 F 3 T 4 T 5 T

2 1 Tourism, farming and food
  2 Half a million people
  3 Long and empty
  4 Mountains
  5 One third
  6 It's mostly a natural wilderness; Europe has big cities, many people, a high density of population, and roads and buildings everywhere.

The words you need ... to talk about tourist attractions and accommodation

2 1 scenery 2 wilderness 3 cuisine 4 wildlife 5 culture
  6 environment 7 sights

3 1 farmhouse 2 guest house 3 self-catering accommodation
  4 campsite 5 house swap 6 villa 7 hotel 8 youth hostel
  9 caravan 10 bed and breakfast

7 From Mexico to Germany

Listen to this

Work is fun

1 1 F 2 T 3 F 4 T 5 T

2 1 Two years
  2 Senior managers
  3 Mexican Spanish contains older forms of Spanish and some American English words
  4 An open and friendly style
  5 Mexican food is closer to Spanish food than German

Check your grammar

Adjectives and adverbs

1 See Grammar reference on page 114.

2 badly – worse   well – better

3 b

Do it yourself

1 1 They drive a lot faster.
  2 I don't speak Spanish as well as I want to.
  3 I work more effectively in the morning.
  4 For me, the bus is not as convenient as my car.
  5 The most important thing to remember is not to forget anything!

2 1 carefully 2 easily 3 important 4 later 5 lower
  6 better

3 1 Petra speaks English more fluently than Kurt.
  2 Petra isn't as interested in working abroad as Kurt. / Petra is much less interested in working abroad than Kurt.
  3 Petra is more experienced overseas than Kurt. / Kurt is less experienced overseas than Petra.
  4 Kurt didn't work as hard as Petra in the team-building task.
  5 Petra didn't do the logical tasks as quickly as Kurt. / Petra did the logical tasks less quickly than Kurt.
  6 Kurt's social skills aren't as good as Petra's. / Kurt's social skills are worse than Petra's.

Sounds good

Stress patterns in long words

2 1 Mexico / languages 2 employer / another
  3 engineer / underline 4 complicated / educated
  5 analysis / competitor 6 absolutely / conversation

8 Globalisation

Read on

Can Zac save the planet?

1 1 B 3 A 4 D 6 C

2 1 100 multinational companies account for 70% of world trade.
  2 The national debt of Ghana.
  3 The richest 20% of the world's population consumes 17 times more energy than the poorest 20%.
  4 580 million people travelled abroad in 1996.

5 By 2020, 1.6 billion people will travel abroad.
6 Zac says that if everyone lived like the average American, we would need six planets to meet the energy needs.

The words you need ... to talk about trade and the economy
1 1 c   2 d   3 i   4 e   5 a   6 g   7 f   8 b   9 h
2 1 environmentally   2 economic   3 politics   4 developing
5 interest   6 invests   7 exporter   8 multinational

Emails 1: Formal and informal writing
1 Neither email is better than the other. The first one is informal, the second is formal.
2 1 i, b   2 l, e   3 h, f   4 a, d   5 j, c   6 k, g
3 *Model answers*
Hi Tom,
How's it going?
See attached report and send me your opinion when you can.
See you soon.
Val

Dear Ms Rivers,
I am writing to confirm our meeting on 15 July at 10 am in the SAS Executive Lounge at London Heathrow. I should be grateful if you would send me some product information. Please let me know if you would like me to help you to prepare for the meeting.
I look forward to seeing you again soon.
Kind regards,
Ramón da Silva

9 Here is the news

Talking about news
1 1 f   2 g   3 c   4 h   5 a   6 d   7 i   8 j   9 e   10 b

Listen to this
Finding out what's going on
1 1 F   2 F   3 T   4 F
2 1 analysis   2 entertainment   3 interactive   4 research
5 newspapers and the radio

The words you need ... to talk about newspapers and news stories
1 1 f   2 g   3 i   4 h   5 j   6 b   7 e   8 d   9 a   10 c
2 1 wonderful   2 terrible   3 disappointing   4 worrying
5 interesting/excellent   6 boring   7 excellent/interesting
8 exciting

10 Executive search

Listen to this
Finding the right people
1 1 Paris   2 for 10 years   3 solve problems
4 to know his clients' needs well
5 the job is different every day
2 1 In the USA
2 He joined the US army
3 1979
4 Everyday management skills
5 People with vision and leadership

Check your grammar
Past simple, present perfect simple and present perfect continuous
1 1 c   2 a   3 b
2 We form the present perfect continuous with *have* + *been* + the *-ing* form of the verb.
We form the present perfect simple with *have* + the past participle.
3 1 for   2 since   3 ago
for – we can use it with different tenses to describe how long an activity lasted
since – we can use it with the present perfect to indicate the starting point of a past activity which continues to now
ago – we can use it with the past simple to say when something happened

Do it yourself
1 1 Maria has lived in London for three years.
2 How long have you had this problem?
3 I came here three years ago.
4 When did you arrive? Last night?
5 How long have you been working for Microsoft?

2 1 has enjoyed   2 joined   3 worked   4 took
5 moved   6 became   7 was   8 has established
9 has been trying / has tried   10 has been building
3 1 for   2 ago   3 for   4 for   5 ago   6 since
4 2 When did his career begin?
3 How long did he work in banking?
4 How long was he CEO of Vodafone?
5 When did Vodafone buy Mannesman?
6 How long has the mobile phone sector been experiencing problems?

Sounds good
Weak forms of *have* and *for* with the present perfect
1 How long <u>have you</u> worked in Paris?
How long <u>have you</u> been living here?
How long <u>has he been</u> working in sales?
2 I've worked in Paris <u>for</u> five years.
I've <u>been</u> living here <u>for</u> a few months.
He's <u>been</u> working in sales <u>for the</u> last four months.
3 We link 'for' and 'a' because a consonant proceeds a vowel.
4 1 for a few months
2 for four weeks
3 for a year
4 for a couple of days
5 for ten hours
6 for the last two weeks

11 Making money

Read on
Alternative investments
1 1 Put money in the bank or invest in stocks and shares
2 Buy a second house to let; buy a share in commercial property
3 Any of the following: buy art; invest in furniture or antiques; play the lottery; gamble on horse racing
2 1 Check that the rent will cover the mortgage and maintenance, and give you a profit
2 Location and demand for property
3 Someone who invests money in a new business
4 You have to know about art and art fashions
5 It's high risk and you need to know about fashions here too
6 It is very rare that you win anything

The words you need ... to talk about finance and investments
1 1 d   2 h   3 j   4 a   5 c   6 g   7 i   8 b   9 f   10 e
2 1 property   2 mortgage   3 interest rates
4 bonds, investment   5 shares   6 shareholders, dividends
7 assets   8 commercial property

Meetings 1: Asking for and giving opinions
1 Developing new markets
Alex does not make his points very well because he sounds aggressive and too direct. The phrases *I disagree* and *You're wrong* can often sound too direct in a business meeting. *Yes, but ...* or *I'm not sure about that ...* or *Don't you think ...?* are more usual ways to disagree.
2 What do you think ... ?   I think ...
(Using a name) Alex?   But ...
That's true, (yes).   I'm not sure about that.
Yes, but ...
3 *Possible answers*
1 My view is   2 What do you think   3 In my opinion / I think
4 Actually, I don't agree   5 What about
6 I'm not sure about that   7 You're probably right

12 Ecotourism

Getting directions
1 j   2 i   3 e   4 a   5 g   6 h   7 c   8 f   9 d   10 b

Listen to this
Tourism and the environment: the Eden Project
1 1 T   2 F   3 T   4 F   5 T
2 1 You can learn about the natural environment
2 Think about the relationship between plants and people
3 Money

4 It has created jobs, tourism, and brought money to the local community; helped to rebuild an area badly damaged by industry; an educational benefit as well as a leisure resource

5 He created the Eden Project.

The words you need ... to talk about the environment

1 1 c   2 h   3 b   4 a   5 e   6 f   7 d   8 g
2 1 fossil fuels   2 energy consumption, global warming
   3 farming   4 pollution   5 infrastructure
   6 the natural environment

13 Changing culture

Listen to this

Norway sets female quota for boardrooms

1 1 T   2 F   3 F   4 F   5 T
2 1 More women will mean better corporate leadership.
   2 Companies need time to find the right women.
   3 Less than 10%
   4 He doesn't think there are enough qualified women to fill a 40% quota.
   5 You can't make a cultural change quickly.

Check your grammar

Future 1: *will, going to* and the present continuous

1 1 I'll call you at the end of the month.
   2 Are you going to push this process in Norway immediately?
   3 I'm seeing our directors tomorrow.
   4 I'll check and I can get back to you on that.
   5 Companies in Norway are going to fix quotas for women in management.
   6 We're introducing this change next year.
2 *will* c   *going to* a   present continuous b

Do it yourself

1 *Suggested answers*
   1 Don't worry. I'll solve the problem immediately.
   2 Sorry, that's my phone ringing. I'll turn it off.
   3 I can't come to lunch with you. I'm going to do some training in the gym.
   4 You look stressed. I'll help you with that report, if you want.
   5 I'm flying to Brussels tomorrow at 8.55.
2 1 I'm going to watch   2 I'll do   3 I'm going to work
   4 I'm going to discuss   5 I'll do   6 I'll have
3 1 I'll help   2 am I presenting   3 I'll change
   4 Everyone is staying   5 I'll tell
   6 I'm going to send / I'm sending / I'll send
   7 I'll let   8 we're meeting
   9 I'm just going to finish / I'm just finishing
   10 I won't forget

Sounds good

Contractions with pronouns and auxiliary verbs

1 1 haven't   2 Didn't   3 don't   4 I'm   5 Don't   6 I'll
   We use contractions, which generally have weak stress, in order to speak more fluently and so that we can place the main stress on other key words in the sentence.
2 Contracted forms in **bold**.
   MARK: Hello, **I'm** calling to check you got the schedule. Have you got it?
   EMMA: Yes, I have. **It's** here in my mailbox but I **can't** open it.
   MARK: I **don't** understand.
   EMMA: **It's** very strange. **I've** never had any problems with emails from you before.
   MARK: Did you save the document first?
   EMMA: Yes, I did. It **didn't** make any difference. Can you resend it?
   MARK: OK, **I'll** send it again straightaway. Please phone me if it **doesn't** open.
   EMMA: **Don't** worry. I will!

14 The customer is always right

Read on

Ten foot attitude

1 1 C   3 A   5 D   6 B
2 1 Associates (This word gives the idea that the company values them as equal partners and as an important part of the company.)

2 Sheila who jumped in front of a car to stop a little boy from being hit, and Annette who gave up the toy she wanted for her own son so that a customer's son could have it for his birthday

3 The fact that associates show they are grateful to customers for their business

4 Whenever associates come within ten feet of customers, they should look the customer in the eye, greet them and ask if they need any help

5 At university, Sam Walton spoke to everyone near him and soon got to know more students than anyone else

6 It helps in ways that its customers want, for example, it gives help to local schools, hospitals and groups in need

The words you need ... to talk about customer service

1 'Service' occurs four times:
   extra service; the service was as simple as a smile; better service; customer service
2 1 great: exceptional, five star
   2 poor: unsatisfactory, below standard
   3 cheap: low cost
   4 expensive: pricey, costly
   5 rapid: fast, quick
   6 individual: personal
3 1 at your   2 offer   3 range   4 tailor   5 station
   6 charge   7 agreement   8 sector   9 standards

Telephoning 2: Making and changing arrangements

1 Wednesday 10th May: Oakwood House, Smith Square at 10 am
2 Referring to last contact: I sent you an email about our meeting.
   Suggesting a meeting: Can we meet next week sometime?
   Fixing a time: What day would suit you?
   Confirming: I'll send an email to confirm.
3 Problem: Charlotte can't make the meeting on Wednesday because she has to be out of the office all day.
   Solution: They change the appointment to Thursday at 12 noon.
4 1 I've got a problem now
   2 I have to be out of the office
   3 the following day
   4 is that all right with you
   5 it's not a problem for you

15 An interesting place to live

Visiting someone's home for dinner

1 h   2 e   3 g   4 f   5 d   6 b   7 c   8 a

Listen to this

Living in a windmill

1 1 F   2 F   3 T   4 F   5 F
2 1 (news)paper   2 eight metres across
   3 the location   4 the door is in the floor   5 a field
   6 expensive

The words you need ... to talk about houses and homes

1 1 e   2 i   3 f   4 h   5 j   6 g   7 c   8 b   9 k
   10 a   11 d
2 1 c   2 h   3 a   4 f   5 g   6 d   7 e   8 i   9 b
3 1 washing   2 washing-up   3 housework   4 ironing
   5 put ... away   6 lay   7 clear   8 make   9 take
   10 put out

Revision 1 Units 1–15

Grammar

1 1 work, manages, provides
   2 am / 'm planning, is, are coming
   3 was just reversing, heard
   4 have / 've been writing, has just crashed
   5 have / 've worked, have / 've been working, is almost finished
2 1 Seville is hotter than Paris in summer.
   2 Bill Gates is the world's richest man.
   3 London is not as big as Tokyo.
   4 The 2002 World Cup was the worst ever.
   5 Wal*Mart has the biggest turnover of any retail business in the world.
   6 Yesterday I played squash but I played badly.
   7 My friend Sam plays squash better than I do.
   8 The weather in northern Spain is not as hot as in the south.

Pronunciation

1 1 ✓ ↑ Oh, really?
  2 ✓ ↑ Three? Only three?
  3 ✗ ↓ I'm sure.
  4 ✗ ↓ Is it?
  5 ✓ ↑ Oh, right.
  6 ✓ ↑ The Snowball? Fine.

2 Where <u>do you</u> work?
I work <u>for a</u> film company in Bristol.
What <u>do you</u> do?
I'm <u>an</u> editor.
How long <u>have you been</u> working there?
<u>For about</u> six years.
How long <u>have you</u> lived in Bristol?
<u>For</u> ten years.

Business vocabulary

1 1 founded 2 produces 3 factories 4 turnover
  5 worldwide 6 market share 7 organised 8 employs
2 1 g 2 c 3 e 4 i 5 d 6 a 7 b 8 f 9 h

Business communication

1 1 like to speak to
  2 you through
  3 could I speak
  4 to leave a message
  5 got a problem now
  6 Could we meet
  7 it's not a problem
  8 ask him to phone

Social phrases

1 1 f 2 a 3 j 4 c 5 i 6 d 7 e 8 g 9 b 10 h

General vocabulary

1 1 culture, scenery
  2 performance
  3 travel
  4 recycle
  5 housework, washing-up
  6 contemporary
  7 bed and breakfast, hotel
  8 wonderful
  9 switch off
  10 shelves

16 Taiwan – still a tiger

Listen to this

Real competitive advantage
1 1 T 2 F 3 F 4 T 5 F
2 1 30%
  2 The hotel is in a banking district
  3 10%
  4 The US
  5 It keeps personal information on a database

Check your grammar

Quantifiers
Each and *every* combine with singular countable nouns.
1 most / a lot of 2 a lot of / most 3 much 4 Most / A lot of
Most and *a lot of* combine with both plural countable and uncountable nouns.
5 a little 6 a few
A little combines with uncountable nouns.
7 any 8 no

Do it yourself

1 1 How many years have you lived here?
  2 How much information do you have about Taiwan?
  3 We only have a little information about our customers. We need more for our database.
  4 We have many / a lot of things to talk about.
  5 There are no / aren't any tourists here in the winter.
2 1 All 2 Each 3 many 4 Much 5 some 6 Most
  7 a few
3 1 any / a lot of 2 many / all 3 a lot of / much
  4 much / a lot of 5 many / any

Sounds good

Linking
1 A: Shall we go and get some lunch? I need something to eat.
  B: Sorry, I don't have a lot of time. I've got an important report to finish.
  A: OK. Don't work too hard. I'll see if Jo's free for a little lunch.
3 1 Did it cost a lot of money?
    /j/ /r/ /r/
  2 Shall I order a taxi for Anna?

  3 Do you need any help?

  4 Did you have a nice evening?
      /j/ /w/
  5 Could I ask you a few questions?
     /w/
  6 Are you interested in art?

17 RoboDog

Read on

Barks and bytes
1 Receive emails, play football, greet the kids, balance, understand its location, hear and see, make decisions, find its way around a house or office, do useful tasks, understand and act on up to 60 instructions
2 1 T 2 F 3 F 4 F 5 T 6 F

The words you need ... to talk about technology and gadgets

1 1 colour 2 high/tall 3 long 4 wide 5 weigh 6 cost
2 1 b 2 f 3 c 4 e 5 a 6 d

Emails 2: Handling customer enquiries

1 1 f, g 2 a, h 3 d, l 4 e, i 5 c, k 6 b, j
2 1 e *or* i 2 k 3 d *or* f 4 a 5 c 6 b 7 g 8 d *or* f 9 l
3 *Model answers*
Dear Sam,
I'm sorry about the late delivery. This was due to a production problem. I can assure you that the goods will be ready for despatch on Monday. We are confident that you will have them by the end of the week.
Best wishes,

Dear Mr Amis,
I would like to apologise for the wrong delivery. I can assure you that we will collect and replace the goods this week. Our courier will telephone you later today.
Thank you for your understanding.
Kind regards,

Dear Susanna,
We have good news about the production problem we told you about. I am pleased to tell you we have now resolved this, so everything is running normally again.
Regards,

18 Learning styles

Asking for and giving help

1 g 2 c 3 f 4 d 5 a 6 h 7 e 8 b

Listen to this

Teaching people how to learn
1 Thinking positively
Different kinds of learners
Working with companies
Teaching memory techniques
Good teachers
2 1 Nicholas talks about people's lack of confidence about speaking in front of people – they say, 'I can't speak in front of 20 people'; and about learning languages, they say, 'I'm no good at languages.'
  2 Students learn about themselves and their learning styles by doing this.
  3 Microsoft has a visual culture; Marks & Spencer has a more practical culture.
  4 It shows people how good their memory can be.
  5 Learners, though teachers can help.

The words you need ... to talk about learning a language

1 1 knowledge 2 remember 3 revise 4 translation 5 memory 6 mean 7 made 8 study

2 1 translate 2 Pronunciation 3 vocabulary 4 word families 5 dictionary 6 mistakes 7 record 8 opposite

19 Britain at work in 2010

Listen to this

Vision of the future

1 Richard agrees with 1 and 3.

2 1 South East Asia, especially China
  2 Job security
  3 Heavy traffic and pollution
  4 People will travel more and try to enjoy life more
  5 It will be on personal life, on pleasure and enjoying what they can

Check your grammar

Future 2: *will, can, may* and *might*

1 1 Sentences a and c 2 Sentences b and d

The first conditional

1 *Will* expresses certainty that the action in the clause will happen. *Can* expresses the idea of ability.
May and *might* both express the idea of possibility. Some grammar books state that *might* indicates that the speaker feels an action is more improbable than when using *may*. However, most native speakers indicate their expectation of probability by emphasising uncertainty with appropriate intonation and voice tone rather than through the selection of either *may* or *might*.

2 The present simple

3 *If* indicates that the action in the *If* clause is only a possibility. *When* indicates that the action in the *When* clause is sure to happen.

Do it yourself

1 1 I'm sure we won't have any problems.
  2 I'm not sure where Juan is. He may / might be in the canteen.
  3 If we take more time, we might not make so many mistakes.
  4 If you don't send me a new brochure, I can't place an order.
  5 When I have time, I promise to send you the report.

3 In sentences 1 and 3 *When* is the most realistic choice. In the other sentences, both *If* and *When* are possible depending on the person's work–life context.

Possible answers
  1 When I retire, I'll be able to travel more.
  2 If my organisation offers me the chance to work abroad, I'll definitely go.
  3 When I go home this evening, I may watch TV.
  4 If my company moves to offices 150 kilometres from our current location, I might leave my job.
  5 When I have to use English for my next meeting at work, I can try out some new expressions.
  6 If I drive to work tomorrow, I might get stuck in heavy traffic.

Sounds good

Using stress when giving opinions

1 The speakers stress the underlined words in the sentences.
Speaker 1: But if we cut marketing by twenty per cent, we can save more money.
Speaker 2: But if we cut staff by just one per cent, we can save even more money.

2 1 Speaker 2: But if we increase salary by twenty per cent, staff will be very happy.
  2 Speaker2: But if we invest more, we can increase turnover.
  3 Speaker 2: But if we keep the party, staff will be really motivated.
  4 Speaker 2: But if we reduce quality just a little, we can save millions.

20 How the rich travel

Read on

Selling jet travel for €8,000 an hour

1 c

2 1 Paying by the hour for a jet aircraft to fly where you want
  2 If it helps you to win a big contract

3 A game of golf and a dinner, or a gastronomic evening, with a short presentation to promote Flexjet
4 A man wanted to get off at 7,000 metres because a fly stopped him from sleeping
5 It was harder because Germans prefer not to show they have a lot of money
6 A 'killer instinct' (to be completely focused on reaching your objective)

The words you need ... to talk about sales and selling

1 1 b 2 c 3 h 4 a 5 g 6 d 7 f 8 i 9 e

2 1 keep down 2 break into 3 come down 4 take off 5 look through 6 put up 7 give away 8 sold out

It's time to talk

Sales quiz

Most people can be successful sales representatives. However, the quiz can tell you a lot about your motivation. How many points did you/your partner score?

Less than 13 points
People who mostly choose the second answers have a strong Win–Lose mentality which will stop them being successful in the longer term. If this was your score, change your ways!

13–16 points
People who mostly choose the first answers are strong on motivation and energy but not so strong on how business works. If this was your score, you need to develop more knowledge of business or you will be quickly frustrated by poor results. Good luck!

17–21 points
Bravo! People who mostly choose the third answers should do well. If you scored 17 or more you have clear thoughts about the selling process, the customer focus, and the balance necessary for success. Well done!

Meetings 2: Leading a meeting

1 Meeting 1
  Objective: To fix location and date of next sales workshop
  Decision: Greece; date to be agreed
  Meeting 2
  Objective: To decide on colour for brochure
  Decision: Red

2 Meeting 1
  Opening
  Shall we get started?
  Does everyone have a copy of the agenda?
  We need to discuss ...
  What do you think?
  Controlling
  Thanks for that.
  So you want to ...
  Closing
  So we've decided to ...

  Meeting 2
  Controlling
  Sorry to interrupt.
  Can we let (*Stefan*) finish?
  Closing
  Can we agree to ... ?
  I think we can finish there.

3 Julie wants a new colour – blue – to make more impact in the market. The chairman handles the disagreement well, firstly, by politely stopping Julie's interruption and, secondly, by taking Julie's opinion into account for discussion in the future.

21 Great cinema

Making recommendations and giving advice

1 1 f 2 c 3 h 4 a 5 j 6 i 7 e 8 b 9 d 10 g

Listen to this

The big screen experience

1 1 F 2 T 3 T 4 T 5 F

2 1 Nice films about relationships with happy endings
  2 About 50 times
  3 De Niro and Jack Nicholson
  4 When you change the actors' voices by dubbing, you change the feel of the film

5 The big screen, the community atmosphere, the experience of going out and meeting friends for a drink

The words you need ... to talk about film and cinema

1 1 g   2 h   3 j   4 a   5 l   6 f   7 d   8 b   9 i
   10 c   11 k   12 e
2 1 actor   2 actress   3 entertaining   4 plot   5 plays
   6 cast   7 character   8 directed   9 set   10 ending
   11 violent   12 subtitles

22 Your personal brand image

Listen to this
Image Counts
1 Jenny talks about:
   appearance, voice, etiquette, clothing, working internationally, shaking hands
2 1 She helps with their appearance, their voice and their behaviour
   2 Pop groups
   3 Write on it; put it in your back pocket
   4 Shaking hands
   5 You must listen to people and you must be nice to look at

Check your grammar
Must, have to and *need to*
1 must   2 have to, need to
3 don't have to, don't need to / needn't   4 mustn't

With *mustn't*, the speaker expresses the idea that he/she opposes the person going to the meeting OR that it is forbidden for the person to go to the meeting.
With *doesn't have to*, the speaker expresses the idea that it is not necessary for the person to go to the meeting.
The past of *must* and *have to* is *had to*.

Do it yourself
1 1 I really must stop smoking.
   2 Do you have to go to the meeting tomorrow?
   3 She doesn't have to go to the meeting if she doesn't want to.
   4 Did you have to take a later plane yesterday because of the delay?
   5 We don't have to work late on Friday after all.
2 1 don't have to   2 must   3 have to   4 have to   5 have to
   6 doesn't have to   7 didn't have to   8 had to
3 1 mustn't   2 don't have to, need to   3 mustn't, need to
   4 mustn't   5 don't have to   6 don't have to, need to
   7 mustn't   8 don't have to

Sounds good
Strong and weak stress with modal verbs
1 In the second sentence, the speaker uses 'really' and stresses 'should'; stressing the modal gives it more urgency.
2 1 A: W, B: S   2 A: W, B: S   3 A: S, B: W   4 A: W, B: S

23 Managing people

Read on
We listen to what they say
1 HR activities: attracting, developing and keeping the best people; recruitment; staff development; negotiating with works councils and unions on working conditions and salaries; pensions planning; company strategy; staff appraisal; downsizing; expatriation
2 1 Laying people off or downsizing
   2 A system of monitoring employees' performance at work by interviewing them
   3 Two-way communication, to listen to employees
   4 Staff moving abroad to work
   5 Because of relationship problems, especially if the employee's partner is unhappy
   6 Women like the personal aspects and the communication

The words you need ... to talk about managing people
1 1 e   2 h   3 g   4 f   5 i   6 c   7 d   8 a   9 j   10 b
2 1 lay off   2 unemployment   3 early retirement
   4 voluntary redundancy   5 recruit   6 development   7 skills
   8 training   9 trade unions   10 works councils   11 policies

Emails 3: Making travel arrangements
1 1 h   2 f   3 g   4 d   5 a   6 c   7 i   8 e   9 b
2 *Model emails*
   Dear Get There Travel,
   Please book three flights from London Heathrow to Budapest on 14 March. Dep. 10.00, arr. 12.30. Names Anthony Bowden, Ingrid Kepper, (your name). Return 15 March. Dep. Budapest 14.00. Thank you.

   Hello Janina,
   Anthony, Ingrid and I will arrive on March 14 at 12.30 at Budapest Airport. Flight No. CR1663. Please arrange for a car to meet us.
   Thanks. See you soon.

   Dear Hotel Ibis,
   My colleague Anthony Bowden booked three single rooms for the night of 15 March in your hotel. Please change the reservation to 14 March, for one night only.
   Sorry for any inconvenience. Thank you.
   Best wishes,

   Dear Ingrid,
   Here are details for the Budapest trip.
   LHR – Budapest 14 March Dep.10.00, arr. 12.30
   Return 15 March Dep. Budapest 14.00
   Hotel Ibis, Budapest, 14 March (same hotel as last time)
   See you soon,

24 Social issues

Receiving international colleagues
1 1 g   2 j   3 i   4 h   5 a   6 c   7 b   8 e   9 d   10 f

Listen to this
Social issues in Britain
1 1 d   2 c   3 e   4 a   5 b
2 1 Football
   2 More jobs and more money
   3 Three million
   4 Better education, more hi-tech industries
   5 Incredibly high
   6 Houses and flats people can afford
   7 At weekends
   8 More police, more black police
   9 Single parent families and divorce
   10 More tax for the rich, more spending on the poor

The words you need ... to talk about social problems and solutions
1 1 unemployment   2 street crime   3 ethnic violence
   4 homelessness   5 begging   6 poverty   7 car theft
   8 football hooliganism
2 1 improve   2 better   3 conflict   4 solve   5 make
   6 worse   7 solution
3 1 e   2 d   3 f   4 a   5 c   6 b

25 The coffee business

Listen to this
Douwe Egberts – coffee producer and seller
1 1 F   2 T   3 T   4 F   5 F
2 1 Receiving the correct data
   2 The price would rise
   3 It guarantees enough production, more producers means more coffee
   4 By paying market or higher prices
   5 Because they don't publish or communicate the fact that they work ethically

Check your grammar
The second conditional
1 The first conditional suggests that the idea in the *if* clause is possible.
   The second conditional suggests that the idea in the *if* clause is less likely.
2 The past simple

3 *would* indicates certainty: (if A, then B is sure)
could indicates ability: (if A, then someone/something is able to do B)
might indicates possibility: (if A, then B is possible)

Do it yourself

1 1 If we increased her salary, she would be more motivated.
2 If we did that, we would meet the target.
3 If we changed our office around a little, people could work more efficiently.
4 If we decreased our prices, I think it would start a price war.
5 Would you work on Saturday if we gave you next Monday off as a holiday?

2 *Model answers*
1 If we banned motor cars in major cities, we would reduce urban pollution significantly.
2 If we introduced a 35-hour working week, employees could create a real work–life balance.
3 Companies would be able to find qualified people more easily if we had a better education system.
4 If we made criminals wear microchips, we could stop a lot of crime.
5 If we had to give 2% of our income to developing countries, we would reduce poverty significantly.
6 Our staff would be much healthier if they did 30 minutes of regular exercise every day.
7 If we worried less about money and material possessions, we might be happier.
8 If politicians listened to the people, the world would be a much better place.

3 1 pay   2 did   3 will   4 would   5 will   6 created
The man uses the first conditional to suggest that the ideas are possible. The woman uses the second conditional to make them seem less likely, and to communicate her disagreement with the man's ideas.

Sounds good
Silent letters and difficult words
2 1 Crossing out the silent letter(s): would, might, climb, who, doubt
2 Noting down a word with the same sound as the problem word: would, climb, know
3 Writing the phonemic transcription from the dictionary entry: who, doubt
4 Noting a pronunciation rule: might
5 Writing personal notes on how to pronounce words: honest, science

26 Intelligent skis
Read on
Intelligent ski technology
1 1 C   2 B   4 E   5 D   6 A
2 1 They make it easier to turn and increase speed
2 They vibrate more
3 Adapt to different conditions
4 They send an electrical signal to the computer chip and the fibres become hard and stiff
5 The skis are very expensive

The words you need ... to talk about products
1 1c   2g   3d   4h   5a   6f   7b   8e
2 1 designed for   2 includes   3 user-friendly   4 enables
5 You can   6 ensures

Telephoning 3: Handling complaints
1 1 D   2 B   3 C
2 1 I'm very sorry about that   2 Let me check
3 get back to you   4 There was a computer error
5 Is that OK?   6 Sorry again   7 I really do apologise
8 We had a lot of problems   9 We'll talk next week

27 You are what you eat
Food talk
1 b   2 g   3 c   4 f   5 a   6 i   7 d   8 e   9 h

Listen to this
How do you like our food?
1 Food is really important to the Japanese.
2 1 A beautiful picture.
2 Fresh food, top quality and presentation.
3 She used to send him boxes and boxes of food from Japan.
4 'How do you like our food?'
5 Because the Japanese eat whale meat (some of which, the people who get angry believe, comes from endangered species).

The words you need ... to talk about food and cooking
1 1 d + v   2 c + vii   3 f + viii   4 g + vi   5 h + i   6 i + iv
7 e + ii   8 j + x   9 a + ix   10 b + iii
2 1 overcooked   2 spicy   3 rare   4 medium   5 ripe
6 rich   7 tender   8 salty   9 off   10 sweet   11 savoury
12 sour

28 That's entertainment!
Listen to this
From strongmen to look-alikes
1 1 T   2 F   3 T   4 T   5 F
2 1 Product launches and promotions
2 A product launch with a fireworks display
3 One day
4 The heat
5 Every week

Check your grammar
The passive
Describing processes
Firstly, any possible contract is discussed internally.
Then performers are contacted.
If they are available, they're hired immediately.

We form the present simple passive using the verb *to be* + the past participle.
We use the passive when we focus on the action more than on the person.
Other uses of the passive
Speaker A uses the passive because it is not important to say who recruited the singers or who gave them the wrong music (or it is not known).
Speaker B uses the active because it is important to specify who is responsible for the action.
We form the past simple passive with the past simple of the verb *to be* and the past participle.

Do it yourself
1 1 The coffee is normally made by our secretary.
2 The report was prepared by a colleague yesterday.
3 He was asked by his boss to meet a client at the airport.
4 I am fascinated by your ideas.
5 The email was sent yesterday.
2 1 Firstly, a meeting is arranged with the client to identify needs.
2 Secondly, the freelance people we want to use are contacted.
3 Thirdly, a second meeting is organised to discuss the proposal.
4 Then a detailed schedule is agreed.
5 After that a price is negotiated.
6 Finally, the contract is signed.
3 1 was established   2 were used   3 was started
4 was also seen   5 is normally held   6 are turned up
7 is now managed   8 were trained   9 were also used
10 is expected

Sounds good
Corrective stress
1 Actually, it's fourteen years.
No, she runs the company.
She was, but now it's Sinatra.
Speaker B stresses these words in order to draw attention to mistaken information used by speaker A and to give the correct details.
2 No, it's an entertainment agency.
Not really. Most of our work is corporate.

We <u>did</u>. Now we work all over the <u>world</u>.
Actually, we have almost <u>no</u> employees. We use <u>freelance</u> people.

29 Life coaching

Read on
Do you need a change?
1 A a   B b   C b   D a
2 1 Around New Year
  2 Better working relationships and reduced stress
  3 70% of people are doing jobs that they don't want to do
  4 To help people to realise where they want to go and then make them think about their own solutions to get there
  5 They can expect to earn £4,000 a month = £48,000 a year
  6 The rise in the membership of ICF from 5 to 400

The words you need ... to talk about changes and trends
1

Verb (infinitive)	Past simple	Past participle	Noun	Adjective
reduce	reduced	reduced	reduction	reduced
fall	fell	fallen	fall	falling
grow	grew	grown	growth	growing
rise	rose	risen	rise	rising

2 1 b   2 c   3 a   4 e   5 f   6 h   7 d   8 g
3 1 due to   2 resulted in   3 due to   4 a result of   5 lead to

Presenting 2: Handling questions effectively
1 1 Budget   2 Training   3 Upgrade costs
2 1 Does anyone have any questions?
  2 OK, if there are no more questions, I'd like to go to the next point.
  3 Does that answer your question?
  4 It's an important question.
  5 Right, if there are no more questions, I'll finish there.

30 Work or lifestyle?

Listen to this
Work, belief and lifestyle
1 1 No   2 Yes   3 Yes   4 Yes
2 1 Media and marketing.
  2 Leather, anything that comes from an animal.
  3 Sugar, salt and fat.
  4 250,000
  5 It's World Vegan Day.
3 1, 3, 4 and 5 are important to him.

The words you need ... for continuous learning
1 1 e   2 c   3 d   4 a   5 b
2 a save   b competitive   c commission   d advertise   e responsibility   f narrow   g tailor-made   h tiny

Saying goodbye
1 h   2 c   3 d   4 a   5 b   6 i   7 f   8 e   9 j   10 g

Revision 2 Units 16–30

Grammar
1 1 some / a few   2 a few/ some   3 some / many / most   4 any   5 no   6 a little / some   7 much   8 each   9 much
2 1 11 billion bananas are eaten by Americans every year.
  2 20 billion hot dogs are consumed by Americans every year.
  3 Six billion Oreos are produced by Nabisco every year.
  4 100 billion M&Ms are manufactured by the Mars M&M factory in Hackettstown, New Jersey every year.
  5 Mars's first candy was sold in 1911 by Frank and Ethel Mars.
3 *Possible answers*
  1 If I take early retirement, I'll move to a smaller house.
  2 If I had more, money I'd buy a new car.
  3 If I could have dinner with anyone in the world, I'd choose Zac Goldsmith.
  4 If I could work in another country, I'd try to learn the language first.
  5 When I next go on holiday, I'll take lots of books with me.
  6 If I said that to my boss, I'd lose my job.

Pronunciation
1 1 A: Did you say 51 88 57 83 / five one, double eight, five seven, eight three?
    B: No, it's 51 88 <u>97</u> 83 / double oh four seven, five one, double eight, <u>nine</u> seven, eight three.
  2 A: Is that M–A–R–K–U–S?
    B: No, it's a <u>C</u>. M–A–R–C–U–S.
  3 A: One hundred and thirty-five?
    B: No, not thirty-five. It's one hundred and forty-five.
  4 A: The second?
    B: No, the <u>twenty</u>-second.
2 1 Shall we go and get some lunch?
  2 Can I have a cup of coffee?
  3 I'm afraid I'm a bit too busy.
  4 I've been working here for over a year.
  5 Maybe I should take that job after all.
  6 How about trying that new Indian restaurant?

Business vocabulary
1 1 appraisal   2 pension   3 recruit   4 trade union   5 workforce   6 downsizing

Business communication
1 1 Shall we get started?
  2 Does everyone have a copy of the agenda?
  3 Our objective today is to review all our projects.
  4 What do you think?
  5 If I understand you correctly, you think it's a good idea.
  6 Sorry, can you let him finish?
  7 Can we fix a date for the next meeting?
  8 Are there any further points?
  9 I think we can finish there.
2 1 details   2 flight   3 flight number   4 arrange   5 pick me up   6 take a train   7 return flight   8 hotel reservation

Social phrases
1 1 f   2 b   3 a   4 h   5 g   6 d   7 e   8 c

General vocabulary
1 1 rise   2 poached   3 rich   4 Subtitles   5 violence   6 thriller   7 memory   8 reduction   9 situation   10 poverty